Sufism
and
Psychology

LYNN WILCOX, PH.D.

ABJAD

Book Designer
Liaquat Ali

Library of Congress Cataloging in Publication Data

Wilcox, Lynn
   Sufism and Psychology.

   Includes bibliographical references.
   1. Psychology, Religious. 2. Consciousness. 3. Sufism. I. Wilcox, Lynn
   II. Title
   BL53.U45   200'.1975.16302
   ISBN: 1-871931-47-8

Published and Distributed by:
ABJAD Book Designers and Builders
P. O. Box 18374
Chicago IL 60618

CONTENTS

FOREWORD

"It's in everyone of us to be wise." So goes the song. Lynn Wilcox has discovered that wisdom within and manifests it in the writing of a "complete" psychology. Dr. Wilcox begins with the original definition of the word psychology, the study of the soul, and wisely gives consideration to its source, God, something not done by traditional psychology.

The neglect of the origins of "mind" and "soul" in American psychology is incongruous. Since William James early on focused on "states of consciousness," American psychology has been more a behaviorology than a study of the mind, a departure from its roots. This prompted William McDougall, a follower of James, to observe that with the coming of John B. Watson, psychology lost its mind. In fact, Watson made up his vocal cords that there was no mind, having no mind to make up. In many ways psychology has not only lost its mind, it has lost its vision, or more accurately, has had a very limited vision. In its attempt to be objective, to be a science, psychology has most often studied persons as objects from a distance, trying to quantify individuals instead of understanding them experientially and existentially in a more personal, subjective way. That is, subjects have become objects to know about rather than persons to know in a deeply personal manner, including the most important dimension of all, the area of "spirit."

The psychology explained in this book is not familiar to most westerners and naturally is looked at askance by persons conditioned from birth by their culture to believe that linear, rationalistic, objective thinking is the true way of knowing. Some persons have been resistant to a non-rationalistic system of thought because it emphasizes submission rather than control, such being at variance to an allegiance to the pre-eminence of freedom. Ironically, much of this resistance to the notion of submission has come from Christians, who in their private lives purport to follow a religious leader who emphasized that "He who will find his life must lose it.," a paradoxical teaching affirming the centrality of surrender of the ego over a psychology of control and dominance.

Dr. Wilcox, herself a westerner, also believes in the concept of freedom and individual responsibility and demonstrates that freedom by having the courage to present an alternative psychology. Her purpose is not to deny the advances of traditional psychology, or to put down the efforts of researchers, but rather to help open our eyes and awaken us to the reality of our true identity which lies beyond our learning. Her psychology is a more inclusive, comprehensive view which affirms the whole person. She follows the way of the Pirs, the Spiritual Masters, but recognizes that variations may appear over time. However, "the essence always remains," particularly the concept of selfless love of God.

In this book, Dr. Wilcox notes that Sufism has existed in human history for at least 1400 years, predating modern psychology by many centuries. As evident in the Contents, she skillfully deals with traditional psychological concepts but reconceptualizes them based on the ancient wisdom of the School of Sufism, which in large measure has been ignored by psychologists bound to "science."

The attainment of Wisdom, she contends, comes from going beyond the human mind to the universal mind of God. When traditional psychology has had a concern for human "identity," it has either tended to focus on human behavior or descriptions of "personality." Sufism is concerned with the essence of human identity, the experience of knowing one's true self.

It seems fair to say that the various "schools" of psychotherapy have neither been fully aware of their basic assumptions about the nature of reality and human identity nor have given adequate consideration to the influence of those assumptions, on their work as researchers or on their clinical practice. In particular, "the psychology of the empty organism" has held that all behavior is learned, that psychology should deal only with observable phenomena, that reason should be the *sine qua non* of psychological intervention, that human development proceeds in a relatively predictable sequence, and that non-operationally defined terms, such as love, wisdom, altruism, intuition, virtue, identity, empathy, caring, good, evil and freedom, are suspect and not proper psychological subjects for scientific scrutiny. However, the assumption that the knowledge gained from such a psychology will lead to the betterment of the human race has hardly been proven to be accurate, given the state of the world today.

Psychology's attempt to be a science, to virtually worship science as a god, is understandable considering the many deviations from and perversions of organized religious groups from the basic teachings of their founders, whether Muhammad, Jesus, Moses, Buddha or others. Also, the successes of the physical and biological sciences have enhanced the reputation of science and increased public confidence in it. Thus, as a science, traditional psychology has most often focused its efforts on observable behavior rather than on subjective experience arbitrarily limiting the scope of its field of inquiry. It has even closed its eyes to recent findings of quantum physicists, who have found that the very presence of the researcher alters the nature of what is being studied. What has been missing is a theory of metaphysics and the development of an epistemology, the study of knowledge itself. The psychology of Sufism includes a physics, a metaphysics, an epistemology and an elaborate set of techniques to attain self-realization, which is the highest goal of life. Sufism relies on direct transcognitive experience. The True Self has the capacity to observe or witness the transient self and to know that what appears to be individual souls are at once the soul of humanity itself.

Western psychology has tended to be body-bound, ego-bound, and culture-bound. The Sufic psychology of Wilcox enlarges its field of inquiry and is a more open and comprehensive science, and thus a more true science.

This book is both a passionate and compassionate statement about what it means to be a person. That is, it is a psychology which is alive and related to the natural impulses and rhythms of the universe, the dynamic creative divine energy which we call God, which paradoxically is always in the process of expressing itself.

The psychology of which Dr. Wilcox speaks is a human science inextricably related to the basic question of what it means to be human, that is, the question of human identity and the source of human existence. It is a science or mode of inquiry that does not reject the subjective but instead enthusiastically embraces it. All of reality begins in the "subjective," the understanding of which is a precondition to understanding "objective" physical reality. In fact, it is a psychology that transcends arbitrary boundaries, taking as its subject persons who image the human and the divine.

In my judgment, Dr. Wilcox must have had the experience of being close to the source of soul, having transcended the prisons of rationality and rationalistic thinking. Like Pascal, she undoubtedly has experienced that truth that "the heart has its reasons which Reason does not know." However, there is no necessary irreconcilable conflict between science and Sufism. Indeed, Wilcox's task seems to be one of reconciliation, of bringing peace to the profession of research psychology and applied psychology. That accomplishment requires being at peace with one's self, and being close to Peace itself. Her task, then, is to bring psychology home. She lifts the study of psychology to a higher plane, beyond mechanism and rationalism, to the experience of life and its creative source.

Thomas H. Elmore, Ph.D.

Dr. Elmore is Professor of Counseling Psychology and Director of Counselor Education at Wake Forest University. Widely known and respected for his extensive work in Holistic Psychology and Psychotherapy, he has traveled widely and also taught in Spain, Italy and Germany. The author of numerous professional articles and papers, he received his Ph.D. in Counseling Psychology from Ohio State University, where he was Phi Beta Kappa. He is a certified Marriage and Family Therapist and Licensed Psychologist with more than thirty-five years of clinical experience. He has served as president of several professional associations, and has received a Carnegie Fellowship in Teaching, as well as awards for Mentor of the year, Outstanding Leadership in Counseling, and Outstanding Professional Leadership.

CHAPTER I
INTRODUCTION

T hrough the long years of human history, learned persons of all times and places have pondered the answers to the eternal human questions: Who am I? What is the purpose of life? What is Truth? What is Beauty? What is Love? What is Goodness? Is there life after death? How can I find peace? Who or what is God? Since such questions have not been the focus of Western psychology, the answers to them have not been addressed.

Hazrat Pir, in *Peace*,[1] states two fundamental questions that are the key to human behavior exist: How can the perfect human be developed? How can the perfect society be developed?

Modern Western psychology does not have the answers to these questions, either, for it has not dealt with the fundamental questions of human existence. Rather, it has focused on describing behavior, without having examined the basic, underlying principles governing human behavior. Psychology has therefore become the purview of those studying small and quantifiable segments of human behavior. Psychologists have provided useful information and descriptions of human behavior, but have not been able to provide answers to the deepest questions of the human "heart."

Despite the presence of thousands of psychologists, counselors, social workers and psychiatrists attempting to help them, modern western psychology has been unable to demonstrate the ability to teach people how to change dramatically and permanently in a positive fashion. Nor has it been able to show people how to live in peace and contentment. Several psychologists, most notably Abraham Maslow, have described persons they consider as models approaching the ideal—the self-actualizing, fully functioning human being. But psychologists have been unable to demonstrate the means to enable people to attain and function at these or higher levels.

Wherever we are, in whichever society we live, and whatever language we speak, we are all systematically taught to accept the cultural consensus about "the way things are" and "how we are supposed to be" as reality. We are taught the social conventions from the moment of birth, and as infants and young children, simply accept them, usually unquestioningly. These social norms and conventional ways of viewing the world become everyday habit, comfortable as well-worn shoes. We forget that they also become blinders, boundaries limiting our vision. The social rules and regulations, whatever they might be, control all aspects of any society, and the members of the society come to consider them as "truth." This includes the respected positions or professions and the "hallowed halls of learning" of the society, whose members tend to be the epitome of the norms and conventions of that particular society. One need only look at the history of science in the western world, in which there are numerous cases of strong resistance to new ideas, including life-saving ones, to recognize the social arbiters as frequently keeping the gates to new learning tightly shut, bound within the confines of socio/cultural thought. This is as true of psychology as it is of every other field. If every society has its own bounds and every language has its own limits, where does one look for something different?

Historically, there has been one source which has traditionally and consistently transcended societal rules for more than 1400 years. Its view of the human and of psychology is far broader and brighter than the usual Western "psychological" view point. It is not just a hopeful idea; it has been able to systematically produce the desired results: an outcome of motivated, competent, content, creative, productive, fully-functioning human beings who are at peace with themselves and with Existence. This result is beyond the capability of present day Western psychology. Called "*irfan*" in Persian, it is little known in the Western world. What little is known has been called "Sufism."

Hazrat Pir (the Spiritual Master of the School of Islamic Sufism)[2] uses the simple example of a lamp to illustrate the difference between Western psychology and Sufism. It is as if psychology studies the characteristics of the lamp, such as its height, its weight, and the materials from which it is constructed. Is it a table lamp or a floor lamp? Small or large? A "night light" or reading lamp? How heavy is it? How is the weight distributed? What shape is it? Is it constructed of ceramic, wood, plastic, glass or metal? The size, color, material and shape of the shade might be of concern, and perhaps the condition, length and color of the cord. Psychology would examine the wiring and the maximum allowable bulb voltage. The location and type of the switch, whether it is analog or digital, might all be noted. All these aspects are changeable.

To continue the analogy, psychotherapy would then be concerned with any change that would be necessary to make the lamp appropriate for the position in which we wished to put it. Does the color match the room? Is the lamp attractive? Does the style fit the decor? Does the shade allow enough light? Is the base high enough? Is there enough weight at the bottom so that the lamp is not easily tipped over? Is the wiring frayed? Can you reach the switch easily? The various types of psychotherapy attempt to alter different aspects of the outer characteristics of the lamp— color, size, shape, weight, type of bulb, shade, cord or switch. This is useful. We need and want different lamps for different purposes.

However, no matter how much one studies or changes the characteristics of the lamp, it will not work unless it is plugged in. To provide light, the lamp must be connected to a source of power. Changes to the lamp are unimportant if there is no connection to the Source. Without connection to a source of power, the lamp cannot provide light.

In this example, Sufism is concerned with the reason for making a lamp in the first place. It is concerned with lighting the lamp, with providing a connection to the Source so that the lamp will fulfill its function. Sufism is concerned with the power that provides the light, not with the shape or color of the lamp. Sufism is concerned with the one stable, unchangeable aspect of the lamp—the connection to the Source.

Sufism is the way to healing the sickness of the soul, the alienation from one's true being and from God that afflicts modern persons. That healing lies in connection with the Source of Life. Sufism offers what modern psychology and psychotherapy do not and cannot offer, for they do not have it to offer—the way to fundamental change, to transformation, to harmony, unity, tranquillity and survival. Sufism is not an explanation. It is finding and traveling The Way to meaning, the way to connection with the Source of Light.

CHAPTER 2
HISTORY
DEFINITION OF PSYCHOLOGY

The original meaning of the word "psychology" differs markedly from the ordinary meaning of the word today. The term "psychology" comes from the Greek terms "psyche" and "logos." Psyche meant breath, "...hence, life (identified with or indicated by the breath); the animating principle in man and other living beings, the source of all vital activities, the soul or spirit" or "the animating principle of the universe as a whole, the soul of the world or anima mundi."[3] Logos meant the word or form which expresses a principle; in theology, logos meant the Word of God. So psychology originally meant the word or form expressing the principle of life, the soul or spirit.

The word psychology is first found in English usage in the 1600s, referring to the soul. Early psychology was a branch of metaphysics, dealing with the concept of the soul. A gradual change in the meaning of the word psychology began only relatively recently. In the 1830s, psychology began to be used to refer to the soul or spirit and states of the mind, or self, or ego as well. What caused this expansion in meaning is not clear, but it continued. By 1897 Huxley would state: "...so the psychologist studies the so-called 'faculties' of the mind.," and by 1900, some psychologists would deny the existence of the soul.

Surprisingly, most current works on contemporary psychology do not even attempt to define psychology. The most widely used psychological dictionary, *English & English*[4], defines psychology as: A branch of science dealing with behavior, acts, or mental processes, and with the mind, self, or person who behaves or acts or has the mental processes; a branch of philosophy, generally regarded as a part of metaphysics.

HISTORY OF WESTERN PSYCHOLOGY

Western psychological historians consider the "anticipations" of modern psychology to lie in the thoughts of the early Greeks and of seventeenth and eighteenth century Western European philosophers, and the work of nineteenth century physiologists. Like many historians, they find specific ideas to cite which agree with their own concepts.

However, only in the latter part of the last century did three different methods of examining human behavior, with three different goals, become the real foundation of the new field of study. In Germany, several researchers were attempting to systematically study perception and other sensory responses, thereby establishing experimental psychology, the basis for today's theories of "Behaviorism." In Vienna, Freud and his followers, who were interested in the mentally ill, began recording their thoughts about abnormal psychology (psychopathology), which developed into the theory of "psychoanalysis." A little later, the Frenchman Alfred Binet developed what came to be the first "intelligence test."

EXPERIMENTAL PSYCHOLOGY

Wilhelm Wundt (1833-1920) is considered the "father" of modern psychology, perhaps because he did two things. He denied the existence of the soul, and he established the first psychological laboratory in 1879, where he attempted to measure and record the responses of subjects, often to sound and light. He considered the basic method of psychology to be experimental self-observation, that is, introspection.[5] He made his subjects practice thousands of times before the results were accepted.

The Gestalt school believed, "The whole exceeds the sum of its parts.," and studied perception of patterns, forms or wholes (Gestalten). Gestaltist Wolfgang Kohler (1887-1967) later described the importance of "insight," the sudden appearance of a complete solution involving an entire situation, and Kurt Lewin developed the concept of the human as an element in a general field with forces within the field attracting or repelling the individual. The forces then determine the individual's behavior.[6]

John B. Watson (1878-1958) originated "Behaviorism" in the US. He adopted the concepts of Pavlov, famous for training his dog to salivate at the sound of a bell, and insisted psychology should be objective and only study the relationship between stimuli (whatever stimulates) and an animal's or human's response to the stimuli. He threw out the concept of mind. B.F. Skinner later added the idea that consequences were crucial in determining future behavior, and he utilized a method called "successive approximations" to teach animals new behaviors. He taught chickens how to play baseball, and other animals to perform very unusual tasks. Why he did so is not clear. Skinner admitted the mind exists, but since mental processes are unmeasurable, he focused on observable behavior.

PSYCHOANALYSIS

Sigmund Freud (1856-1939), Carl Gustav Jung (1875-1961) and Alfred Adler (1870-1937), the primary contributors to the psychoanalytic approach, were trained in what comparatively little was known about medicine in the prior century. Psychoanalysis is based on clinical work with troubled people who sought help. Using an iceberg, most of which is hidden from view, as a model, Freud described the conscious mind as the small, visible part of the iceberg, and the unconscious mind as the submerged and invisible other nine-tenths of the iceberg. Analysts encouraged patients to talk while they interpreted or "psychoanalyzed" the real meaning of the words, which came from the patient's unconscious level. The goal was to make what was hidden in the unconscious, and thereby unknown to the patient, emerge into consciousness, so that its interference could be stopped, and the patient could function in everyday life. Freud insisted that everything was determined; nothing happens by accident. He emphasized the importance of childhood experiences, "The child is father to the man.," and described the various "defense mechanisms" people use to protect and continue whatever their internal mental structure and dynamics are.

INTELLIGENCE TESTING

In 1905, commissioned by the French government, Alfred Binet (1857-1911) published a series of questions which could be used to predict whether or not children would be able to do well in schools. This first "intelligence test" was the forerunner of the various types in use today, notably the Stanford-Binet and Wechsler tests. World War I saw the development of the first "group intelligence test," the Army General Intelligence Test, used to determine whether or not individuals could function adequately as soldiers. Today there are many kinds of psychological tests available.

OTHER APPROACHES

These three separate and distinctly different approaches to examining human behavior became the basic foundation for the "psychology" of today. Many others also contributed. Franz Mesmer (1734-1815) first worked with the electro-magnetic fields of the human body, then called "animal magnetism," and induced trance like states that eventually became known as "hypnosis." Galton (1822-1911) published *Hereditary Genius* in 1869, discussing the inheritance of mental ability. Hans Berger (1873-1943) recorded the electrical nature of the human brain in 1903, then developed a method of recording the electrical waves, the electroencephalograph (EEG).[7]

BRIEF HISTORY

We can put psychology in its present form in historical perspective by realizing it emerged after the American Civil War. It is the "baby" of what is referred to as the "social sciences." In the United States, early psychologists[8] also held chairs of philosophy. Gradually, separate departments of psychology were founded. The first US. psychology texts were written close to the turn of this century. An 1886 text included a chapter titled: "Interaction of Soul and Body."[9] William James (1842-1910), the founder of American psychology, in 1890 described the general situation in psychology. He noted psychologists used two ways of unifying the diverse and complex phenomena observed. The first view was to assume a common agent, the soul, *behind* the behaviors. The second viewpoint was to examine the parts of the phenomena, like examining the bricks and stones in a building. He stated that the latter group, called the associationist schools *"have thus constructed a psychology without a soul."*[10]

Psychologists wanted the respect of the academic world. They wanted to be scientists, and wanted psychology to be a science like chemistry and physics. For this and other reasons, the second viewpoint prevailed.

Western Psychology lost its soul, which was eliminated from the text-books and the curriculum. As psychology re-defined as study of the mind and/or behavior became increasingly accepted, and an integral part of college and university studies, the various strands remained separate and sometimes became competitive. Departments proliferated as "Clinical" psychologists, practitioners using various therapeutic methods on clients, and "Experimental" psychologists, usually researchers using a behavioristic approach, often disagreed.

In the middle of the twentieth century, another strand was added, of "humanistic" psychology, which attempted to study what adherents considered to be positive, healthy, growth-producing aspects of human behavior. Carl Rogers and Abraham Maslow are probably the best known. Rogers, in *Client-Centered Therapy*[11] espoused the self-healing ability and capacity for growth of the client. Maslow, (1908-1970) brought Western psychology the first real positive models when he described exceptionally healthy, creative, and well-functioning people, whom he called "self-actualizing."[12] Many texts refer to the "three forces" in psychology as Psychoanalytic, Behavioral, and Humanistic, expanding humanism to include "Existential" psychotherapists such as Rollo May and Victor Frankl.

A new area, Transpersonal Psychology, has been attempting to become the "fourth force" but has met marked resistance, for transpersonal psychologists are interested in metaphysical topics, such as the soul, spirit, mysticism, love, meditation, extra-sensory perception, and life after death. However, traditional psychology does not like to accept what is not measurable, and thus far has not recognized the legitimacy of this point of view.

As information proliferated, more and more subdivisions in psychology have occurred. The American Psychological Association now has forty-seven divisions, which reflect only a portion of the diverse interests covered by the field of psychology today.

Today a doctoral degree is expected for membership and recognition as a professional "psychologist." Psychological "knowledge" is normally obtained through study, by reading the professional literature and listening to papers presented at professional conferences. Quantitative research, based on measurable behavioral observation, is most highly valued and accepted. More than 1900 different journals are included in psychological abstracts. In addition to presenting new information, publication in professional journals is of great importance for psychology professors who want to be promoted and gain tenure.

Today, most people are familiar with psychologists as professors and researchers or as psychotherapists, and the field is about evenly divided between the two categories. A competent psychotherapist is expected to have practical experience in psychotherapy as well as familiarity with the literature. As indicated in the earlier quote, both researchers and practitioners have been unable to determine any basic, underlying mechanisms of human behavior, and have therefore chosen to focus on and specialize in small, specific aspects or characteristics. In the original analogy of the lamp, researchers and professors describe the lamp, and the psychotherapist attempts to make the lamp more suitable for the spot in which it is placed.

DEFINITION OF SUFISM

The word "Sufi" appears in print in the ninth century. The possible derivations of the word "Sufi" were outlined by Hujwiri (d. 1071) in the eleventh century. He indicated that the name may have come from the word "*suf,*" meaning wool, because of the woolen garments the Sufis wore, or from "*ashab-i suffa,*" the name given to "the people of the porch" who gathered around the mosque of the prophet Muhammad, or from "*saf'i,*" meaning purity. Perhaps the correct answer is "all of the above."[13]

The closest word to Sufism in English is gnosticism. An agnostic is one who does not know. A Gnostic is one who knows; in this case, one who knows God. Sufism is not an explanation, it is an experience, the experience of coming to cognize one's own true identity, which is synonymous with cognition of God. The prophet Muhammad (peace be upon him) stated: "He who knows himself, knows his Creator." Sufism is the way of returning to the original state of being, a path by which one can find meaning and purpose, attain tranquillity and everlasting life, a path by which one can again "Come Home."

In Western literature, Sufism is frequently characterized as Islamic mysticism, for it is the way to the personal experience of Divine Love with which God graces the human being, which often includes the ecstatic experience described as mystic. The true student of Sufism learns through the intuitive experience of the heart opened to a spiritual master, not through words or books, which are simply roadsigns along the way.[14] It is necessary to be guided by the *arif* (Pir, Spiritual Master) who has attained the state of absolute cognition through annihilation in God, and who must be inwardly introduced by God. The idea of a spiritual master, familiar to those in other parts of the world, is strange to Westerners. Intellectual acceptance of the meaning usually requires the formation of a new category in one's mental processes, like opening a new file for a new topic.

Sufism is experiencing and living the reality of religion, the discovery and reality announced by each of the prophets. Each person is given the potential to discover this secret of existence. It cannot be accomplished through reason and logic, but must come from the innermost recesses of the heart. For every person, the Pir provides the experience necessary for their progress, just as a gardener cares for each of his plants. Cultivation and development are necessary for the plant to reach its potential.

ORIGIN OF SUFISM

Sufism has existed since the beginning of human history, for in every time and place, God has sent Prophets to lead mankind to knowledge of Him, and Sufism is the Way of the Prophets. The great Master Bayazid Bistami (d. 878) stated: "Its seeds were set at the time of Adam, they sprouted under Noah and flowered under Abraham. Grapes formed at the time of Moses, and they ripened at the time of Jesus. In the time of Muhammad, they were made into pure wine."[15]

Historical records date back more than 1400 years to the time of the Prophet Muhammad (peace be upon him). The basic teachings are found in the Quran, the Word of God spoken to and through Muhammad in poetic form, recorded as he recited it. The founder of the School of Sufism is Oveys Gharani, who lived in Yemen at the time of the Holy Prophet of Islam. Without ever meeting the Prophet Muhammad, Hazrat Oveys had received the teachings of Islam inwardly through his heart, and lived by the principles taught by him. At times the Prophet would say of him, "I feel the breath of the Merciful, coming to me from Yemen."[16]

Shortly before the Prophet passed from this life, he requested his cloak be sent for Hazrat Oveys. In so doing, the Prophet confirmed the method of heart to heart communication through which Hazrat Oveys had received the essence of Islam. Since that time the cloak, symbolizing the highest level of Divine Illumination, and conferring honor, recognition and respect, has been handed down through forty-two successive spiritual leaders and teachers. This simple act creates the only hierarchy within Islamic Sufism. The designated spiritual teacher, called the Pir in Persian, meaning "light of the path," is the essence of the Sufi Way.

Figure 1 depicts the genealogy of Maktab Tarighat Oveyssi Shahmaghsoudi, the School of Islamic Sufism. Since later Sufi students often left their homeland and settled in other areas to teach, additional groups have also come into existence over the centuries. The School of Sufism, sometimes called an order or fraternity, may therefore appear to vary somewhat over time, just as water is flavored by the earth through which the spring emerges, but the essence always remains the same. Sufism is Islamic, for Islam means submission to God, and the goal of Sufism is the submission to God necessary for union with the Divine Beloved.

The Pirs (*urafa'*), due to their remarkable and elevated spiritual level, have served as revered and esteemed teachers and as inspiring models. Dramatic stories describe their backgrounds, from simple shepherds and butchers to kings who gave up their kingdoms to heed the call of God. They have been talented artists, philosophers, scientists, and often, prolific writers.

HISTORY OF SUFISM

In marked contrast to the newness of psychology, Sufism has 1400 years of history of works in art, crafts, music, literature, architecture and the sciences. The history of Sufism is traceable through the written works of those extraordinary spiritual teachers, the Sufi *Arifs*. They have written thousands of volumes, dealing with all aspects of human behavior, but only a few works have been translated into English. They described human psychology perfectly a thousand years before it came into existence as a separate area of study. The greatest works—those of Attar, Rumi, Hafiz, Sadi, and Nizami, to name a few—were written in Persian, others in Arabic. While seeming outwardly accurate, comprehensible and enjoyable, they are actually written in a technical language first developed in the ninth century. The true meaning of the works are known only to those who have received the necessary illumination from the Pir.

In the first two centuries immediately following the death of Mohammed, many Sufis were described as ascetics. Ebrahim Adham (d.742), a prince, gave up his family and his kingdom to find gnosis[17]. The best known early Sufi "saint" was a woman, Rabi'a (d. 801), who lived and taught the concept of selfless love of God.[18] The theme of the lover and the Divine Beloved is central in Sufism, and since in annihilation in God the lover no longer has a separate existence, no distinction can be made between man and woman. Women have been important figures in the history of Sufism.

During the European Dark Ages, Islamic science and literature flourished, and Sufi scholars proceeded in scientific and mathematical experimentation and discovery while Europeans who attempted the same were being tried for heresy. While the richest Christian monasteries them might be endowed with 300 to 400 books, the Muslim University at Granada had 105,000 volumes. Interaction between Judaic, Christian and Muslim scholars was widespread, particularly in Spain, where Muslims ruled from 711 to 1492, and allowed freedom of religion even during the Crusades. Sufi teachings were made known throughout the "Western" world through Spain and provided the foundation for the Christian mystics—St. Theresa, St. Catherine, Meister Eckhart, Richard Rolle and others—who began to appear in the eleventh century. The best known, St. Francis of Assisi, visited the Sufi-influenced court of the Sultan of Egypt in Damietta in the midst of the Crusades.

The renowned works of medieval Islamic civilization—the art, architecture, crafts, jurisprudence, philosophy and science may be traced back to Sufi sources or the effects of Sufi influence. What Westerners think of as "Spanish" architecture, typified by arches, courtyards, and fountains, is Islamic—Moorish—architecture. The most beautiful architecture of India, including the Taj Mahal, is Islamic, brought to India by Sufi teachers in the fifteenth and sixteenth centuries. When the Renaissance finally began in Europe, its primary fuel was from the discovery and rediscovery of the arts, literature and sciences in the world of Islam.

During this centuries long period, the influence of Sufism spread. In the eighth century, the Sufi master Balkhi (d. 779 or 799) was renowned as an expert in the sciences of physics and metaphysics. In the midst of a battle, he deliberately slept between the two lines of the enemies.[19] The great Shaykh Nakshabi (d. 850) is described as performing miracles and going without food for 21 to 31 days. Several well known Sufis lived during the ninth century—Dhu'n Nun in Egypt, Muhasibi in Iraq, Bayazid Bistami of Persia, famous for poetry and paradox, as well as Kharkhi of

Baghdad, who taught that one cannot learn love, since it is a divine gift. Muhasibi wrote of mystical psychology and developed the highly technical language of Sufis, emphasizing uninterrupted spiritual training.

Over the centuries, many Sufis were martyred by the more orthodox. When charges of heresy were brought against the Baghdad Sufis in 885, Abul-Husayn an-Nuri offered his life to save his companions. Touched, the Caliph set them free.[20] Mansur Hallaj (d. 922) became known as the epitome of martyrdom, executed for stating: "I am the True Reality." Ultimately, a precedent-setting ecumenical trial acknowledged that Sufi behavior, including the poetry of love for which they were famed, was unorthodox, but a unique expression of the reality of Islam. Since then, Sufis have usually been accepted, although often begrudgingly, by the preponderance of Islam.

Some Sufis were well known in the West. Ibn Rushd (d. 1198), known as Averroes, was a court physician famed as a philosopher. Palacios considers Dante's *Divine Comedy* to be based on the descriptions in al-Arabi's (1165-1240) works. Al-Arabi, profoundly influenced by two women saints, wrote more than 250 books. Al-Ghazzali (1058-1111) cooperated with the regime in power while Sufis like Ansari were being persecuted, then had a breakdown and left teaching to enter the spiritual life. Ghazzali's teachings combined mysticism and law, and made him the most influential theologian of medieval Islam, exerting a profound influence on Christian thought.[21]

In the twelfth century, more than 100 works were produced by Shaykh Ruzbahan (1127-1209), who invited his Beloved to enter his heart to see the manifestation of pure love in the rose petals of his soul, where thousands of nightingales burned the wings of their high ambition in the fire of love[22]. Shaykh Najmuddin Kubra (1145-1220), became renowned for his psychology of mysticism and ecstatic experiences. Nizami (1141-1202) contributed *The Story of the Seven Princesses*, and wrote the famed epic love story of *Layla and Majnun*.[23]

Allegories have been a favorite mode of expression, and the best known in the West next to *The Thousand and One Nights*, which includes the currently popular story of Aladdin, is Farid ud-Din Attar's (d. 1220) *The Conference of the Birds*.[24] The tale tells how all the birds wish to seek a king, but most quickly turn back, and few birds survive the arduous journey. Those who successfully complete it discover that the great Simorgh they have been seeking is none other than themselves. Another famed allegory is ibn Tufail's (known as Abubacer in the West) The Story of *Hai bin Yaqzan* (retitled The Journey of the Soul). Originally published in the 12th century, it is based on a still earlier work, and is considered the model for Dafoe's *Robinson Crusoe*.[25] The English translation was published in 1708, and Dafoe's in 1719.

The great and most beloved Sufi poet in the West is Jalal al-Din Rumi (1207-), also known as Mehlavi. A conventional religious teacher, he was transformed at age 37 by the unexpected appearance of a wildly eccentric wandering dervish named Shams al-Din Tabrizi. He found in Shams a mirror of the Divine Beloved, and the two were inseparable until jealous students forced the dervish to flee. Thousands of odes of poetry flowed from Rumi, and his followers recorded them as he recited them. His *Mathnavi* alone comprised six volumes, and expresses the love of this lover: "Whoso falls into Love's hands weeps like a cloud; whoso dwells far from Love freezes like snow."[26]

The noble Semnani (1264-1336) left the court to devote his life and his vast wealth solely to God, writing extensively both poetry and prose: "When I picked up the flower of love, I wounded the Intellect's eye with a hundred thorns."[27] Amir Seid Ali Hamadani (1318-1385), known as "the second Ali" for greatness of rank, migrated to Kashmir with 700 followers. Ghohestani (b. 1392) was sometimes in bonds, put into wells twice, and forced into exile for 24 years by the Sultan because of his honesty and refusal to compromise himself. Sheik Hasan (d. 1855), known as Bahaudin, used the imagery of the drop of water losing itself in the boundless sea to describe annihilation in God.[28]

Molana-al-Moazam Hazrat Jalaleddin Mir Abolfazl Angha (1865-1915) introduced the translation of the delicate knowledge of Sufism into scientific concepts. Almost all his numerous works are preserved only as handwritten, unpublished manuscripts. His son, Molana-al-Moazam Mir Ghotbeddin Mohammed Angha (1887-1963), continued the tradition. He remarked on how Rumi described the particle as if he could have observed conditions in the atom. Speaking of scientists, he stated: "But they do not know that sublime existence does not fit into the bounds of the inferior human brain, and heavenly identity cannot be weighted by a laboratory scale with electron and proton weights." Only two of his many books have been published. The best known is *Az Janin ta Jenan*.[29]

His successor and son, Molana-al-Moazam Hazrat Shah Maghsoud Sadegh Angha (1916-1980) pursued advanced studies in law, philosophy, literature, mathematics, physics, chemistry, nuclear physics, biochemistry, and astrophysics as well as Iranian alchemy, which is entirely different from Western versions. The great Pir wrote more than 150 works in both poetry and prose; those in English translations include *Dawn, The Mystery of Humanity, Al-Rasa'el, Hidden Angles of Life,* and *Manifestations of Thought.*

Molana Hazrat Salaheddin Ali Nader Shah Angha was invested with the Holy Cloak by his father on September 4, 1970, and became the forty-second Pir, Oveyssi. Born in Tehran on September 20, 1945, Hazrat Pir was trained from birth in Sufism by his father and grandfather and did graduate study and taught mathematics and physics in the U. S. He is a bridge between ancient and modern, science and religion, East and West. The author of more than 50 works, only three books of poetry, *The Approaching Promise, The Secret Word,* and *Masnavi Ravayeh,* have been translated into English, as has *Peace,* a book illustrating the way to attain peace. He today heads the School of Sufism, where students from all religious, ethnic and cultural backgrounds come to study at classes held in centers throughout the world.

Genealogy of the School of Islamic Sufism
Maktab Tarighat Oveyssi Shahmaghsoudi

Prophet Muhammad
Imam Ali
1. Hazrat Oveys Gharani
2. Hazrat Salman Farsi
3. Hazrat Habib-ibn Rai
4. Hazrat Soltan Ebrahim Adham
5. Hazrat Abu Ali Shaghigh Balkhi
6. Hazrat Sheikh Abu Torab Nakhshabi
7. Hazrat Sheikh Abu Amr Estakhri
8. Hazrat Abu Ja'far Hazza
9. Hazrat Sheikh Kabir Abu Abdollah Mohammad ibn Khafif Shirazi
10. Hazrat Sheikh Hossein Akkar
11. Hazrat Sheikh Morshed Abu-Esshagh Shahriar Kazerouni
12. Hazrat Khatib Abolfath Abdolkarim
13. Hazrat Ali-ibn Hassan Basri
14. Hazrat Serajeddin Abolfath Mahmoud-ibn Mahmoudi Sabouni Beyzavi
15. Hazrat Sheikh Abu Abdollah Rouzbehan Baghli Shirazi
16. Hazrat Sheikh Najmeddin Tamat-al Kobra Khivaghi
17. Hazrat Sheikh Ali Lala Ghanavi
18. Hazrat Sheikh Ahmad Zaker Jowzeghani
19. Hazrat Noureddin Abdolrahman Esfarayeni
20. Hazrat Sheikh Alaodowleh Semnani
21. Hazrat Mahmoud Mazdeghani
22. Hazrat Amir Seyyed Ali Hamedani
23. Hazrat Sheikh Ahmad Khatlani
24. Hazrat Seyyed Mohammad Abdollah Ghatifi-al-Hassavi Nourbakhsh
25. Hazrat Shah Ghassem Feyzbakhsh
26. Hazrat Hossein Abarghoui Janbakhsh
27. Hazrat Darvish Malek Ali Joveyni
28. Hazrat Darvish Ali Sodeyri
29. Hazrat Darvish Kamal Sodeyri
30. Hazrat Darvish Mohammad Mozahab Karandehi (Pir Palandouz)
31. Hazrat Mir Mohammad Moemen Sodeyri Sabzevari
32. Hazrat Mir Mohammad Tghi Shahi Mashhadi
33. Hazrat Mir Mozafar Ali
34. Hazrat Mir Mohammad Ali
35. Hazrat Seyyed Shamseddin Mohammad
36. Hazrat Seyyed Abdolvahab Naini
37. Hazrat Haj Mohammad Hassan Kouzeh Kanani
38. Hazrat Agha Abdolghader Jahromi
39. Hazrat Jalaleddin Ali Mir Abolfazl Angha
40. Hazrat Mir Ghotbeddin Mohammad Angha
41. Hazrat Shah Maghsoud Sadegh-ibn-Mohammad Angha
42. Hazrat Salaheddin Ali Nader Shah Angha

Figure 1

ABSOLUTE KNOWLEDGE

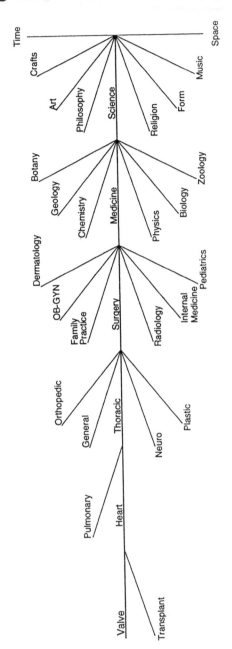

From Absolute Knowledge to Super-Specialization

Figure 2

CHAPTER 3
GOALS

The goal of psychology is that of all science—description, prediction and control—in this case, the description, prediction and control of human behavior. This is a rather chilling concept if one stops and considers it seriously. To that end, psychologists seek knowledge. Knowledge is defined by them as that information which is obtained through the physical senses and is measurable and quantifiable.

Only within the short span of written history has man attempted to categorize knowledge. Previously, everything was viewed as part of an interconnected whole, as different aspects of Unity. Men were knowledgeable or they were ignorant, and the ignorant did not survive. The early Persian, the Egyptian, and the better advertised Greek writers wrote about all conceivable topics as a unitive part of a whole, a totality. Knowledge included all of existence. All areas of human behavior, as well as physical and mental healing, were included.

Division of knowledge into the fields of today came very slowly. An example from medicine may help us visualize what has occurred as man has moved from Absolute Knowledge to specialization. Most of us have had experience with the various medical specialties. If you look at Figure 2, taking surgery as an example, you can see how super-specialized and narrowly focused some medical practice has become. When your professional life is devoted to a very specific and highly technical area, how difficult is it to see all the way back to Absolute Knowledge? It is a long, long way. How could one see? The same type of super-specialization pattern appears in psychology. How can one see the tree for the leaves, or even dream a forest exists?

The consequence of super-specialization in psychology is that the psychological scholar hunts for pieces of information about man. Different kinds of psychologists study different aspects of man. Psychology, in its areas of specialization, usually studies individuals, or specific characteristics of individuals, then "averages" the results. For example, psychologists study the vocabulary of twelve month old babies, the EEG's of people asleep, and the mathematical ability of college freshmen. This approach is simply not capable of dealing with the multifaceted reality of the entirety of the human being. Each psychological theory as well as psychological research deals with a small fragment of the totality, one or a few pieces of a trillion cell jigsaw puzzle called "Human."

The psychologist usually wishes to serve man and the society in which he or she lives. The psychologist, whether aware of it or not, is a representative of the society, presenting its norms and conventions. Psychology itself is a tool of society, and as such, has to have the same social goals as the society. It does not matter which society, for, as Hazrat Pir has pointed out: "Societies and their leaders plan the different systems with only one goal in mind. That goal is the double one of the acquisition and protection of economic profits, and of providing for the natural needs at any price."[30]

As in every aspect of psychology, different theorists have very different ideas about what the more specific goals of psychology should be. A very obvious division occurs between practitioners and researchers, for example. Although both ultimately desire to do work which would benefit mankind, they go about it in very different ways, with very different short-term goals. Many researchers are primarily interested in the accurate description of behavior. In the table lamp analogy, their job is to describe the various characteristics of the lamp—height, weight, color, material, light angle, etc.

The same is true of the study of man within his society, his social reality. One area of psychology is called "social psychology" and attempts to study various social behaviors, but again, it studies only specific characteristics, often with specific practical goals in mind. For example, industrial psychology studies the behavior of people in industry, and is specifically interested in the process of acquiring and keeping competent workers, in order to save money and increase production. There is, of course, an overlap in this area with the field of sociology, which studies behaviors within society, looking at man from the other end of the telescope, so to speak, gazing from the social field toward the individual.

Psychologists are often concerned about social problems, and wish to assist in eliminating them, but have so far not brought forth any resolutions to the problems. Some encourage involvement in social action causes, but such groups have not yet demonstrated any solutions. Psychology simply has no answer to the question of how man can attain the ideal society. Psychology does not know the way to the perfect society.

In US culture there has recently been a strong humanistic influence, and pressure within psychology to adopt a humanistic stance. Humanism basically teaches that the answer to problems, both personal and social, lies in other people. There is an implicit, and sometimes explicit, denial of the reality of God. Humanism urges us to look to other human beings, *rather than*, and in place of, looking to the Creator.[31] Robert Ardrey states contemporary social thought, which includes psychology, ". . . rests on an article of faith, that man is sovereign. And the Greeks had a word for it: hubris (inordinate pride)."[32]

Numerous social critics, including Laing and Szasz, have pointed out that the primary goal of psychotherapy includes adjustment to the society, to the culture; the goal is for the patient to learn how to live within the culture and be of it. When individuals become perturbed and agitated by the current state of affairs, whatever it might be, a goal of psychotherapy, often hidden, is to calm them down and keep them functioning and contributing to the society.[33] The therapist, whether with awareness and willingness or not, functions as a social agent. It is not difficult to discern how many are covertly concerned with maintaining the social order. Using the table lamp analogy, they are concerned that the lamp is appropriate for and fits into the place selected for it.

Each of the more than 250 well-established schools of psychotherapy state differing goals. A few examples from the oldest and best-known will illustrate.

Behaviorists are usually concerned with how to change specific behaviors, particularly how to teach new behaviors and to stop old behaviors. The question of values, of who decides what behaviors are most appropriate to teach, is usually not addressed. Behaviorists see the goal of psychotherapy as "adaptive behavior" or good adjustment.

The goal of the Freudian psychoanalyst is to make the unconscious conscious; to help the client learn to cope and adjust; to work through unresolved developmental stages. Freud was basically concerned with symptom alleviation. His stated goal for patients was that they become capable of work and enjoyment. Other analysts have different goals.

Adlerians cultivate social interests by correcting faulty assumptions and mistaken goals, and help the client develop insight. Adler saw the goal as perfection, expressed through the development of a positive capacity for social living. Once developed, social interest assures a constructive life. Karen Horney redefined the goal of analysis as: "by rendering a person free from inner bondages, make him free for the development of his best potentialities."[34] Erik Erickson's Psychosocial Theory sees the goal as resolution of conflicts between individual needs and social demands, resulting in the development of ego integrity. To Jung, the aim of one's life is to "know oneself," and to reconcile the many opposites of our life through the Transcendent Function. His goals differ radically from those of most therapists, for he emphasized the crucial importance of the spiritual realm and the necessity for a spiritual connection.

Person-Centered Therapy perceives health as a goal, health defined as the ability to perceive realistically rather than defensively, to accept responsibility for one's own uniqueness and behavior, to evaluate experience through one's own senses, to accept others as unique, to prize oneself and others, and to live comfortably in a flowing process of experiencing, with particular emphasis on experiencing emotions.

For the Gestaltists, the primary goal is awareness and congruency. Health is maturation, that is, moving from environmental support to self-support; assuming responsibility for one's own actions, resolving the past, growing up mentally, and attaining authenticity.

Family therapists, who usually use a "systems" approach, have the smooth and efficient functioning of the family system as a goal.

Psychotherapists often linked together and labeled "Existential," including Rollo May and Victor Frankl, among others, state they work toward helping clients realize their responsibility, awareness, freedom and potential, to help them shift from an outward to an inward frame of reference.

Rational-emotive and other "Cognitive" therapies focus most strongly on elimination of self-defeating habits, with particular emphasis on defeating thinking "irrationally," in order to increase tolerance and acceptance of self and others.

Transactional Analysis sees the goal as attainment of health and autonomy, achieved by increased awareness, intimacy, seeing self and others as "OK," and becoming "game free."

In the lamp analogy, all the forms of psychotherapy essentially focus on changing the external attributes of the lamp—the visible manifestations.

GOALS OF SUFISM

The goal of Sufism is entirely different. In the lamp analogy, we stated Sufism is concerned with making the necessary connection with the Source of Power that will allow the lamp to fulfill its function—to provide light. This symbolic goal encompasses the two goals also mentioned earlier: to develop the perfect human being, and to develop the perfect society.

The central teaching of Sufism is that each being has within itself all knowledge of its being, just as the seed contains all knowledge of the tree. Each being has within knowledge of its course in presenting itself as a being, and knowledge of where it will go. Each being is a complete book, a book that can only be read by the being itself. Attaining this knowledge, reading this book, is the goal of Sufism. It is the epitome of "Self Knowledge," and is a Self Knowledge beyond the appearance of reality conceived and understood by the mind. We all yearn, whether or not we are aware of it, to open this book, to discover our inner knowledge, and we are all called to do so, sometimes quietly, sometimes in unexpected ways.

Hazrat Pir defined it specifically in the introduction to *The Mystery of Humanity:*

> If, with an open and sincere mind, one considers the teachings of the Arifs and the results of their search for cognition, it will be apparent that they invite man to a truth which

transcends time and place. That is to say, they show man the path that will lead him to discover the truth, a truth that will free him from the bondage of his natural and physical existence and ultimately lead him to the cognition of his true identity. Thus, the essence of the Arifs' message is that each man, through personal experience and inward discovery, is able to cognize and establish the truth of his own being. As the Prophet Muhammad has said: "Whosoever cognizes his true self has cognized God."

In *Dawn*, Professor Angha describes the goal as cognition of God and annihilation of everything:...except that everlasting, divine and tender being that everyone calls "I," the true self.

> "I" is constant and does not change. "I" is not dependent or subject to change through time or with place. Every self knows "I" briefly in witnessing the manifestations of "I." Each person's personality is rooted in "I," and whenever this cognition penetrates and expands, that person attains true knowledge of self and finds refuge from death. "I" is that divine inspiration of God's spirit breathed into Adam, making him alive. This inspiration of the spirit did not take place once in the beginning without a beginning, but continues without ceasing, making the tomb of the body alive so that "selves" can survive in a divine state.

Symbolically, the goal is poetically presented in various forms—as the moth perishing in the flame, as the drop becoming one with the sea of Existence, and most frequently, as union with the Beloved, God. The goal may be seen as a "death" which is entirely different from physically dying. The moth becomes one with the flame. The drop loses its boundaries in the ocean's depths. The lover is annihilated in union with the Beloved. When this "death" is attained, then there is no longer any fear of physical death. Once you have experienced death, then you know there is nothing to fear. There is instead peace and serenity.

Psychotherapy usually works to increase the ego, to build "ego-strength." Sufism works to obliterate the ego. Psychology concentrates on the self—modifying, changing, "improving" it. Sufism concentrates on diminishing the socially constructed self, until it gradually disappears. The ultimate desire of every salik is union with the Beloved—the complete obliteration of self in God. Union with the Beloved requires an absence of ego, and a giving up of notions of a separate, egotistical self, in order to become one with the Beloved. Union provides complete illumination and enlightenment. In the lamp analogy, union with the Beloved is making the connection with the Source of Power that will provide the Light.

The way to the perfect human being has been outlined in hundreds of volumes of Sufi literature for more than a thousand years. The way to the perfect society has been most recently outlined by Hazrat Pir in *Peace*, his invited address to an audience of diplomats and scholars at American University in Washington, DC.

After first describing the sad state of affairs of the world today, Hazrat Pir quotes his father, Professor Angha:

> Most people (and therefore ultimately human society) remain alien from their true selves and from the truth of life. They neither recognize their true identity nor are in touch with the true values of their spiritual reality. At the same time they become entangled in earthly illnesses that infect their character and behavior, then continuously reinforce their personal indulgences and attitudes so that they are enslaved to temporary and insatiable desires that create an unhealthy mental state. [35]

Any society is the reflection of the people within the society. If you wish to create the perfect society, then you have to find a way to perfection for the individuals within it. He states that national or international social justice is unlikely to occur until each member has been educated and learned to be just. Hazrat Pir states:

> The thinkers and leaders of the world, instead of persisting in designing and implementing an illusory idea known as society, should put aside their past techniques and endeavor to construct a balanced human being and guide him to know his true values. These societies will then enjoy prosperity, happiness and equality, and make available to each of its members educational and developmental opportunities so that they can realize all their creative abilities.

To love and serve humanity, first one must have his own way clear.

We must first be connected with the Source of Power in order to give light that will help others to see. We must heal ourselves before we can heal others. To use another analogy, we dig a well to receive water. This means life for ourselves, then it is what we can give others. When our own cup is filled, the final goal is to give to others. Hazrat Pir is the living example of the pure fountain which has no expectations from the people who draw water.

CHAPTER 4
METHODS

The methods of psychology can be divided into two types: research methods and methods of psychotherapy. Let us first consider research methods, which should ideally lead us to knowledge and to truth. Is not the purpose of doing research to discover truth?

Historically and cross-culturally, in almost all societies, the true scientist, the true scholar, the true researcher, is invariably in a small minority, and is often criticized or even persecuted for speaking the truth. As mentioned previously, Socrates, Galileo and Sammelweis are classic examples. New ideas are rarely welcome. People prefer recitations of the past. Obviously, these perceptions and behaviors affect psychological researchers and research, exerting an ever present hidden force, which tends to adversely affect the search for truth in many subtle ways.

The key to research lies in properly formulating the question to be asked or investigated, and in using the appropriate method to find the answer. What is the question, how it is defined, and the method used to find the answer determine the value of research. To return to the analogy of the lamp, contemporary psychological research methods ask and answer questions about all the measurable physical characteristics of the lamp—the size, shape, color, weight, height, etc. All the methods currently used in psychology are physical, based on the five physical senses and their more sensitive mechanical extensions. Such research may be impeccable, "safe" from attack. It also has not resulted in many major contributions to knowledge.

Psychologists attempt to set up "objective" experiments, in which the researcher does not affect the results in any way. This has proved to be impossible, for several reasons. First, the initial selection of a topic or question involves a value choice—there are countless numbers of areas that could be investigated. Second, as quantum mechanics has so clearly illustrated, the mere act of observation affects the results. Third, no scientist is value-free, and our own personal biases, perceptions, and past experiences affect whatever we do. Today, psychologists attempt to minimize these sorts of influences. Different areas of psychological study use different research methods. *All* the methods are based on information obtained through the physical senses.

Experimental psychologists work primarily in laboratories, usually in colleges or universities. When they have a question they wish answered, they attempt to set up an experiment to determine the answer. They are infamous for using rats and/or college students as subjects. They use very diverse kinds of experimentation, from testing the neural impulses of a squid, to the electrical patterns of the brain, to eye movements during sleep, to memorization time of nonsense syllables, to the behavioral effects of drugs. An experimental approach requires a method of measurement, a quantitative evaluation. Behaviorists belong in this category, and they are concerned with observable, measurable behavior, not with any subjective experience, such as thoughts or emotions. Behavior is treated as an object. Famous experimental psychologists include B.F. Skinner, who taught pigeons how to bowl, and Harry Harlow, who took baby monkeys away from their mothers and gave them "surrogate mothers" of wire or terry cloth, then studied the monkeys' behavior as adults.

Developmental psychologists, who tend to focus on children, frequently study their behavior in the natural environment, observing and describing behavior as it happens. Piaget began his developmental theory by carefully observing and noting the behavior of his own children. Jane Goodall's observations of chimpanzee behavior "in the wild" is another example of naturalistic observation. Other developmentalists compare various specified tasks or activities for groups of children which differ in some way, perhaps in age. Developmentalists also study a group of subjects over time, with some sort of assessments or measurements being made at specific time intervals. One famous example is the Terman study of gifted children, nicknamed "Termites." The children were initially tested and described, then periodically re-tested throughout their lives, to see how they fared, and they fared well.

In cross-cultural research, groups from different cultures are described and compared. A former head of the National Institute of Mental Health did a fascinating cross-cultural study of the roles of American psychiatrists and African witch-doctors. He found that they played precisely the same role in each society, and had about the same degree of effectiveness. There were even similarities of method, including the use of mind-altering drugs. They simply explained what they did in entirely different terms, using completely different conceptual frameworks.

Harry Stack Sullivan insisted that all we could learn of personality, and what formed it originally, were the human relationships in which it was involved and the reciprocal patterns that these relationships formed. This necessitated examining the social interactions as well as the statements of the client or patient. Generally, social psychologists study how the groups or institutions within which human beings function affect their behavior. It is sometimes difficult to discern where social psychology stops and sociology begins, and vice versa. Social psychologists often "set up" situations to determine what people will do, just like "Candid Camera." For example, they might have a "student" drop a big load of books and see how many people stopped to help her.

Physiological psychologists work primarily with animals, not humans, for they study the mechanics of physical functioning, and people are usually not available to be cut open and examined, except as cadavers. They also study and describe the functioning of the various sensory organs—vision, hearing, touch, etc. The results from animal experiments are then extrapolated to humans. Neuropsychologists study the actual physical characteristics of the central nervous system and do experiments to see how it functions. For example, in rats and cats, electrical stimulation of certain parts of the brain is so pleasurable that they will give up everything else, including food, to obtain the stimulation. Information on neuropsychology is also obtained from neurosurgeons and neurologists who work with individual patients who have sustained brain or other central nervous system injuries of various types. Broca discovered the speech center of the brain through the autopsy of a man unable to speak intelligibly. Penfield's brain surgery patients have demonstrated fascinating hemispheric differences.

Clinicians most often use the clinical method, carefully analyzing all the information and materials gathered about a single case. It should be noted that "single-subject" designs are not limited to clinical work, but have a broader prominent history. Two of the most famous "behaviorists," Skinner and Pavlov, based their conclusions on experiments on a single animal, which were then repeatedly replicated on other animals.

Two other methods are popular. One is correlation, that is, using statistical techniques to see how two activities or events co-relate. Clinical psychologists have found, for example, that emergency room admittances go up when the moon is full. Another is the survey method, in which questions are asked of numbers of people, who hopefully answer truthfully, describing their own behavior after the fact, or their expectations about future behavior.

In all cases, the information garnered through the use of these methods is based on the physical senses. Since many methods are dependent on some form of statistical tests, they give us no answers, but only a probability that the answer given may be correct. In most cases, the concern is with measurement. Psychologists want quantifiable data.

Psychotherapy has been called "the talking cure." The numerous different therapeutic approaches use a number of different methods, although most rely primarily on words. Even those using non-verbal techniques, such as art, talk about the works produced. The widely used and also criticized use of prescription drugs will not be considered as a form of psychotherapy.

Figure 3 indicates a number, but by no means all, of the methods utilized in psychotherapy. They are used with individuals, families and groups, depending on the theoretical orientation.

THE METHODS OF SUFISM

Professor Angha teaches that the sciences really can be divided into two categories: "investigating and studying nature," and "cognizing realities."[36] The first is the physics with which we are familiar, and the second is the science of metaphysics. We can think of the dual particle\wave qualities of light as a model. How one observes and measures determines which quality will be manifest. Molana-al-Moazam Hazrat Shah Maghsoud Sadegh Angha teaches that "in order to cognize life and its mysteries, the material laboratory experiences should be used as an introduction." One begins with the physical realm, then progresses to the metaphysical. "Although the experimental sciences do provide solutions

FIG. 3: SOME METHODS USED IN VARIOUS APPROACHES TO PSYCHOTHERAPY

Method	Major Users
Words, Talking	**All: Primary Method**
Art	Art Therapy
Bibliotherapy (reading books)	Selected Therapists
Bodywork, Body Manipulation	Body Therapies (Rolfing, etc.)
Breathing Exercises	Selected Therapists
Concentration (called Meditation)	Transpersonal, selected Therapists
Dance	Dance Therapy
Diet, Exercise	Holistic Therapies
Dream Analysis	Psychoanalysis, Gestalt, Psychodynamic
Genograms (family histories)	Family Systems
"Homework" Assignments	Behaviorists, Cognitive Therapists
Mind-altering Drugs (non-medical)	A Small Number of Therapists
Movement	Movement Therapy
Music	Music Therapy, Psychosynthesis
Pet Therapy (having pets)	Humanistic
Play Therapy	Many, for Children
Poetry	Eclectic, Humanistic
Projective Techniques	Psychoanalysis, Psychodynamic
Psychodrama	Selected Therapists
Relaxation	Selected Therapists
Script Analysis	Transactional Analysis
Tests: Personality, IQ	Selected Therapists
Visualization	Selected Therapists
Words, written: logs, autobiography, etc.	Selected Therapists

to the problems of physical life, they are limited in their research to specific natural phenomena. At times they are subject to exaggeration and error, and they make no reference to spirituality in order to enhance their search for the discovery of truth."[37] Science, including psychology, simply cannot explain, and thus ignores, countless observable phenomena attributed by religious persons to the soul. In order to understand these phenomena, physical and metaphysical research methods must be used.

"Know Thyself." has been the dictate of wise men for millennia. In Sufism, the individual human being is the subject, the laboratory, and the researcher. The *salik* (seeker) is taught by the teacher how to conduct the experiments so that the desired results may be attained. The totality is studied—mentally, physically, emotionally and spiritually. The salik studies him or herself, carefully and precisely, internally and in interaction with the environment and various environmental circumstances, physically and metaphysically. All the research methods of science are used. Every aspect of human behavior, and every important element affecting human behavior, is examined in detail. All the human emotions and the circumstances which appear to produce them are surveyed. The functioning of all physiological systems, including the brain and central nervous system, is examined. The role of "intellect" and how the organism best learns and retains what is learned is studied, and the results incorporated into future research work. All aspects of external influence on the individual are carefully examined, from the varied and often subtle effects of consuming various types of foods to the impact of sun spots. Of course, all types of human interactions, including familial, friendship, organizational, community, and cultural interactions markedly impact us, so they are also carefully examined. Emphasis is placed on study of the spiritual or religious realm, and the role of the Creator in the life of the individual human. The teacher ensures studies are repeated over and over again until there is no doubt about the results, for they have been oft replicated. No statistical tests are necessary, for there is no question of probability. The *salik* learns and knows, from their own repeated experience. The research process itself, as it is experienced, stimulates and alters, and shows the way to God.

Through this method, the *salik's* inherent abilities are developed and trained. Hazrat Pir emphasizes that all of one's energies need to be concentrated and directed toward the goal in order to attain it. Through concentration and meditation, one is able:

...to overcome the disturbances and dispersion of energies. Focusing—meaning concentration—is gathering all the energy on the sources. Remember there are thirteen sources which are extremely active in this system and work both ways, in the metaphysical and physical states. That is, if there is a certain illness or weakness in a certain organ of the individual, that source for some reason is not functioning well. Either it has been disconnected from outside energies, or it has been mis-used by the individual, who then is not able to direct the ener-gies toward that organ. The main source is the source of life, which is sitting in the heart.

Concentration and meditation are two steps. What is com-monly called meditation—the body, the mind, and so forth—is concentration. Meditation is a very delicate state. When the individual is able to reach the state of proper concentration, that's the first step toward meditation. Meditation means absolute awareness. Absolute awareness does not mean that my eyes are able to see beyond this wall. That's not absolute awareness. Absolute awareness means that the body is intact, as is the metaphysical state. In other words, whatever does exist from the lower level to the higher level, all as one unit, in harmony, presents itself. What direction do you want to use it? It will give you any answers. Concentration and meditation direct the individual to describe and discover the source of life.[38]

Metaphysically, cognition of truth is possible by the light of faith and heart discovery. The most important and the essential element of the Sufi method is the presence of the Teacher. *Arif*s have used the analogy of a mirror for centuries in their teachings, and it is still useful today. The Sufi *Arif* acts as a mirror, reflecting everything about the salik, internally and externally, so that the *salik* can see himself, and may be cleansed and purified. As the salik describes the *Arif*: "You are the mirror of my heart."

Sufism has been described as the alchemy of consciousness. It is the human experience of the ancient art of transmutation of base metal into shining gold. As the medieval alchemist patiently worked to transform the metals, utilizing sulfur and mercury, so the modern Pir patiently, slowly and gradually, transforms the *salik*, turning the baseness of physical desires and motivations into the shining gold of spiritual enlightenment. The medieval alchemist did not display the results of his work until it was completed, and pure gold was visible. The work of the Pir is constantly visible, and the slow and gradual change occurring is obvious both to the participant and observers.

Returning to the analogy of the lamp, psychological research describes all the different kinds and sizes and shapes of lamps, and the different kinds of bulbs and switches and shades. It describes the materials and the finishes, and the possible placements or most appropriate usage. It compares and contrasts different kinds of lamps. In contrast, Sufi research methods are a process of experiential discovery of preparation for making the connection with the source of power that lights the lamp.

The therapeutic methods used in Sufism are unlimited, for they differ for each and every individual. Depending on the unique genetic heritage and personal experience, as well as wants and needs, the Pir sees that each person receives exactly what is necessary for their own healing process to occur, as a good gardener cares well for each plant.

In *Wealth of Solouk*, Hazrat Pir presents the eight principles of Sufism essential to reaching the final goal:[39]

Zikr	(to remember)—remembering God at all times	
Fikr	(to think, meditate)—being in the state of wondering	
Sahar	(to awaken)—awakening of soul and body	
Jui"i	(to hunger)—having exterior hunger (mind) and interior —hunger (Heart) to persist in the search and to obtain the truth.	
Suamt	(to observe silence)—ceasing to think and talk about worthless things	
Saum	(to fast)—fasting of body and mind	
Khalvat	(to observe solitude)—praying in solitude, externally and internally	
Khidmat	(to serve)—dissolving in the truth of the master and dissolving in the truth of existence, God	

In an interview, Hazrat Pir was asked: "What do I have to do" (in order to change)? He replied: "Nothing. All you have to do is not do what you are doing." [40]

Chapter 5
The Central Nervous System

Physiological psychology studies the physical aspects of the human being. The human body has eleven different systems recognized by medicine, twelve if the immune system is included. These are the nervous system, skeletal system, muscular system, cardiovascular system, integumentary system (the skin), lymph system, endocrine system, urinary system, digestive system, reproductive system, and respiratory system. For the human body to function, each of these systems is necessary, with the exception of the reproductive system. It is necessary for survival of the species, but not for survival of the individual. Our body cannot survive without any one of the other systems.

Psychology focuses its attention primarily on the central nervous system because psychology generally assumes that the mind and brain are synonymous, or at least that the brain is the home of the mind. They also assume that the mind is who we are, and that the way to truth and knowledge is through the mind. This belief is not limited to psychologists, but is widespread in the Western world. This assumption is based on the belief that we are limited to our physical body, our physiological apparatus, and that we do not have a soul. In the lamp analogy, it is as if psychology focused its attention on the wiring and characteristics of the bulb in the lamp, without consideration of the necessity for connection to the source of power.

Neuropsychologists, with the use of information gained from neurologists and neurosurgeons, try to describe the brain and central nervous system and its functioning. They can tell us it is about the size of a grapefruit and weighs about as much as a head of cabbage. It contains one hundred billion neurons or nerve cells, and a greater number of possible interconnections between these cells than the number of atoms in the universe.[41] Although it composes only 2% of our body weight, it uses 20% of the oxygen. The brain is designed primarily to run the human body. They describe the basic and most crucial functions of the central nervous system as being:

* Regulation of bodily activities (temperature, blood flow, digestion, breathing, etc.)

* Stimulation of movement, including speech[42]

* Serving as the communications network

* Maintaining balance (homeostasis)[43]

The peripheral nervous system relays information about the body to the central nervous system, which interprets them and may initiate any action necessary to ensure balance is maintained in many physical aspects, such as acidity\alkalinity and negative-positive electrical potentials. This balance is essential, even at the cellular level. This maintenance of homeostasis is shared with the endocrine glands. Another important activity is to stimulate movement, for muscles cannot contract without stimulation by a nerve impulse, and the digestive glands, if not stimulated, cannot digest food.

It is theorized the nerve impulses travel electro-chemically. A wave of electrical negativity travels along the membrane surface of the nerve cell (neuron), reversing the polarization, at a speed varying from 1.5 feet per second in a small neuron to 368 feet per second in larger ones. The negativity travels the length of the neuron. At the end of the neuron specialized cells (synaptic vesicles) discharge messenger molecules across the tiny gap (synapse) to the next neuron. This causes negativity in the next neuron, and so on. This simple change relays complex information in the same manner that a digital computer does.

An illustration of the complete nervous system resembles nothing so much as the roots of a tree. Various parts of the brain have different jobs. The lower parts of the brain serve as a highway and traffic control center, directing information from the peripheral nervous system. They also control involuntary behavior—behavior we cannot stop through our own will, like breathing. As we travel upward, there is a change to control of voluntary behavior, like taking a drink of water, in the cerebral cortex.

Portions of the brain stem control breathing and heartbeat and help to maintain equilibrium and control such reflexes as swallowing, vomiting, coughing, sneezing, and hiccuping. All incoming information from the body, with the exception of the olfactory bulb, passes through a core of neural tissue called the reticular formation which warns the organism of important incoming information and is a highly selective gateway for sensory data. One author suggests it is: "our source of knowing, and of knowing that we know."[44] The cerebellum, attached to the rear of the brainstem, maintains and adjusts posture and balance and coordinates muscular movement.

The thalamus is the interpretation center for pain, temperature and pressure, and deals with certain emotions and memory. The hypothalamus is only about the size of a pea, but it controls body temperature, regulates thirst and food intake, and helps maintain waking and sleeping patterns.[45] The pineal gland, which reacts strongly to environmental light and is most active at night, acts as a general synchronizing, stabilizing and moderating organ in several physiological processes. These include melatonin secretion, electrical activity of the CNS, locomotor activity, wakefulness/sleep and body temperature cycle.[46, 47] The limbic system is responsible for maintaining homeostasis and also appears to deal with emotional aspects of behavior related to survival, such as pleasure and pain, rage and affection, as well as with memory. On each side of the limbic system are the basal ganglia, which are concerned with control of movement, particularly with initiating movements.

The most fascinating portion of the brain is the intricately enfolded one-eighth inch thick cerebral cortex. Although much descriptive data has been gleaned, medicine and psychology have so far been able to determine almost nothing about how it works. It is considered the "Executive," receiving new information, analyzing and comparing new data with stored information accumulated from prior experiences, making decisions, and sending out orders. The sensory areas interpret sensory impulses, the motor areas control muscular movement, and the association areas are concerned with emotional and intellectual processes. There are specific portions of the cortex dealing with different aspects of eyesight, with movements of the mouth, legs, arms, etc. There are also specific areas dealing with language and speech. Sensory information about different parts of the body is represented in corresponding parts of the brain, in direct proportion to the amount of usage. Our hands are very important to us, so a large amount of space is devoted to them. In contrast, a cat's brain has little space devoted to its paws, but a great deal to its whiskers. In the rat, specific cells respond to specific whiskers.[48]

"Pop" psychology has recently popularized the idea of two brains, the left brain being devoted to certain tasks, the right brain to others. However, this concept is an oversimplification. The hemispheres are specialized to handle different tasks, but the division is not complete, and the two hemispheres are in constant communication. Most complex activities involve both hemispheres. The left hemisphere is primarily involved in language and logic, while the right is much more involved in spatial abilities and "artistic" activities, but both hemispheres are usually involved in these types of activities. These two hemispheres are interconnected by a bridge of some three hundred million nerve fibers, the corpus callosum, which is the largest fiber pathway in the brain.

The electroencephalogram (EEG), has been used to record the electrical current the brain produces, recorded from the surface of the skull. The voltage is very low, only a few millionths of a volt, and "The EEG is a very crude measure, something like recording the overall noise that a city produces."[49]

Despite its crudeness, EEG's have produced interesting results. Writing, supposedly a left-hemisphere task, produced alpha waves at approximately 10 cycles per second in the right hemisphere. Block arranging, supposedly right-hemisphere, produced alpha waves in the left hemisphere. Alpha waves in this case indicate "quieting down," a sort of "turning off." Another study found the right hemisphere "resting" while subjects read technical passages, but active while folk tales were read. Emotion is also reported to be hemispherically connected, with anger in the right hemisphere, and happiness in the left, even in ten month old babies.

Brain Wave Patterns
BETA: 14 to 30 hertz or vibrations per second
ALPHA: 7 to 14 hertz: relaxed, meditative state
THETA: 4 to 7 hertz: facilitates learning & creativity
DELTA: 1 to 3 hertz: Deep sleep

If you do not like your brain wave patterns, you can purchase a "Brain Machine" equipped with opaque goggles with pulsing light and headphones with pulsing sounds, coordinated by a cigarette-pack-sized computer. The theory is that when the synchronizer's lights and sound pulse in alpha range, the user's mind falls in step and slows down. And so on down to deep sleep.

Diet can strikingly affect the brain. MIT studies found eating protein increased serotonin production in the brain. Eating egg yolks or other substances rich in choline dramatically increased the neurotransmitter ACh throughout the brain. Tryptophan, an amino acid, increases the production of the neurotransmitter serotonin. Diet may affect us even before birth. Diets fed to nursing mother rats significantly affect the food preferences of the young; they prefer what the mother ate. Experiments with rats have also demonstrated that malnutrition retards growth, and results in brains with lower weights and less DNA, RNA, lipids and proteins in the brain. There is less exploratory behavior, and increased emotional reactivity. Stimulating environments for young rats have accelerated brain growth, accelerated development, and increased cortex and brain weight. Exploratory behavior is increased, emotionality is decreased, and the survival rate is increased.[50]

The central nervous system is involved in the functioning of all the other systems. A new field of research, Psychoneuroimmunology (PNI) is carefully documenting how these three areas—the mind, the nervous system and the immune system, affect each other, particularly in recovery from disease or injury.[51] Most of the research is being done in medical facilities. Gerard Renoux states: "The brain controls the immune system the same way it controls behavioral activities."[52] They are demonstrating that what we think and feel influences our other systems, specifically our immune system, mediated by the endocrine system. Several best-selling books have addressed this topic.[53] In addition to standard treatments, as well as diet and exercise, methods which have been found to induce a positive effect on the immune system and/or healing include relaxation, visualization, biofeedback, prayer, and meditation.[54]

Theorists have proposed various models for how the brain functions. The computer model is most popular. The anatomical description accepted by most of psychology is that of the brain as an electrochemical biocomputer that is part of our physical body, which is precisely how National Institute of Health researchers envision it. Since we tend to think of our brain as who we are, we may be inclined to dislike such a seemingly mechanical concept.

Karl Pribram has postulated the idea of holography as a model. In holograms, laser light is used to produce a three dimensional image which allows a large number of patterns to be stored on the same plate, and, astonishingly, every portion of the plate reproduces the whole. The entire interference pattern of any scene is recorded simultaneously on all parts of the plate. If you had a screen containing the image, and cut part away, the entire image would still be present, but be fuzzier. The more is cut away, the fuzzier the picture becomes, but it is always present. This model "solves" paradoxes about the brain, including the fact that memories are often left unimpaired by massive destruction of brain tissue. However, it has been pointed out that at every stage in the history of neurology, the brain has been likened to the most complex technology available at the time.[55] Likening it to holography is continuing a time-honored tradition, which will undoubtedly give way to the next appropriate technological discovery.

Laughlin & d'Aquili, in their book, *Biogenetic Structuralism*, propose a neurognostic model, defining neurognosis as "biogenetically given rudimentary information about the world." The neurognostic models are like seeds or crystals around which form universal behavior patterns like sucking, grasping, music, and primary social group identification.[56] An example is Stockholm's Karolinska Institute discovery that the cries of normal infants and the cries of infants who are diseased or brain-damaged are different, recognizable, and give reliable indications of the type of abnormality. They assume this to be due to genetically based neurognosis.

This idea explains the deep similarities found in various human societies by Levi-Strauss, Piaget, Chomsky and others, and the universalities in unconscious production described by Jung. Levi-Strauss and Jung both maintained that the "primitive" mind orders things in terms of opposites. The social process then is a magnification of this initial mental process of binary opposition onto the structure of social institutions."Social institutions then are behavioral exemplars of an underlying neurophysiological structure that regulates human social behavior in a biologically adaptive manner."[57] There are regularities underlying diversity in human society. Social and linguistic universals are manifestations of genetically determined neurognostic models in the deep structure of the brain.

The authors envision normally functioning adults as possessing a number of models of reality that are genetically preconditioned. In other words, we are born with them—we come "pre-wired." Any learned skilled activity, such as writing or tying one's shoes, is said to be laid down in "motor engrams," the engram being the definite and permanent trace left by repeated stimuli in neural tissue. One problem with the idea is that researchers have been searching for engrams, examining DNA and protein molecules, for more than 25 years, with little success.

THE VIEW OF SUFISM

Psychology limits itself almost exclusively to specific physical manifestations. Sufism includes the physical manifestations in a vaster vision of the human being. The methods now being utilized in Psychoneuroimmunology have been used effectively by Sufism for centuries, and are today, under the supervision of Hazrat Pir and in conjunction with other techniques and a spiritual foundation, helping AIDS patients stay healthy. Sufism recognizes and utilizes another system of the human body, the electromagnetic system or field. Various electromagnetic measures, including the EEG already mentioned, and the EKG or electrocardiogram, are standard diagnostic tools in medicine. Several major universities are studying the electromagnetic fields of the human heart and brain, which requires extremely sensitive and expensive equipment. Sufism also considers external influences on the central nervous system, particularly electromagnetic influences.

The view of Sufism is that the brain is not who we are. Our real identity is beyond the physical level. The brain should be a tool used in the service of our true being, an instrument in the service of what many call the soul. In *Al-Rasa'el*, Professor Angha makes an important and extensive comparison between our brain and a computer. Although very fast and precise in computational ability if properly used, it does not possess an innate intelligence to allow it to make decisions, to analyze facts and figures, or to create and construct logical theories. It has only the information and program which has been fed into it, and various processes by which it can manipulate these numbers and symbols.

Psychology appears to mistake the bio-computer for the Intellect which created it. Computers come in different models, for different purposes, and the programs that are fed into them vary enormously. They may or may not be properly cared for. Modern mechanical computers can receive input in typed form, visually through scanning written documents, and in auditory form. The bio-computer receives information through the senses of taste and smell as well. All the input is from sensory data, from the externalities, the form, shape, size and appearances of things. For example, when we see, we actually see no objects, only the reflection of light off whatever we are observing. Our brain receives the messages, and how it responds is dependent upon what has come into it. Output is dependent on input. The computer transmits the wave patterns that the senses relay through their interaction with the environment. Therefore, "It is incapable of differentiating between good and evil, truth and falsehood, because its sole source of knowledge is the input it receives from the physical comparisons."[58] Its outputs, inputs and responses "depend on its inherent program, the forces influencing it and the existing universal order." [59]

The memory of the unit, considered to be its "personality," is limited, and reflects a specific computer language which is decoded on tapes or discs. The computer does not have an innate intelligence; it functions according to the program. Even when the computer is given the correct program and data, if the temperature of the unit is not at its point of balance, either it will not function or it will not give the correct response. Professor Angha tells us: "If the given inputs are incorrect, its output is also incorrect. As its information is based on the superficial understanding of appearances and on the capabilities of the senses, and because knowledge is based on physical observations and comparisons and results in images formed in the mind, the brain cannot discover the truth."[60] The brain cells and the logic of nature are useful in everyday life, but they are not sufficient for inner guidance, and knowledge based on such activity cannot discover the truth. Its teachers are not acknowledged for inner guidance by the enlightened. The salik must learn to still and relinquish his mind. He must learn to let his brain perform its primary function, the physiological management of the body. The Holy Quran states: "With Him are the Keys of the Unseen, the treasures that none knoweth but He." They are not in the brain or the mind.

Relinquishing the mind means removing all the images, concepts, fantasies and imaginings that exist through relationships, associations and recollections from sensory data registered in the memory. The enlightened have called these temptations, for they are the creation of the mind and the self, and are thus desires. This is not true of inner cognition, which is the result of Divine Guidance.[61] For inner cognition to occur, physiological changes are necessary, and occur gradually, over time. The salik changes physically as well as mentally, emotionally and spiritually, and the various types of physical exercises taught in the Meditation classes assist in this process.

An interviewer, describing how her mind refused to be quiet when she tried to meditate, told Hazrat Pir that her brain was her enemy.[62] He agreed with her. He uses the analogy that the brain is like Pharaoh when Moses tried to lead the children of Israel out of Egypt. God gave Moses numerous miracles, which he performed, but Pharaoh refused to believe in God, no matter how much evidence was amassed, no matter how many miracles occurred. He stubbornly insisted on his own superiority. Moses defied Pharaoh and led his followers out of Egypt. Pharaoh's army pursued them until the Red Sea, which had parted to allow Moses and his followers to pass through, drowned Pharaoh's forces.

In addition to sensory input, we cannot avoid being constantly influenced by many external forces of which we are unaware. Gravity holds us to the earth, air pressure is constantly exerting force upon us, but we rarely, if ever, even give their influence a second thought. The new interdisciplinary field of bio-electro-magnetism studies electromagnetic phenomena between and within biological systems, including human beings. Physicists speak of unified electromagnetic interaction as one of the four fundamental forces of nature. Biophysicists consider electromagnetism the essential force responsible for all atomic and molecular (chemical) interactions, and therefore for all life. However, although Faraday and Maxwell demonstrated in the mid 1800's that electromagnetism was a single fundamental force, science was quick to apply the ideas to machinery, but is really just beginning to study the influence of external fields on humans.

Research done at Northwestern University by Frank Brown "suggests that man may be a more diversely sensitive creature, more subject to the invisible influences of the surrounding universe than Western science usually considers him.[63]" He found many aspects of behavior to be influenced by forces in ways of which we are probably totally unaware. Brown found many organisms respond to cosmic radiation and electromagnetic fields. He believes "all living organisms gain information about time and orientation in space from weak electromagnetic fields in the environment." In his terms, these fields are used by the central nervous system and provide a kind of medium enabling the bioelectric activity of the brain. This concept gains importance when we realize that the earth itself is a huge magnet, with bands of magnetic force whose lines of changing field strength lie between the North and South poles. His work is supported by that of the physicist Y. Rocard at the University of Paris. He planted electric coils underground to create changes in magnetic strength, and was able to condition the ability of people to detect very tiny (.3 to 1.0 milligauss) changes in the magnetic field.

In addition to the external forces, we have our own "pre-wired" and persistent internal influences. Biological rhythms have been found in all plants, animals and humans. High-frequency rhythms (millisecond to second range) appear in individual cells, specific tissues and single organs. Medium frequency (minute and hour range) arise in regulatory processes and complex functional systems. Low frequency rhythms involve the whole organism or even entire populations. In this range, there is a close relationship between biological and environmental rhythms.[64] These cycles mirror fluctuations in cosmic radiation, such as solar flares and geomagnetic disturbances.

Responses to some of these influences are mediated by the brain. However, the primary effect occurs in the thirteen major electromagnetic centers of the body. Strengthening these centers, and concentrating on attaining harmony, unity and balance between them, is a major focus in the Concentration and Meditation methods of Sufism. All living organisms, plant and animal, have measurable energy fields. The human energy field has been depicted for centuries in art, most often as the halo around the heads of saints and prophets. However, the direction of the field is actually from front to back rather than across the top of the head. This field is generated by thirteen electromagnetic centers, which "are constantly in contact with the currents of existence."[65] These centers are entirely different from "chakras." The magnetic body cannot be felt. We have to see it with the inner eye. Most of us have met someone we loved or hated almost instantly. This is the result of fields of power, not "vibrations." Most people waste their magnetic powers.

The most important magnetic source in the body is the solar plexus, located just below the end of the breast bone or sternum. Its magnetic particles are directly fostered by sunlight. The brain is another, and the heart a third. Connection and unification of these three centers opens the gate to the celestial and incorporeal world. Concentration and focusing of magnetics on the source located between the eyebrows produces the potential for telepathy and most of the subjects related to the "sixth sense." Other sources include the last vertebra of the spinal column (kundalini), and the fontanels, which can serve as a sort of radar, as well as the head of the medulla oblongata, which, when in proper communication and unification with the spinal column, enables one to perform extraordinary actions.

The process of concentration in Sufism is "performed on the source of life in the heart and the magnetic source which is located under the sternum, and then will be expanded to the brain."[66] When a state of true concentration is attained and sustained, then the forces of Pharaoh will be drowned, and the journey to the promised land can be completed. As Professor Angha tells us in *The Mystery of Humanity*: " Gather all your energies and concentrate them on the source of life in your heart for your findings to become imperishable so that you will live in balance and tranquillity and know eternity."[67]

CHAPTER 6
SENSATION AND PERCEPTION

We learn about the physical world through the information relayed to us by our five senses. Psychology and biology describe the physical characteristics of the sense organs, and can partially describe how they function. It is clear that we come "pre-wired"—we are born with built-in reactions to specific smells and tastes and with the knowledge of how to use the senses. Very young infants respond to stimulation of each of the five sensory modalities—taste, touch, smell, sight and sound.

TOUCH

Some experts say the most important sense organ is our skin, which most people probably do not think of as a sense organ at all.[68] We can survive without the use of our other sense organs, but cannot survive without our skin. Touch is often little noticed until some extreme sensation is experienced.

The layer of skin on the outside, the wrapper around our bag of fluid, is completely dead. There are no nerve endings, and hence, no feeling. Feeling starts at the inner layer of the epidermis, utilizing some 640,000 receptors distributed unevenly over the body. In addition to these skin or surface receptors, we also have deep receptors buried within our muscles that tell us the size, weight and shape of objects.

There are only four primary qualities of touch which are actually experienced. These are pressure, cold, warmth, and pain. All the tactile sensations, the silkiness of satin, the roughness of sandpaper, the softness of a fuzzy stuffed animal, the coolness of marble, are simply variations on these four qualities.[69] There are secondary qualities, but these are dependent on either intermittent stimulation of primary qualities, as in itching, which is intermittent pain, or tickling, which is intermittent pressure, or on combinations of the primary qualities. The nerve endings then relay the information received to the brain, which "translates" it based on prior experience. The information sent to the brain is limited to location, quality—pain or pressure, quantity or strength, and the duration of the stimulation.

We may not think of it as touch, but pain receptors are found not only in the skin, but in practically every tissue of the body. Excessive stimulation causes pain. When stimuli for other sensations, such as pressure, heat, or cold, reach a certain threshold, they stimulate pain as well. Muscle spasms or prolonged contractions, inadequate blood flow and the presence of certain chemical substances can also cause pain. Pain receptors therefore perform a protective function by identifying changes that may endanger the body.[70] The ability of the brain to locate pain is based on past experience. With somatic, or surface pain, it usually accurately projects the pain back to the stimulated area. If you burn your finger, your finger hurts. However, in most cases, visceral pain is "referred," that is, it is felt somewhere else rather than the point of stimulation. For example, the pain of a heart attack is usually felt in the skin over the heart and along the left arm. One phenomena which science has not been able to explain is the "phantom pain" experienced by patients who have had a limb amputated. They still feel pain in the extremity as if the limb were still there.

High-voltage sparks may be jumped to the skin to stimulate receptors. If the amperage (rate of current flow) is kept small, no shock will be felt. Instead, the subject will feel pressure, warmth, cold, pain, or combinations of them.[71]

TASTE

Taste buds are located throughout the mouth, upon the tongue, palate, pharynx, larynx, tonsils, and epiglottis, but the most receptive region is the upper surface of the tongue. Taste buds are grouped on the tongue into some 9000 small mounds, called papillae. These cells live only about eight days, constantly regenerating. The taste buds within these mounds are connected to two nerves, which come together at the back part of the brain stem. They then travel to the thalamus at the front of the brain stem and thence to the cerebral cortex of the brain. Here the signals are interpreted, and we become aware of taste.

We relish rich ice cream or imported chocolates, or a fine cheese, and pride ourselves on being "gourmets." But we only have four tastes: sourness, sweetness, saltiness and bitterness. That's all. A great deal of what we consider the "flavor" of foods is dependent on smell, not taste. Newborn infants react strongly to taste, preferring sweetness. Taste changes as we grow up, for previously unpleasant tastes later come to be enjoyed.

SMELL

The least studied sense is that of olfaction or smell. We detect smells by breathing air that carries odors. The aroma of fresh-baked bread, lemon rind, a rose, or French perfume, all come from molecules of gas that have been released into the air from differing substances. The olfactory receptors are located at the top back of our nostrils. Each time we inhale through our nose, the air passes the protruding olfactory cilia (hairs). Information about the gaseous molecules is carried by neurons to the olfactory bulbs, which lie directly beneath the frontal cerebral cortex.[72] Olfaction, or smell, is the only sensory modality which does not have to travel through the various parts of the brain lying below the cortex, for stimulation of the olfactory receptors is directly relayed to the cortex of the brain.

The processes by which we smell, distinguish between smells, recognize smells, recall memories associated with smells and react emotionally with feelings of delight or utter disgust to certain smells are little understood. What limited research has been done indicates that our sense of smell is 10,000 times more sensitive than our sense of taste. Some theorists divide smell into four types, others six, still others, into seven detectable primary odors: camphoraceous (mothballs and camphor), musky, floral, minty, ethereal (dry cleaning fluid), pungent (vinegar), and putrid (rotten egg).[73] The human nose is extremely sensitive to the smell of rotting meat, and can detect 1/400-billionth of a gram of this odor in a quart of air.

At birth, babies who have never eaten react visibly to certain strong smells. A one month old infant can distinguish and prefers its own mother from others on the basis of smell.[74] Women have a better sense of smell than men, due to higher levels of the female hormone estrogen, known to activate the olfactory receptors. The sensitivity of women varies with their hormonal cycle, becoming enormously greater during periods of high estrogen production. Most people can recognize several hundred odors; a skilled chemist may distinguish between several thousand.

Some fragrances have a calming effect, and can actually lower blood pressure. Yale has taken out a patent on an apple-spice fragrance because it stops panic attacks in some people. The smell of a beach decreases anxiety levels.

SIGHT

The beauty of a sunrise, an exquisite seashell, or a perfect blossom are all dependent upon a one inch watery ball, of which only 1/6 is exposed. Light rays enter the eye through the cornea and pass through the lens and the jelly-like substance behind the lens. The innermost layer, the retina, lines the rear 3/4 of the eyeball. The retina includes a layer of light-sensitive nerve cells, called rods and cones because of their shape. The 125 million rods in each eye are very sensitive to light intensity and enable you to see in dim light. The 7 million cones of each eye detect color and fine detail, and are stimulated only by bright light, which is why we cannot see color by moonlight.[75] Cones are most concentrated in the fovea, a depression in the macula lutea or yellow spot in the exact center of the retina, at the back of the eye.

As light waves enter, they pass through the pupil and lens to the retina, forming an upside-down image of whatever is being looked at. The rods and cones receive the light waves and translate the information into nerve impulses. The impulses are transmitted along retinal nerve fibers, to the optic nerve, a stalk-like collection of nerves that connect the rear of the retina to the brain. At what is called the optic chiasma, about half the nerves cross over into the other side of the brain from the eye from which they come, and half continue on the same side of the brain, until they terminate in the thalamus. The information received is then relayed from the thalamus by more neurons, finally reaching the visual area of the cortex, which is in the occipital lobes at the very back of the brain. The brain then interprets the impulses received from each eye, reverses the images, and integrates them into one image.

It is not known how we see color. None of the theories advanced adequately explain the phenomena.

Hearing

The sounds of chalk scraping on a blackboard, a crying baby, and a Beethoven symphony are produced by the motion or vibration of some active body, which sends waves through the atmosphere. If the vibrations occur regularly, a musical sound if produced. Irregular sounds experienced by the ear are considered "noise." Generally, a noise has a rapid alternation of different kinds of sensations of sounds. Musical tones, in contrast, have an undisturbed, uniform sound, and are considered the simplest and most regular elements of the sensation of hearing.

The various sound waves have three qualities. The higher the number of vibrations, the higher or shriller is the sound produced, the lower the number of vibrations, the lower the sound, or pitch. The deepest sound we can hear is around 16 hertz (vibrations per second). If we double that frequency 10 times, (add 10 octaves), we attain 16,000 hertz, which is about where our hearing ends. We can visualize sound as producing waves just like a pebble thrown into a pond produces waves around its point of entry.

The width, or amplitude of the wave, corresponds with the loudness of the sound. The form of the wave corresponds with the quality of the sound. Loudness of sound is measured in decibels. Zero decibels is barely audible. Normal conversation is about 60 decibels and a power mower or subway over 100. Prolonged exposure to sound over 85 decibels can damage the inner ear and cause deafness. Sounds over 130 decibels, which is the threshold of pain, are an immediate threat to hearing.

When the sound waves reach our body, the external ear helps channel the waves down the ear canal, until they hit the eardrum, which begins to vibrate. It is so sensitive it can register amplitudes less than the diameter of a hydrogen atom. The vibrations pass through the tiniest bones in the body, the hammer, anvil, and then the stirrup, which taps on the oval window and vibrates the fluid of the cochlea. Tiny hairs that line the cochlea change the vibrations in the fluid into nerve impulses (in some undiscovered manner), which are transmitted to the brain by the auditory nerve. The brain then translates the impulses. This basic hearing is supplemented by vibrations conducted through the bones of the skull to the inner ear, which is how we primarily hear the sound of our own voice.

Our ears also serve another function. In the labyrinth of our inner ear, known as the semi-circular canals, is the most important receptor of balance. It regulates all the others distributed through the body, and is the only receptor that can measure angular velocity, and never sleeps. All our other senses switch off in sleep, except the inner ear.

Sound is numerical—computational. Music is precisely arithmetic. For hundreds of thousands of years sounds have fed us with number—with an immediacy and directness unparalleled in our other senses. The old Indo-European linguistic root ar signifies both harmony and number, as in the Greek harmonia and arithmos. Leibniz stated: music is "the concealed art of computation for a soul unaware of its counting."

Our eyes cannot inform us that the wavelength of purple (760nm) is twice that of violet (about 380nm). The eye can only compare and estimate. The ear measures. There are three times as many nerve connections between the ear and the brain as between the eye and the brain. How is it, then, that some of us hear conversations, the garbage truck and the neighbor's cat, and others hear God?

The role of the brain in the "translation" of the data received from the various sensory mechanisms is of crucial importance. The nerve endings from the sensory modalities are simply providing information. The brain gives meaning to that information, and the interpretation of the mind may be affected by numerous factors. A psychology text gives a simple example. Suppose we are going to bed, and just before we lie down, we see a spider run down the wall behind the headboard. Then we lie down, and a thread from the pillow case lightly touches our cheek. How will our brain interpret that? It is likely we will think: "Spider!"

PERCEPTION

Perception is not just a visual phenomena, whatever we "see," physically. Developmentalists consider perception to be the element of understanding of the sensory input provided to the brain by the senses, relayed through our central nervous system. In other words, perception is the brain's translation of information provided to it by all the physical senses. Whatever already exists in our minds, all our wants and desires and prejudices and needs and past experiments, help to define our perception. Often these mental elements may affect our perception more than our senses do. Our "software," our computer program, determines what we think we see, hear, feel, taste and touch. Many experiments demonstrate the effects of perception, but its development and the method of its operation are surrounded in mystery.

Our culture systematically teaches us not only what to perceive, but which sensory modalities to use to perceive. For example, in the United States, most children enter school with stronger auditory strengths. But between kindergarten and sixth grade, vision becomes the dominant modality, as teachers suppress audition in an effort to maintain a quiet classroom, and encourage the visual modality.[76]

Attention is the first stage of perception, for attention is the means of selecting incoming messages from the mass of data. Very intense stimuli —those that are louder, brighter, larger, more irritating—gain attention. Repetitious stimuli gain attention. Attention is also related to contrast or change in stimulation. We quickly habituate and then respond less to an unchanging stimulus. Motivation strongly affects attention. If we are hungry, we notice restaurants and food ads. Advertisers take advantage of this by using sex and anxiety over sexual attractiveness in many ads.

Expectation (perceptual expectancy) is probably the largest element of perception. We are creatures of "perceptual habit." We see what we have learned to see and expect to see, and we hear what we have learned to hear and expect to hear. And if we do not, our totalitarian ego simply filters it out, so it does not even register. Through our life experiences, we learn to expect certain behaviors from others, as well as from ourselves. Through expectations, we feel reasonable, satisfied and safe in making assumptions about ourselves, others, and the world around us. Most of these assumptions are based on the notion of constancy of the physical world, which is a false assumption. There is nothing in the physical world which could not be gone tomorrow.

Typical human perception has certain characteristics. We tend to perceive objects rather than the sensory qualities registered. In other words, we see green trees instead of just patches of green. We also think of objects as remaining like they were when we perceived them. So we still think of our childhood friends as young, even years later, unless we see them in the meantime. We do not react equally to all stimuli. To do so would be impossible, so we focus on a few. We may pay attention to certain preferred stimuli, and ignore others. A mother can hear her baby's faint cry despite distracting noise. We may listen to music in the midst of loud background noise. Labeling strongly affects our perception of ambiguous figures. Many studies indicate what figures are seen depend on what words they are called. Another study documented how psychologists who viewed a fifteen minute videotaped interview saw the person in the video one way when he was described as a job applicant, and entirely differently when he was described as a mental patient.

Most introductory psychology texts have examples of common visual misperceptions. They show two lines of the same length, but one has arrow points on each end. It looks shorter than the same line without points. Another popular example is a top hat. The width of the hat brim and the height of the hat are the same, but it looks taller. Cross-hatched lines make the lines they cross appear shorter. As, for example, Є and C. An old party game illustrates what happens with auditory perception. A sentence is written down, then whispered into the ear of the next person, who repeats it to the next person, and so on, until everyone has heard the sentence. The difference from beginning to end is almost always marked, and may be amazing.

It is well documented that we hear and see what we want to, and make judgments and decisions according to our own preconceived notions. As one psychologist titled his chapter on perception, "Believing is Seeing."[77] And our perception can fool us in many other ways. McConnell flatly states: "your sensory receptors lie to you constantly, and your brain knows it. Your eyes are particularly bad about lying—which is to say that the world is full of visual illusions. And if you are to survive, you have got to find a way to perceive the difference between illusion and reality."[78]

If we become knowledgeable in physics, we discover just how illusionary our perceptions really are. Max Born states: "Matter as given by our senses appears as a secondary phenomenon, created by the interaction of our sense organs with processes whose nature can be discovered only indirectly through theoretical interpretations of experimentally observed relationships. (I see something in my environment—I touch it and it feels solid.) To designate the result of this operation by the old word "matter" seems to be wrong."[79] Our sense organs actually experience waves. We do not see an object, we see the light reflected from it. From these waves, our intellect creates "things." However, according to quantum physics, when we move to the microscopic level, subatomic particles are not matter, but energy waves of varying frequencies that interact to create the illusion of matter. The effect of energy vibrating at different frequencies coincides with our sensory perceptions of solids, liquids and gases, as well as heat, color and sound.[80]

THE PERSPECTIVE OF SUFISM

Our physical senses cannot discover truth because they are changeable, unstable and inconstant. "Sensual observations and experiences happen repeatedly, and every time they happen, they acquire special characteristics completely different from those they had before."[81] For example, our idea of something so simple as what is blue changes with each additional sight of a new hue we think of as blue. Since they are changeable and inconstant, the patterning set up within the brain on the basis of them must also be changeable and inconstant. It is important to understand that the senses and their different levels of contact with the environment are solely for the purpose of survival and social interaction and do not define the individual nor define reality. They are unable to convey the delicate spiritual truths.[82]

Professor Angha tells us: "What causes man's eminent position to be degraded is his dependence and his reliance on his perceptions, on sense organs that distort them in proportion of their limited capabilities and shun the ultimate reality, that veils of ignorance cover, that prevails!"[83] He states, in *The Mystery of Humanity*:

> The eyes see, the nose smells, the taste-buds taste, the ears hear, and the fingers feel roughness and softness, warmth and cold. Senses are for feeling and contact with nature. Mistakes made by them will not be questioned, their task is to feel the outside of things; their pleasure is the unknown states of the nervous system. We will not acquire the true knowledge of life through any findings resulting from the transactions of our sensory organs; the transient faces of nature and their different states are the short-lived, shallow ripples on the sea of life. Remaining attached to them is painful, and parting from them is what brings peace and happiness.
>
> Treachery of the senses and nerves and their natural tendencies is a false shadow of the real you, an unrealistic existence which you refer to as "I," and in this false state of recognition you remain until your death. Breaking away from this delusion is the beginning of your coming upon yourself, and finding the truth of "I" in tranquillity and freedom.[84]

How can we do so? How, then, can we hear God? Psychology does not address this issue. Both The Holy Bible and The Holy Quran are very specific. In them, Jesus and Muhammad both state that the teachings are for those "who have eyes to see and ears to hear." Now Jesus and Muhammad were prophets. They knew that our eyes and ears performed everyday physical functioning. That could not be what they were talking about. The vision and hearing to which the verses allude must be something entirely different, something stable, constant, and unchangeable. As Professor Angha states: It is necessary to know at this point that the activities of the ear, eyes and other organs are different from the nature of sight, hearing, smell, and so on. The calculations of the brain and the responses based on the limited inputs of the senses do not entail eternal truths and thus they are unable to cognize them.[85] It is an inner vision, an inner hearing of the soul, that is the seeing and hearing of which the Prophets speak. Through our five senses, we painstakingly scrutinize superficial things. With vision we observe the essence of the Universe.

Sufism is the Way of the Prophets; it is an experience of the inner vision and hearing spoken of in the Holy Books. God is always broadcasting His Word, but we cannot hear it. We are not tuned in to His channel, or if we are, there is so much interference from sensory data and a chattering brain that we cannot understand Him. Sufism teaches the way to Tune In, to develop the eyes to see and the ears to hear with which were born, but which we have forgotten how to use. Regaining this capacity is learning how to make the essential and necessary connection to the Source of Power for the light in the lamp analogy.

Developing our innate capacity for inner vision and hearing is a gradual process involving substantial physiological change at the cellular level, with a resulting slowly increasing awareness. It requires patience and endurance, and taming our brain so that it does not interfere in the process. The brain is like a young colt that must be trained to accept a bridle, saddle, and rider. When it is quiet, we may tune in to the Divine Melody.

At certain times in our life, the subtle, divine song of the Timeless Player, the voice radiating light, comes. We hear or we do not hear. It comes three times in our life. We may listen and respond. If we do not answer, we are lost forever. The time is frighteningly short—a brief moment in the enormity of infinity.

CHAPTER 7
MEMORY

Psychologists differ on the definition of memory. Psychology does not know what memory is, where it is, or how it works. Many think it is in the brain. For example, Ornstein assumes and states: "The structure or architecture of memory in the brain is almost completely unknown, one of the great unsolved mysteries,."[86] As indicated earlier, a number of scientists have been unsuccessfully searching for physical representations of memories (engrams) in the brain for more than 25 years, examining RNA and protein molecules.[87] Other scientists insist there simply is not sufficient room in the brain for all our memories. Experiments on flatworms showed that if you cut a flatworm in half, both halves remembered, not just the brain half. Both sides regenerated and there was no difference in subsequent memory.

Psychologists state that what is known about memory cannot be described by a few basic laws. Most of what we know is limited to specific bits of information. Memory is considered to be dynamic, and determined by:

* Characteristics of the Learner: attitude, knowledge, etc.
* Nature of the Materials: sensory mode, structure, difficulty, etc.
* Learning Activities: attention, practice, elaboration, etc.
* Type of Memory: recognition, recall, transfer, etc.

"Memory for complex events is sometimes startlingly accurate; it is also frequently incomplete and occasionally highly distorted."[88] Memory can be changed by being influenced by someone else's description.

The central ideas in memory research deal with how we remember new information (encoding), and how we locate what we remember when we need it (retrieval). Numerous theories have been advanced to explain memory. Schema theory proposes that what is stored in memory "is heavily determined by a guiding schema or knowledge framework that selects and actively modifies experience in order to arrive at a coherent, unified, expectation-confirming and knowledge-consistent representation of an experience."[89] In other words, somehow we each individually construct and utilize an internal scheme (script or pattern) which governs our memory. Some researchers insist we have two kinds of memory, explicit and implicit[90]. Explicit memory involves conscious recollection of the past, and most research has been done in this area. Implicit memory involves retention without conscious awareness. In other words, we learn something and retain it unconsciously. Examples include the learning of complicated skills, such as riding a bicycle.

Several investigators have studied memory of complex sentences and stories. Once the meaning of a sentence is grasped, the meaning is retained, but the exact wording is not. Sentences and paragraphs tend to be recalled better when they "go together" than when they do not. Not only the interrelationships, but the learner's general knowledge, affect retention. The meaning of any sentence or story is recalled better than the surface details, even though details are remembered.

Novelty also affects memory. We remember what is typical better than what is atypical or novel. This is probably related to the findings that we remember more information about fields in which we are knowledgeable. For example, physicians remember more about medicine, psychologists more about psychology, etc. Pictures and words are evidently handled differently in memory, but how this occurs is unknown.[91] Drugs can interfere with learning and markedly affect memory. Clustering or chunking material into similar categories and organizing categories improves memory, makes it easier.

Psychologists think we have three different kinds of memory: sensory, which is as if we saw a photo of it in our brain, short-term memory, and long term memory. Short-term or immediate memory, what we can hold in immediate awareness at any given moment, is surprisingly limited—to the "magical number," about seven items for the average adult. In contrast, some visual memory persists remarkably. Students were shown, for two seconds only, more than 2,000 slides of people and scenes. The next day, they were shown the same slides again, each paired with a new slide. They were able to indicate which of the two slides they had already seen with 90% accuracy. Short-term memory is easily erased by any interference, and unless something seems important, it is soon forgotten.

Experiments on rats indicate that electroconvulsive shock (ECS), given immediately after learning, results in no memory of the learning. However, if an hour or more passes after the learning before the shock is administered, it does not affect the learning. Severe trauma can produce the same effect. So there seems to be something different about old and new learning. It almost appears as if new memories require some time to become part of the permanent memory pattern or traces. Some researchers believe it takes some thirty minutes or so for long-term memory to file an item away.

Obviously, long-term memory (LTM) lasts. It is thought to be practically limitless, like an unbelievably large library. Neurosurgeon Wilder Penfield claimed that memory records the past like "a continuous strip of movie film, complete with sound track." Penfield's epileptic patients had vivid memories when certain parts of their brain were stimulated during surgery.

Many stories are told of amnesia, the inability to remember old memories, as the result of head injuries. Such amnesia is usually temporary. Psychology cannot explain it, nor can psychology explain what happens to memory when we are asleep or "unconscious." Psychologists do not know what causes us to forget. They speculate that new learning can interfere with old learning (retroactive inhibition). We also appear to forget because of interference caused by associations from earlier learning (proactive inhibition). Most forgetting occurs just after memorizing. What is remembered best is usually what came last and then what came first in the sequence we are trying to remember. The middle portion is less well remembered.

No one knows how it works, but many insist clear attention is crucially important in memory. Research has shown that recognition depends on the number of eye fixations on the items in question—in other words, on precise attention. They have also found that we are most likely to remember when circumstances are most similar to those of what we originally experienced. Other researchers point out that there is evidence we remember events that occurred during sleep or when anesthetized, indicating memory occurs without awareness.[92]

The brain "processes" or "analyzes" all information received, and large parts of the data are eliminated as somehow not "important." Some psychologists think we form internal images that can be very vivid to help us remember. Tulving states: "what is stored is determined by what is perceived and how it is encoded, and what is stored determines what retrieval cues are effective in providing access to what is stored."[93] Psychologists think we categorize memories, filing them away by identity, class, attributes, context, function, sensory associations, sound and visual patterns and muscle movements needed to reproduce the information. Cataloging, filing and retrieval errors are common.

Our memory is self-centered. "Recent research on the relation of self and memory supports the conception of the self as an active, central structure of memory."[94] "Memory functions well when the self is involved in the encoding or retrieval of to-be-remembered items."[95] In other words, we remember personal information and information we ourselves generated more easily. Material that is expected to be used in the future is more easily retrieved. Material is more easily remembered when circumstances are most similar to those of what we originally experienced.

Clearly, a process similar to what occurs in perception occurs in memory. First we select the focus of attention, and then when information is relayed to it, the brain intervenes, creating its own idiosyncratic reality by filtering, censoring, ignoring, omitting what and when it pleases. Bartlett described memory as a process of reconstruction rather than recollection. His subjects were asked to reproduce material they had read or observed (article or picture). From the details remembered, they created the descriptions rather than reporting what they had seen.

Removal of the hippocampal areas on both sides of the human brain results in the inability to form new "memories." The person simply cannot permanently remember new information, names, labels, or people. Motor learning is unimpaired, but memory of it will not be retained. In other words, such a person would be able to learn how to play tennis, and their game would improve, but they would not be able to learn any tennis terms, and would not remember having had lessons or even meeting their tennis instructor before. Memory of events prior to the surgery would still be remembered as well as before. These lesson was learned when the hippocampal areas on one man were surgically removed to relieve epileptic seizures. The seizure stopped, but the man was unable to function thereafter, for obvious reasons. Medical problems in several parts of the brain have been found to affect memory.

Surprisingly, all humans have almost perfect photographic memories. But the memory only lasts a fraction of a second, then is forgotten. However, most young children have persisting photographic memories which are lost when they begin to learn to read. In pre-literate societies, many adults retain this photographic memory ability. Somehow, reading appears to interfere.

As indicated, neuropsychologist Karl Pribram has popularized the theory that our brain must function like a hologram.[96] He believes that the entirety of any pattern is stored throughout the brain, so that if you have even a small portion of it, you can " remember" and reproduce the whole again.

It is generally taken for granted that our memory is based on sensory input; that is, on information provided by our physical senses. However, Carl Gustav Jung posited the concept of the "collective unconscious"—a level of our being which we not only share with all others, but which somehow also contains our racial history. In other words, the collective unconscious contains our ancestral memory. This concept is obviously radically different from that usually accepted by memory researchers, who tend to be either experimental or educational psychologists.

SUFISM AND MEMORY

The bits of information which psychology has accumulated are useful in everyday life but cannot explain memory. The explanation, although undiscovered by psychology, is relatively simple. Memory is one of the qualitative effects of the magnetic field of the brain. There are five stages in memory: learning, storing, remembering, recognition, and replacing.[97] In each one, the field of activity is the inner part of the neurons of the cerebrum, which creates changes in the RNA of the molecules and consequently causes actions and reactions in the axons. The axons function like magnetic plates, becoming stronger with increasing contact of the brain's electrical current. These billions of microscopic magnetic plates, create a magnetic field which can store and record thousand fold thousands of auditory and visual waves. When necessary, any of the contents of the field, like files of colorful slides, can be visualized—consciously or unconsciously. New and healthy cells are more sensitive and more accurate in both action and reaction, in comparison to weak or fatigued cells.

Our memory system can be compared to a recording. Visualize a cross-section of a tree and the lines within it—this is the electromagnetic field of memory which revolves at the speed of light. Whatever we have heard or read is recorded on these lines. It can also be likened to a tape recorder. On a tape, the metal bits are on the film in random order. The magnetic field organizes them by stabilizing wave patterns on the tape. A key element of the tape recorder is the head, which is magnetic. The tape recorder head functions as our brain does for memory. What is recorded is not stored in the head, but the head is necessary to record or to play whatever is on the tape. The total recorder, including all parts, is the entirety of the body, and the recording is in the magnetic field of the body.

The information received by the brain is recorded in the magnetic body, not in a cell. Anesthesia temporarily disconnects the circuit between the magnetic body and the cells. In a coma, all the circuits are cut off. The reason it feels as if severed limbs are still there—itching or pain may be felt—is because the magnetic body is still there, and the brain connection still functions. It is the magnetic body that registers pain.

The magnetic field or body is blank when we are born. It is programmable. Any and everything can be recorded on it. We record experiences from the physical level as we go through this life. Whenever something new comes, if we accept it, it is recorded. If we do not accept it, then it is not recorded. It is the record of our physical life. A crucially important point is that when we wish to enter the spiritual world, we may try and use what is already recorded. If we do, we will never reach it. God cannot be reached through the physical senses. In order to attain the goal, it is necessary to forget all that has been recorded, for the recording is on the physical level, and not only useless, but confusing when intruding on the metaphysical level.

There is also a tape and recorder for the spiritual world, which must be discovered and used. What is recorded in the way of Sufism will never vanish. You can use it. Happiness is recording the blank spiritual tape.

CHAPTER 8
LEARNING AND COGNITION

How have you learned what you know? Psychology assumes that all learning occurs through our five physical senses. Learning is acquired from outside ourselves, with our senses carrying the information to our brain. As in every other area of psychology, there are descriptions of discrete, specific aspects of learning and cognition, and a great deal of theoretical speculation.The author of a text on Cognitive Development states: "The study of cognition is the study of the knowledge we possess, the organization of this knowledge, and the processes we have available to us for using this knowledge in the everyday activities of attention, learning, memory, comprehension, and problem solving."[98] The assumption is that knowledge is what we have obtained through our five physical senses from the external world. Two basic theoretical orientations have dominated, those of Jean Piaget, and of information-processing. Today theorists attempt to combine the two.

The information-processing approach generally assumes that the mind is a system for storing and processing information.[99] This approach comes primarily from Chomsky's ideas about how we learn language, but, most importantly, from computer science. All information-processing theories have three basic assumptions in common. The first is that humans process environmental information (sensory input) in a series of stages between input and response, and this process takes time. Second, the information is somehow transformed during these stages. Third, there is a limited capacity in terms of the amount of processing that can take place at one time.

PIAGET

Since Piaget's theory of cognitive development is the best known and most popular, let us examine it first. Piaget believed that all babies are born with a set of sensorimotor systems, that allow them to incorporate experience and stimulation from interaction with the environment. He even titled one chapter: "The Construction of Reality."[100]. The child uses these systems to actively construct his or her knowledge of the world, constructing his or her own reality from the relationship of actions and objects, beginning at about age two.

Piaget considered action schemes (whatever actions were necessary for grasping, throwing, rolling, etc.) to be the infant's form of thought—-their primary units of mental organization—like concepts without words. Without language, based simply on motion and intelligence, the first constructions of intelligence are sensori-motor coordination of actions. "This means that intelligence proceeds from action as a whole."[101] One important point is rarely mentioned. Although other forms of intelligence later emerge, there is no reason to suppose that Sensori-motor Intelligence ceases to be used and useful, even in adult life. This period is divided into progressive stages; the sixth stage is a transition stage, in which the infant achieves insight, and suddenly comprehends how to obtain what he wants.[102]

Piaget considered play to fulfill an essential function in the life of the child.[103] The child needs play to transform reality to fit the needs of the self and also needs the self-expression of language or other symbols which are self-constructed.

Piaget saw mental images as NOT necessarily derived from perception, as behavioral psychologists insisted. He cited neurological evidence that measurements of both brain waves and the electrical potential of muscles are the same regardless of whether a bodily movement is imagined, or real. If mental images were derived from perception, the motion would have to actually occur to cause the electrical activity, and the opposite is true.

From about two years of age until seven years, he called the

Preoperational Stage. Piaget considered thought during this period to be intuitive, and not logical. One of the most well-known experiments he did was to pour milk from a wider, shorter container into a taller, narrower container. Young children thought there was more milk in the taller container, even when they had seen it poured out of the shorter container. The Preoperational period includes the dawn of representational thought, when a child can think about objects and people not present.

He named the type of thought he inferred was occurring in seven to 11 year olds Concrete Operational, because it was systematic logical thought, but basically only in regard to concrete objects. Only after about eleven years of age were children capable of what he called Formal Operational thought, which is the abstract, logical thought of the adult.

Piaget's Stages

Sensorimotor	**0-2**	**Thought confined to action schemes**
Preoperational	**2-7**	**Representational Thought Thought intuitive, not logical**
Concrete Operational	**7-11**	**Systematic, logical thought, but only in regard to concrete objects**
Formal Operational	**11 up**	**Abstract, logical thought**

Piaget observed that the stages emerge in a constant order of succession, and neither heredity nor environment alone could explain the progressive development of mental structures.

INFORMATION PROCESSING

Now let's examine the information processing, computer model, discussed in Chapter Five. These models assume that humans receive and process information from the environment. During this process, the information is transformed, which takes time. For example, a visual code could be changed into a verbal one. There is also an assumption that the system has a limit, that it can only process so much information at one time. In a simplified model, there are five major components: sensory registers, short-term memory, long-term memory, a central processor, and a response system which controls output.

David Bronson sees our minds as being designed (or programmed) for finding and making patterns, which is an inherently pleasing activity.[104] From the raw materials, all human brains gradually extract patterns individually, and then we live by the programs, switching on one after another, selecting from those that have been acquired and stored in the brain. Learning is then defined as the acquisition of useful programs, and we can examine learning in terms of what programs are being used.

George Kelly states: "Man looks at his world through transparent patterns or templates which he creates and then attempts to fit over the realities of which the world is composed.."[105] The input is not everything, but rather, whatever is perceived by the individual as bearing on a particular pattern in any way. A program is a fixed sequence for accomplishing some end—a goal, objective, or outcome. We can use only those programs that have already been built and stored. The programs of one individual may be, and usually are, entirely different from those of others. The process occurs automatically and does not require conscious thought. The failure of a program to work calls for recycling. When a high proportion of self-selected programs work well, confidence rises, when too many fail, confidence decreases, and the individual may become poorly able to self-select programs. Once we have laboriously acquired a program, it is easy to forget that other individuals may not have acquired these programs or may have entirely different ones. Some theorists believe the capacity to use old programs in fresh combinations seems to underlie what we call creativity. The learner who can adapt established programs to new tasks, by seeing similarities of patterns involved, learns much more rapidly than one who cannot. Various theories attempt to explain how the program processing actually works.

BEHAVIORISM[106]

Although Aristotle's idea that we retrieve stored information based on principles of similarity, contrast, and contiguity, is still accepted, what is called behaviorism began with the Russian physiologist Ivan Pavlov's description of teaching his dog to salivate at the sound of a bell. This process is now called "Classical Conditioning," for behavioral psychologists have developed their own language to describe learning. They consider such concepts as "self-esteem" and "sense of achievement" to be explanatory fictions. They are concerned only with the stimulus (whatever stimulates us) and the response, which are observable and measurable. To the behaviorist, learning occurs through conditioning. In this country, a man named E.L. Thorndike did animal experiments which he then applied to humans. From observing the behavior of cats try to escape from "puzzle boxes," he derived a "learning curve," which later experiments indicate is the same for animals and men solving such simple tasks. He called the behavior "trial and error." Not knowing how to escape, the animal performed various behaviors until some action was effective in getting them out of the box. Thorndike came up with two laws of learning. The law of exercise states that practice makes perfect, or at least improves. and the law of effect states that learning is strengthened by the effects of what you do—whether what happens is satisfying or punishing. Later experiments proved he was correct about satisfaction (called Positive Reinforcement), but incorrect about punishment (Negative Reinforcement). Punishment was found to suppress responses, but not to eliminate them. Unfortunately, many teachers and parents still have not learned that punishment is not effective in stopping unwanted behaviors. Satisfaction is not the same as reward. For example, experiments with children have shown that if you give them a concrete reward for doing something that is intrinsically satisfying, like drawing with felt tip pens, they tend not to later do it again, but if they receive no reward, they will return to it. Its as if concrete rewards redefine play as work, and the intrinsic satisfaction disappears.

Wolfgang Kohler, a German Gestalt therapist, believed animals were capable of intellectual or problem-solving activities. He described the behavior of a chimpanzee who "figured out" how to fit two sticks together to make a pole long enough to rake in a banana outside her cage but beyond her reach. He dubbed such behavior "insight." To him, insight involved a sudden restructuring or reorganization of the organism's perceptual world into a new pattern or Gestalt. At the same time, E.C. Tolman at Berkeley published articles indicating that even rats, which have a very tiny cerebral cortex, appear to possess some sort of what he called "cognitive map." Rats who were trained to run very complicated mazes would shift immediately to the second most efficient way of finding the reward if the usual route were blocked.

A popular theory in schools today is that of B.F. Skinner's Operant

Conditioning. Most of the time, people and animals tend to change slowly, bit by bit, rather than in insightful jumps. Skinner and his students trained all sorts of animals to do all sorts of peculiar things based on this observation, using the method of successive approximations to teach animals complex behaviors. Behavior is gradually molded in an ordered series of steps which increasingly approximate the desired behavior pattern. James McConnell's text[107] describes how to teach a hungry pigeon how to bowl in two hours using this method.

Reinforcement is what causes the behavior to recur. Generally, researchers begin with total reinforcement, then gradually use less and less, while more and more behavior is required to get it. If you want a behavior to continue forever, reinforce it gradually, and then intermittently, at irregular intervals. That behavior will become very difficult to stop (extinguish). To extinguish fears, behaviorists often use mild forms or intensities, working up to more. An example would be fear of water. The subject first walks through a tiny puddle, and the amount of water is gradually increased, until he will go into the ocean. Making the consequences very unpleasant (Aversive Conditioning) is also used to treat severe fears (phobias). Another technique used to try and eliminate bad habits is called "satiation." The subject performs the undesired act until they are tired of it.

EDUCATIONAL PSYCHOLOGY

The most famous teaching method is that of Socrates. Socrates assumed ideas were innate, and what was necessary was to recollect them. He used a series of sequential questions which allowed the students to discover the correct answers for themselves.

Jerome Bruner lists four key concepts of learning: structure or process, readiness, intuition, and motivation.[108] Intrinsic motivation is an essential key to effective learning. John Dewey said there is "the teachable moment" when motivation and information come together. Bruner recommends *Discovery Learning*, in which the student discovers the answers for him or herself through experience, as most effective, because the learner is able to see how information comes into existence. Successful learning through discovery leads to "intellectual potency" because you get better at it with practice. Discovery is itself a rewarding process, and strategies for further learning on one's own emerge. What is learned through discovery is remembered better. As a Chinese Proverb states: "I hear and I forget, I see and I understand, I do and I remember." John Holt, a teacher, delightfully described how young children learn from actual experience. In so doing, he provides a model for all learning.

> The child is curious. He wants to make sense out of things, find out how things work, gain competence and control over himself and his environment, do what he can see other people doing. He is open, receptive and perceptive. He does not shut himself off from the strange, confused, complicated world around him. He observes it closely and sharply, tries to take it all in. He is experimental. He does not merely observe the world around him, but tastes it, touches it, hefts it, bends it, breaks it. To find out how reality works, he works on it. He is bold. He is not afraid of making mistakes. And he is patient. He can tolerate an extraordinary amount of uncertainty, confusion, ignorance, and suspense. He does not have to have instant meaning in any new situation. He is willing and able to wait for meaning to come to him—even if it comes very slowly, which it usually does.[109]

He contends children learn naturally and well until we train them out of it. He states that we like to say we send children to school to teach them to think. What we do, all too often, is to teach them to think badly, to give up a natural and powerful way of thinking in favor of a method that does not work well for them and that we rarely use ourselves. He feels children fail because they are taught that they do not dare trust their memories. Even when they are right, they feel wrong. Their first hunch is often correct, but they don't trust that hunch. They think: "it must be wrong." Holt recommends that we do not "correct" children, but just keep doing and saying the "correct" thing in front of them. They will catch on. Correction is not needed, nor necessary.

Leslie Hart contends that no part of the brain is naturally logical, and logical presentations usually result in poor learning.[110] Since previous individual experience is the foundation to which more learning is added, logical group-instruction inevitably produces a large degree of failure. We do not all learn best in the same manner. Some people learn information better through one sensory modality, such as hearing, rather than through another. Some learn better visually, some kinesthetically. Kagan[111] and others describe people as having differing cognitive styles, ranging from an analytic-reflective style to a global-impulsive style. An "analytic" child would group a table and chairs together because they all have four legs. A "global" child would group them together because they are both used for dining. Another way of looking at cognitive styles is through field independence or insensitivity and field dependence or sensitivity. The former are more likely to follow internalized values and beliefs, while the latter are far more dependent on others for definition of their own values and actions.

Anxiety has been found to improve performance, up to a point. After that point, performance declines. The terrified person is incapable of functioning cognitively.

The types of cognitive abilities developed vary enormously from culture to culture. For example, in non-literate cultures, photographic memories frequently persist into adulthood. It is as if reading somehow interfered with the ability. In such cultures, auditory memory is highly developed, and extremely long histories, stories, or information can be heard once and retained in memory. What is learned in one culture may be entirely different from what is learned in another. Eskimos become acutely sensitive to variations in snow. New Zealand aborigines are knowledgeable about rocks. As what is important to survival varies from culture to culture, and from geographical location to geographical location, so does what is considered important to learn.

"Brainwashing" is a systematic, methodical attempt to eliminate old mental and connected emotional patterns and substitute new ones in their place. Various forms of physiological mistreatment, including semi-starvation and torture, may be used to break down resistance to the process. When only psychological methods are used, whether these attempts to change thought patterns are considered "brainwashing" or educational is often dependent on how the observer values who is doing it. If we agree with their point of view, then we consider it educational. If we disagree, we may want to label it "brainwashing." Although imprisonment may imply brainwashing, only when deliberate physical abuse is an integral part of the process of acquiring new mental and emotional patterns is there general agreement that brainwashing has occurred.

LEARNING AND COGNITION IN SUFISM

The learning and cognition that psychology studies, that occurs through the five physical senses, is useful, and deals with everyday functioning in this life. It is a learned social process of construction. The ordinary person learns from knowledge acquired through the senses. This learning is based on sensations and observations of external appearances and surfaces. Giving them a rational form, the individual shapes them in his or her mind like a sculptor, and construes them as reality. Societies agree on, and teach their members, how to do so. We are taught how and what to perceive as a necessary basis for accepting the social consensus of reality. This type of learning deals with physical appearances, and not with ultimate reality. "Knowledge based on physical observation is the greatest veil in the discovery of truth."[112] To attain true cognition, this level of learning and cognition must be set aside. The Sufis and the devout receive knowledge from the Source of Existence, which is eternal. "Knowledge is not acquired through study, but is a light which God shines in the heart of whom He wills."[113]

Let us use an analogy in terms of science. In ordinary life, we see or feel an object—a chair or a table—and learn it is separate, solid, and motionless. We also learn to see ourselves similarly. Yet when we later read of particle physics and quantum mechanics, we learn our perception was inaccurate. We discover every atom contains constantly changing subatomic particles. These particles are not independently existing entities. A particle "is, in essence, a set of relationships that reach outward to other things."[114] These subatomic particles are constantly in motion—mass is changing to energy, and energy to mass. Every subatomic interaction consists of the annihilation of the original particle and the creation of new subatomic particles. The theory which describes this "is a successful physical theory, yet it is based on the assumption that *physical reality is essentially non substantial.* Fields alone are real. *They* are the substance of the universe and not 'matter'. Matter (particles) is simply the momentary manifestation of interacting fields."[115]

Everything—light, sound, heat, electricity—is composed of subatomic particles (waves) which are a form of energy. The air we breathe, the water we drink, our own body, and even the planet itself are essentially concentrated energy fields existing at different frequencies. How energy is manifested depends upon the medium of conduction and the frequency of vibration. Almost everyone has seen a chart of the electromagnetic spectrum. It is a table of the known frequencies or rates of vibration. Our physical senses are capable of perceiving only a very minute portion of the spectrum. In this analogy, psychology could be said to deal only with that small portion of the electromagnetic spectrum perceptible to our physical senses. Classic Newtonian physics is its model. The cognition of Sufism then would be said to encompass the entire electromagnetic spectrum.

However, it is not easy for us to "let go" of our brain's construct, to break the boundaries of our well-learned limitations. It is not easy to realize the physical world is "...not a structure built out of independently existing unanalyzable entities, but rather a web of relationships between elements whose meanings arise wholly from their relationship to the whole."[116]

Psychology tries to describe the organism, its physical needs and the exterior forces influencing it. Sufism, in traditional terms, is the way to "cognition of the true character and identity of man, which is his authentic and delicate aspect."[117] Cognition of the true identity ". . .is the way to cognize the attributes and essence of God through the discovery of the heavenly kingdom and the secrets of man's heart through vision and revelation."[118] Cognition is achieved through self-discipline, purification, concentration, and heart meditation. It cannot be achieved through logical analysis, debate, time, space, situation, action and reaction, cause, effect and properties. Most of us have the idea of cause and effect so deeply imbedded in our minds that we evaluate everything by it. It is a barrier, a blinder to Truth.

Jesus tells us that in order to enter the kingdom of Heaven, we need to become again as a little child. In other words, we need to let go of all our pre-conceived notions, all the ideas of others we have accepted as our own, all our assumptions about ourselves and the world, all we have been taught, and simply open ourselves to the experiential learning presented by the prophets. Those cherished creations of our mind, our thoughts, keep us from receiving and cognizing the truth; we mistake mental imagination and illusion for truth. The young child is not so hampered. Not even the most sophisticated, logical, analytical reasoning deduced by our mental faculties can find truth for us. This is the way of philosophers (including many scientists). But it is not the way of the prophets. The philosopher wants to know. The *Arif* knows. The philosopher seeks. The *Arif* has found.

In *Wealth of Solouk*, Hazrat Pir tells us: "Cognition of man's truth is the essence of the message of the prophets, which is the way of release from the confines of nature and the means for the cognition of man's true character and identity, which is the gateway to the cognition of another mysterious level of man."

Professor Angha tells us: "In s*olouk* (the journey), truthful words, a pure heart, sincere intention, honest livelihood, firmness of step and truthful devotion are necessary," so that by the grace of God "the delicate divine truths will be inwardly revealed to the salik without question or doubt."[119] The result is Absolute Knowledge. The drop of water knows only what is within its limited boundary; when it becomes one with the sea, the knowledge is boundless, is that of the sea. We say there are seven seas, but there is only one, for all are interconnected. The result is the eternal Light of Truth.

The most important factor in cognition is desire to know, a deep and sincere seeking for Truth. There are basic and important principles necessary to learning and cognition. If we take an ordinary school as an example, we can examine the important factors entering into learning. Attendance is necessary—we must be present, mentally as well as physically. We need a teacher, lessons, instructions, books, homework, and we need to be a talented student. There are tests.

If we want to cognize Truth, we must stop thinking. Let's return to the original analogy of the lamp and examine how electrical power works to light a bulb. First there must be a source of power—a generator of some type, let's say. It produces electricity of very high voltage, too high to be of direct use in household appliances. However, it is much cheaper and easier to transport power for long distances in high voltage form. We are used to seeing high voltage wires cris-crossing the countryside. These have no external insulation, which is why children are continuously cautioned not to fly kites near them. The high voltage power, when it reaches its destination, is directed through transformers, which transform it from one voltage into another—usually, in the US., to 110 and 220. The electrical power then enters the usual house in these voltages, flowing continuously through the wiring system, where it may be used as needed. Permanent light fixtures are connected directly to the wiring and controlled by a switch. Electrical appliances and lamps are plugged into wall sockets.

Within the lamp is a light bulb. Without it, the gadget called a lamp would be useless. In order for the bulb to receive the current properly, it has to be whole, unbroken. It must not contain water or dust. It has to be intact and the inside must be free of all contaminants. If there is any adulterant in it, it causes a "short," and the bulb cannot produce light.

If we are to cognize, to receive the light of absolute knowledge, we need to be in the same condition as the light bulb. We must listen—without any past or future—without any memory or any prospect, drawing no conclusions. All the *salik* has to do is to hear, to really listen. To do that, and nothing else. It is not possible to listen if our own brain is chattering. We have to really listen in utter internal quiet. But we are distracted and disconnected. We wish and want. The material world continually attempts to create and stimulate more wishes and wants. Man is full of worldly concerns and thoughts. Our "bulb" is not empty. In order to attain cognition, it must be completely clean and pure.

CHAPTER 9
MOTIVATION

Why do you behave as you do? Do you really know why or do you think you know? The word motivation comes from the Latin term meaning "to move." So motivation is what "moves" us. The ancient Greeks thought that self-initiated motion was caused by a spirit. Whenever the "spirit was moved," so was the object or body that the spirit inhabited. We still speak of someone doing something "when the spirit moves him."

Today there are nearly as many definitions of motivation as there are psychologists. One of the simplest states that motivation includes everything which arouses, sustains and directs behavior.[120] A generally accepted definition would be that motivation refers to the processes by which behavior is activated and directed, and these processes vary in direction, intensity, and duration at different points for different individuals.[121] Both definitions assume more than one motivator.

None of the motivational theories is able to answer the simple basic question: "What makes your arm move?" They cannot answer because they do not ask the question, "What is the animating principle in life?" Instead they describe selected small aspects of behavior. It is as if they become so involved with the details of a leaf that they forget both the tree and also the forest. Some theories of psychotherapy do postulate some inner spirit or power which pushes us along life's path—they may call it "mind" or "cosmic force" or "libido." The term "soul" is not academically acceptable, except to Jungians.

The two major categories of theory tend to see motivation as either mechanistic or cognitive.[122] The mechanistic analyses see behavior as begun by either an external stimulus, like a hot stove, or an internal one, like thirst. We then simply react. We move our fingers away from the hot stove, or we do whatever is necessary to obtain water to stop the thirst. If the response produces the desired result, it becomes a habit. Hamilton argues that such notions are inadequate, for they do not include what has been described as the "exploratory drive," the need for sensory or perceptual stimulation, or information seeking.[123] Both animals and humans are curious and seek cognitive activity, that is, to explore, to obtain information, to find sensory or perceptual stimulation. If it is insufficient, they experience what we label "boredom." Cognitive theories consider thinking about incoming information and other factors as important in determining the behavioral response to stimuli. For example, personal attitudes and social influences are most important in decision making and consequently, motivation, but little work has been done concerning the relative importance of each.

Psychology needs basic organizing concepts, such as those of physics and biology—which have the atom, the cell, and the interchange of energy and matter. In trying to determine what makes people do what they do or don't do, many theorists have turned to "need" as such a concept.[124] Theorists then divide various motives into types of needs:

1. Biological: hunger, thirst, sex
2. Emotional: approach, avoidance,
3. Social: affiliation (connection to others), power, aggression
4. Play and Achievement Motivation: play, exploration, seeking stimulation, achievement.[125] A social psychologist named Samuels has even dared to risk discussing the idea that what he calls "the immortality factor" is a need that should be added to the list.

Advertisers use the information to try to motivate people to purchase the products they advertise. Psychologists also use it. For example, they use interest in "gadgets" and technology to motivate people to change certain behaviors through the use of "biofeedback" devices which provide some sort of visual image of a physiological process, such as heart rate. The image is not a necessity, but simply stimulates interest and motivates concentration of attention.

Some have called motivation Push/Pull: we are pushed to act to decrease physical discomfort caused by deficiency of a basic need, such as water, food, etc., or pulled to act in a certain way to achieve a more complex goal, such as competency, or affection.[126] The pull exerted by a goal is called its incentive value. For example, have you ever seen anyone who has just eaten an enormous meal and whose hunger is clearly satisfied, then eat a rich desert? Even if you were very hungry, would you eat live ants? They are considered a delicacy in some parts of the world.

Hunger and thirst are considered key motivators. If we examine the phenomena of hunger as a motivation, we discover it is theorized to be triggered by low blood sugar, possibly in the liver, and is influenced by fat stored in the body. One area of the hypothalamus controls eating. If it is removed, the animal will refuse to eat, and will have to be force fed. If electrically stimulated, the animal will begin eating immediately. A second area seems to act like a "stop center" for eating. If it is destroyed, dramatic overeating results, but the phenomena is not understood. In one experiment, students were fed fluid through a tube directly into the stomach, and controlled the amount by a lever. They could not see, smell, taste, chew or swallow the food, but they controlled the amount as readily as if they were drinking it from a glass. Yet they were totally unable to explain how they did it.

Abraham Maslow saw motivation as stemming from basic human needs, which he considered universal. Physical needs, essential for survival, are basic. He believed higher needs are expressed only when the lower level physiological needs are predominantly satisfied. He considered the lowest two levels basic needs, and the higher levels growth needs. Maslow considered the self-actualization level to be of "meta-needs."

Maslow's Hierarchy of Needs[127]

Self-Actualization
Esteem & Self-Esteem
Love and Belongingness
Safety and Security Needs
Physiological Needs: air, food, water, shelter, sleep

Maslow believed there is a tendency to move up the hierarchy, yet he estimated only about one person in ten is motivated primarily by self-actualization needs. If a person's lower level needs are met, but their meta-needs are unfulfilled, they will experience apathy, despair, and alienation.

What actually motivates us, and what we think motivates us may be two entirely different things."[128] Whether correct or not, our brain will make up some sort of explanation of "why" we do anything in order to satisfy itself. Our brain constantly does this, and our responses are typically based on sensory perception. Interesting examples can be obtained by asking three or four year old children the "whys" of various natural phenomena, such as, "Why is the sky blue?" "Where does rain come from?" or "How can birds fly?" We keep this behavior in adulthood, usually without being aware of it. For example, one woman, seeing numerous planes leaving jet trails, told others to watch the planes practicing sky-writing. Could it be that often we really have no idea, or else totally erroneous ideas about why we do what we do? It is often easy to see that others have a "hidden agenda," another motive for what they do besides the more obvious one. One has only to notice the personally self-serving motives of numerous supposedly altruistic acts. We consider acts hypocritical when people say one thing, and do another. However, is it possible that people are often fooling themselves even more than others?

Samuels sees at least five factors which directly determine the influence of any particular need upon behavior. They are urgency, survival valence, appeal, risk, and availability—all as perceived by the individual. The first four are the motive power. After studying motivation extensively, he came to the conclusion: "I become convinced that free choice may be an illusion, albeit a necessary one. It is important to act as if you are choosing with some freedom——for self esteem if for no other reason."[129]

Most of the psychological research on motivation was begun by David McClelland, who devised the Thematic Apperception Test (TAT), a set of pictures of people doing various things in different scenes, in which it was not clear what was happening. Then people were asked to make up stories about the pictures. McClelland thought the theme of their stories reflected the reasons for their behaviors. He found three motivating needs: a need for achievement, a need for power, and a need for affiliation. In his definition, power included control over others, and affiliation meant the kinds of relationships we usually describe as friendship or love. According to him, we do as we do in order to gain control, or love, to receive some sort of "reward." He saw these motives as influencing each other—that is, if you were high on affiliation, you would be low on power, and vice versa. Not surprisingly women tended to be higher on the former, and men on the latter. However, the effect of the content of the scenes depicted and how strongly they affect possible responses does not seem to have been adequately analyzed.

Theorists often ignore emotions when discussing motivation. Both the word emotion and motive are derived from the same Latin word, meaning to move. Of course, no one can really define what an emotion is, although emotions obviously "move" people. Measurers try to relate them to internal physical aspects, such as hormones in the blood and electrical activity in the brain, but these are descriptions, not definitions.[130] The current psychological state of affairs regarding the study of emotions is summed up in Lazarus' article in the American Psychologist: "There has never been any agreement about which emotions should be distinguished."[131]

Nearly a century ago, Wilhelm Wundt did a large series of studies, and concluded that there are only three pairs of feelings: pleasure and pain, strain and relaxation, excitation and quiescence.[132] These rarely occur alone, but are combined into what he called a "feeling compound." Modern factor analysis strategies have obtained only two (positive and negative) or four (activation, relatedness, hedonic tone and competence) factors involved in emotions.

General excitement is the only emotional response a newborn infant can clearly express, according to some researchers. Fox theorizes a basic emotional dichotomy is present at birth, that of approach or withdrawal. We then label the facial expressions associated with approach as joy, interest or anger. Facial expressions labeled as distress, disgust or fear result from withdrawal action tendencies. Fox states: "identification of distinct patterns of the four primary emotions (fear, anger, joy, sadness) are only reliably coded toward the end of the first year of life."[133] Even after that time, he suggests we give emotional labels to infant facial expressions depending on our perception of behavior.[134] Children are considered more emotional than adults, perhaps because they are more expressive. Most of us are familiar with the "emotional" behavior of two year olds. Emotional outbursts are said to become less intense as people age.

Feelings and emotions are accompanied by physical reactions, particularly respiratory and cardiac reactions triggered by a flow of adrenaline. To a large degree, the physical aspects are innate, built into the body. They are caused by the sympathetic system of the autonomic nervous system. The changes that occur include: pupil dilation, faster heart beat, dilated blood vessels, dilated bronchi, decrease in digestive secretions and movements, retention of bile, release of blood sugar, constriction of surface blood vessels, and perspiration.[135] Wundt insisted that with emotions not only is there an "intensification of the effect on heart, blood-vessels and respiration, but the external muscles are always affected in an unmistakable manner."[136] The movements which result are called expressive movements. As a rule, they are entirely involuntary. Wundt insisted the passions did not differ in any essential respect from emotions, thus differing from Spinoza and Kant, both of whom considered passions to be the result of long continued feelings.

Emotions are primarily in the limbic system, the survival brain. Under strong threat, the brain downshifts to this brain area. In extreme situations, the lower brain takes over, as in great rage, object fear, or panic flight. Since language is in the neocortex, this leaves us literally speechless. The over-threatened person cannot function cognitively. He freezes, seems unable to think, stabs wildly at possible answers, cries, vomits, or "acts up." Cerebral learning and threat conflict directly and completely. Play implies the absence of threat.

Strong emotional reactions have marked physical consequences. A Yale study found that people who react with strong emotions, particularly anger, are especially likely to die of cardiac arrest. However, extreme joy can trigger the same reaction—the surge of stress hormones. Men who scored high in emotional reactivity were three times more likely than more even tempered men to die of cardiac arrest, and five times higher if they also had high cholesterol levels.[137]

Cultural meanings and language appear to have an important place in the emotion process. Some cultures emphasize certain emotions and act as if others are unimportant or even do not exist. For example, if the culture has no words for an emotion, will its people not experience the emotion? People in some Eskimo tribes seem not to even feel, much less express, anger. Tahitians pay little attention to what we would label as sadness, longing and loneliness—they talk about it as fatigue or bodily distress. At the same time, they have many words for shame and anger, which seem to occur frequently. "Schachter and Singer (1962) theorize that we label diffuse arousal by whatever concept characterizes the social context."[138] In other words, emotion is basically an unrefined physiological state which we then proceed to categorize and label, depending upon our perception of what feelings we believe the event ought to cause. The labeling is based on cultural norms.

Jung states that emotions are not an activity of the organism. They are something that happens to it. Emotions do appear to be contagious. Children obviously learn many emotions from the emotional reactions of their caregivers. Research has demonstrated that the intensity of emotional response to a situation is markedly affected by another person's appraisal of the situation. If they appear unemotional, the observer will tend to be less emotional. If they stress emotion, the observer will be more emotional.

Behaviorists define emotions such as fear as an arousal response in the autonomic nervous system. Therefore, "emotional" responses not only can be, but are, conditioned. The best known examples are of fears of an animal caused by a very unpleasant or threatening experience. The original fear can "generalize," so that the person feels fear just hearing the name of what originally frightened him or her. The "lie detector" or polygraph is not a lie detector at all, but an emotion detector, for it notes and records sudden changes in autonomic nervous system activity.

Stanley Schachter developed a cognitive theory of emotion. He thinks emotion occurs when a particular label is applied to general physical arousal. We seem to need to interpret our feelings when we are aroused. "The label (such as fear, anger, happiness) applied to bodily arousal is influenced by past experience, the situation, and the reactions of others."[139] Valines refined the theory by stating that perceptions of emotion depend on what feelings of physical arousal are attributed to. His "attribution" theory predicts, for example, that you are most likely to "love" someone who gets you emotionally upset, even if fear, anger or frustration are involved. Research studies have indicated this is certainly a factor.

How we think about the state of emotional arousal appears to significantly affect behavior. Several psychotherapeutic techniques are based on changing negative thought patterns. Hope seems to be a crucially important, even life-saving, emotion. It can differentiate between those who live and die in extreme circumstances, such as concentration camps. It also is the antidote to "learned helplessness." Learned helplessness occurs when an animal or human learns it cannot escape a painful situation. For example, a dog who receives electric shocks it cannot escape will later crouch, whine and howl if placed in a box where it could avoid electric shock by jumping over a low barrier, but will not try to escape. It has "learned" shock is unavoidable. The only way they found to overcome this learning was to drag the dog across the barrier until it learned that there was "hope," that it had some control over the environment. The same concept is considered to apply to humans, for the symptoms of depression are very similar to learned helplessness. Perhaps people could be "immunized" against learned helplessness and depression by helping them to master extremely difficult situations. The Outward Bound programs, involving mastering physically difficult and hazardous situations, use this model.

A thorough examination of motivation would require that we look at what motivates people strongly enough that they are willing to give up their most valuable possession, their own life, for it. There are extremely rare cases of people who deliberately sacrifice their lives to save the life of a stranger; a very few people who have given up their lives for their loved ones, usually parents giving up their lives for their children. Most of the many cases of people (often called martyrs or saints) who have been willing to give up their own lives are those who somehow give up their lives for their belief in God. They hold in common their intense love of God, and the willingness to sacrifice their life for Him. This would appear to be the highest level of motivation, transcending even the need for physical survival. Yet psychologists usually do not even mention it, much less attempt to study it.

THE REALITY OF MOTIVATION

At twenty-one days after conception, when the fetus is a tiny curved collection of cells, the first, rudimentary heartbeat occurs. One moment, there is no heartbeat. The next, there is a separate heartbeat. What causes the heartbeat? "Electricity" is correct, but does not answer the question. How does the electrical current begin at twenty-one days? What makes a seed sprout? There is only inanimation, and then there is life as the seed sprouts. Stating soil and water is not an adequate answer either. What is the motivation for the heartbeat and the sprouting plant? Psychology cannot answer.

Sufism answers the question: "What is the animating principle of life?" In *Dawn*, Professor Angha tells us that the animating force is the divine radiation of God's spirit. This inspiration of the spirit "radiates constantly. and makes the dead tomb of the body alive."[140] The essence of our being, the prime motivating force, is the spirit of God. All of us have had glimpses of that spirit, if only when we recognized its manifestations. Each of us has had moments when we felt what psychologists sometimes call "peak experiences" or "oceanic feelings"—it may come through a near-death experience, or a beautiful scene in Nature, or viewing our newborn infant, or moments when we felt totally at peace, in harmony and at one with all of Existence. Somehow, each of knows deep within that there is more to us than the trivia of everyday life.

How then, are people motivated to behave so differently? Each of us is born with the capacity to receive the continuing emanation of God's spirit. All of us want access to that Divine Knowledge within. "If you delve into the innermost aspect of people and to the depth of their desires, you will see that they wish to know more and more."[141] Yet in this life we become slaves to our senses, which delude us into the quest for fulfillment of various material desires. As children, we usually accept unquestioningly what we are taught by adults, first our parents, then other teachers—school, TV, movies—all the social forces shape us. We are taught to believe the illusion that men are separate and that the soul of man is separate from God. All societies teach us the prime importance of socio-economic factors. Current bumper stickers read: "Born to shop" and "Whoever has the most money when they die, wins." The children learn prejudices based on blind obedience and remain ignorant. Most grow up and remain that way. If you ask most people why they do as they do, they will tell you: "That's how everyone does it." or "That's the American (French, Italian, Spanish, or whatever) way!" or "That's what I was taught, and if it was right for them, it's right for me." Yet both the Bible and the Quran teach us: "Follow not that whereof you have no knowledge."[142]

Whatever rank or position or beliefs people attain as adults, the goal of all their efforts is to achieve internal peace, to attain tranquillity, whether this effort is expended in material, non material, or spiritual endeavors. People are misled. Do you remember what you wanted when you were 6, 12, 16, 21 and 26 years old? Perhaps a bicycle, or a horse, or a friend, or a car or a job, or your family to behave differently. But if you obtained whatever you wanted, how long did your satisfaction and happiness last before you wanted something else? Has the wanting ended? Will it ever end? The world always gives us more to want—houses, computers, land, more successful children, boats, whatever. Hazrat Ali says: "This world is a thing of great and exclusive importance to those who have no breadth of vision, and who cannot see or substantiate what lies behind it or beyond it."[143]

People without are filled with ambition to get so and so, and they believe that if they just make enough money, or gain enough status, or enough possessions, or designer clothes and gourmet food, or are beautiful enough, or they have enough friends, or they reach a certain rank, then they will be content. But the people already in that position still struggle for more, all giving personal accounts of why they are struggling. If we look closely, the underlying reason for all the struggles is the attainment of tranquillity—each and everyone wants true tranquillity. However, reaching such tranquillity is disrupted by the inevitable arrival of death. This is the reason why the wealthy, despite their wealth, do not have tranquillity.[144]

Children are afraid of entering a dark room because they do not know what is within it. So darkness needs to be illuminated for them. And so it is with the reality of death, which awaits each of us. We cannot escape death, and are fearful, because we do not know what death is. If death is known, then we can move toward tranquillity. If you study the lives of great people who were completely unafraid of death, you will note that they knew death was not the end of the journey. In order to accept this point, they had to truly know death, not just read or hear or accept it. Once people discover this essential truth, they are freed of all fears.

We can therefore summarize what motivates everyone, what everyone wants, in two words: tranquillity and survival. These are the two universal and essential laws that govern the behavior of each of us from childhood to death. We want to survive, and we want tranquillity. Everything we do in this life are attempts, however misguided, to attain one of those two goals.

If the ways societies teach us to attain them are not effective, then how can we attain tranquillity and survival? Sufism teaches that attainment cannot be achieved through the mind or senses. To do so, we must first discover our constant identity or "I," that essence of our being that is constant and unchangeable, that is the Truth we seek, the Divine within us. We must come to know God. Knowing God cannot be achieved through repetitions of words or phrases, or memorizing all the words of famous people, or observing rituals and ceremonies, or punishing oneself, or hunger. To know God, we must prepare ourselves to receive Him, as a lover prepares him or herself to meet the Beloved. The preparation requires discipline, practice, patience, devotion and love.

All efforts mankind uses, in whatever way or through whatever means, are really attempts to live in tranquillity and remove death. Concentration of an individual's entire powers, homed at a heavenly point inside his heart, will acquaint him with his actual being, and assures him of being able to succeed in reaching happiness, an everlasting peace, and eternal life."

Motivation can also be examined at a more basic level. Physically, we are born as a marvelously complex and efficient organism equipped with all the apparatus necessary for sight, hearing, motion, growth, language, learning, etc.,—all the capacities which develop after birth. We are provided with a program for growth and development, just as the program for the development of a mighty tree is provided within the tiny seed.

As indicated in the chapter on the central nervous system, certain physiological phenomena which significantly affect our behavior and thereby "motivate" us, have not yet received the attention of psychologists. As mentioned previously, we are born with "spontaneous" biological rhythms, ranging from high frequency rhythms in individual cells, specific tissues, and single organs to involvement of the whole organism in low frequency ranges.[145] Like every biological system we possess a complex electrodynamic field.[146] Scientists at several major universities studying the electromagnetic fields of the body with super conducting magnetometers have found the heart has the strongest field and the strongest field from nerve tissue is from the brain, which yields its largest fields during sleep.[147]

In *Manifestations of Thought*, Professor Angha speaks of how we, too, obey the "natural" laws. From the moment of birth, we are affected by forces such as air pressure and gravity, yet are usually unaware of their effect. If the moon can make the seven oceans dance, how can it not affect a body which is primarily water? If solar flares can completely disrupt communication systems, how can we avoid being affected by them? The portion of the electromagnetic spectrum perceived by our physical senses is extremely limited. Sufism teaches us how to attain access to a far greater proportion of the spectrum. If however, there is coinciding and coordination between our physical and spiritual abilities and universal dynamics, then our receiving capacity is activated and extended. Sufism leads the way to the superior strengths and energies of nature, to an intuition capable of comprehending truth and reality, of understanding the heart of motivation, the essence of our being, the divine inspiration of the spirit of God.

CHAPTER 10
CREATIVITY

reative talent has intrigued man for centuries. The word create is
derived from the Greek "krainein," meaning to accomplish and
the Sanskrit "kar," to make. To create means to originate, to bring
into being from nothing, to cause to exist. Creativity is defined as creative
ability; artistic or intellectual inventiveness.

Theories about creativity abound. Some, whose ideas are not well-
accepted in academic psychology, insist "the source of creativity is not
the individual but the We—not the individual—but God who manifests
Himself in the We, of which the self is a part"[148] Galton and others
thought it to be purely genetic. In psychoanalysis, Freud and his followers saw creative work as sublimation of the sexual drive, and tried to analyze artistic works in terms of the artists' defense mechanisms and neu-
roses. Later analysts considered creative works as restitution for destructive impulses. Jung protested strongly:

> Should the claim be made that such an analysis accounts
> for the work of art itself, then a categorical denial is called for.
> The personal idiosyncrasies that creep into a work of art are
> not essential;" "What is essential in a work of art is that it
> should rise far above the realm of personal life and speak from
> the spirit and heart of the poet as man to the spirit and heart of
> mankind.[149]

Culture is often suggested as an essential force. Torrance believed that creativity was a learned, conditioned behavior. Many theorists believe interpersonal dynamics, interactions between people, to be the source of creativity. Rogers and others believed creativity to be the result of the tendency toward self-actualization. Transaction theory about the sources of creativity sees creativity as natural, and asks, "What are the origins of uncreativity"?[150] Environmental stimulation is also considered an origin of creativity.

In the early 1960s, the concept of creativity became academically popular, and researchers devoted much time to the topic. J. P. Guilford described two basic intellectual modes, which he called "convergent" and "divergent" thinking. Convergent thinking was defined as being essentially repetition of what most people thought, and divergent thinking as coming up with ideas that were entirely different from those of most people. Divergent thinking was considered creative. Interested in the possible economic rewards of creative thinking, various divergent thinking tests, tasks and exercises were developed, as were workshop techniques designed to accelerate the process of creative thinking. The best known were Paul Torrance's *Creative Thinking Tasks*.[151] One requires that you make as many different "things" as you can out of each of many circles printed on a page. Examples are given of a coin and a ring. Another was to think of as many uses as possible for a brick, such as a doorstop or paperweight.

Investigation indicated the creative differ from the non-creative in several ways. They are more independent, non-conforming, resistant to authority, and usually dislike routine and small detail work. Other researchers have found the highly creative to be also intellectual, expressive, asocial, consciously original, and open to experience. College students scoring high in creativity described themselves as original, versatile, imaginative, ingenious and inventive. Torrance and his associates considered the following adjectives descriptive: adventurous, courageous, curious, determined, dominant, emotional, energetic, fault-finding, humorous, individualistic, industrious, persistent, reserved, self-confident, sincere, stubborn, temperamental, thorough, timid, and versatile.

"Intelligence tests" do not predict creativity, although a certain minimum level of intellectual functioning appears necessary. Achievement test scores and grades in school are unrelated to creativity. Teachers are not fond of creative students. They describe creative students as discovered by tests as less ambitious, less studious, less known, less desirable as pupils, playful, having more naughty ideas, and more disturbing to the group.

Artistic creativity and scientific creativity were assumed to be very different. However, when they studied the actual process that creative people said occurred, they turned out to be very similar. The process of scientific creativity seemed to involve preparation, that is, gathering all the information necessary, then a sort of what was called an "incubation" period occurred, and then finally, and often unexpectedly, the solution would come. Creative ideas are frequently described as coming like flashes of lightning, most often in dreaming or reverie-like states, or when the body is in active motion, as in walking. The essence of both scientific and artistic creativity was described most often as a vision, or the sound equivalent.

The unimportance of and even interference of language and the intellect is often emphasized. Arthur Koestler concluded, after studying creative geniuses in science, that: "their virtual unanimous emphasis on spontaneous intuition, unconscious guidance, and sudden leaps of imagination which they are at a loss to explain, suggests that the role of strictly rational thought processes in scientific discovery has been vastly overestimated"[152]. In essence, the most creative scientists are visionaries and seers. A.E. Housman stated clearly "the intellect is not the fount of poetry, that it may even actually hinder its production, and that it cannot even be trusted to recognize poetry when produced."[153] Albert Einstein insisted words as written or spoken did not play any role in the mechanism of his thought. "Language can become a screen which stands between the thinker and reality. This is the reason why true creativity often starts where language ends." [154]

His statement hints at conditions that seem helpful, if not necessary, in creativity. Modern psychology speaks of altered states of consciousness. Amy Lowell spoke of going into a semi-trance.   Research indicates meditation substantially increases creativity.[155] "Seeing is the problem, or, to be more specific, shifting to a particular way of seeing."... .to experience a slightly altered mode of awareness;....to see things in a different way," "artists speak of feeling transported . . . Awareness of the passage of time fades away, and words recede from consciousness."[156] Edward Hill spoke of emptying one's mind of all thought and refilling the void "with a spirit greater than oneself,," which extended the mind into a realm not accessible by conventional processes of reason.[157] Koestler believed "Every creative act involves a new innocence of perception, liberated from the cataract of accepted belief."[158]

Creativity inevitably invokes the idea of genius. In 1700 genius meant: "an incomprehensible and mysterious force animating certain human beings." It was generally applied, however, to "the individuals manifesting this force." The designation genius is today usually given to a human being who has an extraordinary capacity for desirable originality, or who makes a new and profound contribution to some or all of mankind.[159]

Such people are rare. However, it is well known that they appear in clusters, in particularly large numbers in certain periods of history in given geographical areas, as in the classic Greek period, the Italian Renaissance, and Moorish Spain. The clusters occur at irregular and at times long intervals. Great debate is waged over whether the culture makes the men, or the men make the culture. Arieti thinks the potentiality for creative genius is frequent, and believes some cultures are creativogenic, promoting creativity much more than others.

Another often noted phenomena, particularly in science, is that frequently people in different parts of the globe, seemingly unrelated, "discover" the same thing at approximately the same time.

Psychiatrist Cesare Lombroso insisted genius and insanity were related, and finally decided that the quality of being a genius is associated with epilepsy—in other words, with unusual electrical discharges in the brain. Hirsch stated: "the works of genius are produced by an inner or 'instinctive necessity'; genius never proceeds from intention or choice, nor from utility nor gain. For the genius, his works are an end, sufficient and necessary in themselves; for others a means."[160] Buckminster Fuller thought we are all born geniuses, and then are systematically "degeniused" by our parents and social forces. He attributes his incredible creativity to intuition, which he learned to trust at age nine, when it saved his parents' lives.

Psychotherapists have examined the creative process. They found strong external hindrances to creativity, including social pressure to conform, time limits, performance pressures, over-emphasis on order and discipline, over-emphasis on verbal logical-analytical modes, over-emphasis on practicality, and depreciation or even punishment of creative expression. Internal hindrances, which are considered learned, include concern over others' opinions, excessive involvement with others, judgmental attitudes, freezing of behavior into rigid patterns, and fear.[161]

They also found conditions which favor creativity. The external conditions include a playful, non-competitive, non-judgmental environment, situational motivation, no time pressure, trust, privacy, and process orientation. The internal conditions include receptivity to new phenomena, lessening of defenses and inhibitions, non-habitual responses, self-discipline, realistic self-appraisal, wide interests, rejection of external restraints, self-expression with materials, ability to let capacities flow, and ability to improvise, dance and dramatize.

Kubie compared the neurotic and creative processes, and wrote that the essence of health and normality "is flexibility in all vital ways," and the essence of illness is the freezing of behavior into unalterable and insatiable patterns.[162] He thought creative behavior to be automatic when unhindered. What we need to do is learn how not to interfere with the inherent creative capacity.

SUFISM AND CREATIVITY

Although we use the term, man does not and cannot really create. Man does not bring into being out of nothingness. Man cannot cause to exist that which does not exist. What man can do and does do, is describe, and modify, use and adapt to suit his own purposes and ends. Much of what we consider "discovery" is description. The stars named by astronomers have always been there. Electricity existed millions of years before Franklin put a key on a kite string in a thunder storm, and said so. Einstein's Theory of Relativity describes what already exists. Gravity was present long before Newton described it after watching an apple fall.

The Bible (Ecclesiastes 1:9) tells us "there is no new thing under the sun." There are modifications and improvements and additions. Man combines already existing elements in new and more beneficial ways. In science, work of multiple layers of complexity may be involved, as in development of the polio vaccine, or Magnetic Resonance Imaging. Generations of prior work and discovery may go into the production of some object of everyday use. However, nothing man has invented does not already have a basis somewhere in Nature. All the principles of physics and engineering and chemistry and architecture and all the other fields have been ever present. No art form, however beautiful, is more than a variation of the art of Existence. The most fantastic geometric patterns are present in flowers—one need only to look at the pattern of seeds in a sunflower. No colors are more exquisite than those of the tropical rain forests. No pattern is more delicate than those of the microscopic "snowflakes" of life seen through the electron microscope.

There is only one source, only one Creator. The works of man are manifestations of His creativity, mirrors of His handiwork. Those who are considered creative are those who are able to make and sustain a connection with the creative force of the Ground of Existence, with God. And those who do, whether they be artists or scientists, inevitably sound more like people we label "mystics" than they do the image of the rational, logical, measured mind many of us have been mistakenly taught as essential for scientific knowledge.

Literature has provided clear portrayals of the creative process. The poet Samuel Taylor Coleridge fell asleep in his chair, and "all the images rose up before him as things" which later became *Kubla Khan*.[163] The writer D.H. Lawrence said: "The knowing eye watches sharp as a needle; but the picture comes clean out of instinct, intuition and sheer physical action. Once the instinct and intuition get into the brush tip, the picture happens, if it is to be a picture at all."[164] Mozart slept and dreamt of a far journey, to Syria, Judea, Arabia and Jerusalem: "Now during my dream-journey, the following canon came into my head."[165]

If we move to scientific creativity, Albert Einstein said that: "The psychical entities which seem to serve as elements in thought are certain signs and more or less clear images which can be 'voluntarily' reproduced and combined." "The above mentioned elements are, in my case, of visual and some of muscular type." [166] Nietzsche spoke similarly: "When my creative energy glowed most freely, my muscular activity was always greatest. The body is inspired."[167] Henri Poincare, felt understanding higher mathematics required a "special intuition."[168]

Contrary to what most believe, Einstein taught us that scientific theory should not be based on observable, measured data. "On principle it is quite wrong to try founding a theory on observable magnitudes alone. In reality the very opposite happens. It is the theory which decides what we can observe." Albert Einstein said this to Werner Heisenberg, who changed his ideas and began to "assume" that relationships existed. The resulting work led to concepts which changed the world of science for Heisenberg won the Noble Prize in 1932 for his "uncertainty principle." The words he used and those invented as a result of quantum theory changed all of science. Since then scientists are allowed to be uncertain about the ability to measure everything. But many psychologists have not yet realized this.

The English physicist Michael Faraday "saw" the stresses surrounding magnets and electric currents as curves in space and "saw" the entire universe as made up of these lines of force. From his visions, numerous mathematical theorems were developed, and the dynamo and electric motor invented. The inventor of the electron microscope, Max Knoll, was fascinated with the often sudden emergence of new ideas. He described the process: "Always unmistakable are the suddenness and activity of the intuitive event, and its tendency to occur in a state of relaxation, and after a protracted 'period of meditation .This cannot be attributed.to higher thinking functions."[169]

Creative people often experience creative activity as "inspired." Jean Cocteau felt that "when the work that makes itself in us and in spite of us demands to be born, we can believe that this work comes to us from beyond."[170] Jung envisioned art as "a kind of innate drive that seizes a human being and makes him its instrument. The artist is not a person endowed with free will who seeks his own ends, but one who allows art to realize its purposes through him."[171] Nietzsche described:

> one is the mere incarnation, or mouthpiece, or medium of some almighty power. The notion of revelation describes the condition quite simply;... One hears—-one does not seek; one takes—-one does not ask who gives: a thought flashes out like lighting, inevitably without hesitation—I have never had any choice about it... Everything occurs quite without volition, as if in an eruption of freedom, independence, power and divinity.[172]

Thomas Wolfe tells us "I actually felt that I had a great river thrusting for release inside of me and that I had to find a channel into which its flood-like power could pour."[173] Jung felt the artist: "has penetrated to that matrix of life in which all men are embedded, which imparts a common rhythm to all human existence."[174] His concept of creativity as deeply connected with the spirit of all men is often echoed. Roger Sessions tells us "music goes deeper (it) reproduces for us the most intimate essence, the tempo and energy, of our spiritual being."[175] The philosopher Suzanne Langer spoke of " the concept of the human mind as a creative entity not belonging to physical nature but to a different order of reality."[176]

Psychology, despite valiant efforts, has been unable to teach us how to become creative. A few psychotherapists have accepted the effectiveness of Concentrational practices (which they call meditation) in increasing creativity, but essentially, psychology has described, and assessed, but has no real means for developing creativity. Sufism teaches the way to make the connection with the Source of Life which is the essential ground of creativity.

Creativity requires listening very, very carefully, to the love songs of Existence. The listening must be open, untainted by the conceptions and perceptions of others, the open listening of the young child. The poet Amy Lowell said:

> Let us admit at once that a poet is something like a radio aerial—he is capable of receiving messages on waves of some sort; but he is more than an aerial, for the possesses the capacity for transmuting these messages into those patterns of words we call poems... Some poets speak of hearing a voice speaking to them, and say that they write almost to dictation. I do not hear a voice, but I do hear words pronounced, only the pronouncing is toneless. The words seem to be pronounced in my head, but with nobody speaking them.[176a]

The waves are always being broadcast, but most of us cannot hear them. God is always speaking, but we are not always listening. As both The Holy Bible and The Holy Quran teach us, we must have eyes to see and ears to hear that are beyond those of ordinary sensory perception. These capacities require development. Creativity entails letting go of the boundaries, like a drop of water becoming one with the sea. When we have opened ourselves to Existence, then we can see the beauty, harmony, and order of the Universe, and let the pattern of creation of the Creator move through us.

Through many centuries, the creative flow has repeatedly emerged in saliks. The earlier quotations are accurate, but not complete descriptions of the experience for many seekers. A state of ecstasy, of rapture, of being "carried away," often occurs. Rumi recited his famous love poems while in a rapturous state, often being unable to remember what he had said. Thousands of volumes of poetry, works of science and art, attest to the efficacy of the methods of Sufism. Working on concentration, meditation, and with the electromagnetic fields of the human body, many devoted seekers, with the guidance of the Pir, have been able to attain an unprecedented creativity.

In *Manifestation of Thoughts*, Professor Angha tells us that if all man's natural powers, strengths, senses, perceptions and other faculties can be concentrated on a precise, sensitive, metaphysical point of existence — or become accustomed to comprehending truth and reality, superior to sensory limitations and animal habits, he can then cognize more clearly and precisely natural principles which have metaphysical terms. When one reaches this concentration, then he will be able to comprehend and recognize even the energies beyond the waves, and will be able to comprehend the spirit and divinity of himself and those materials in the depth of his mind and soul. A different level of reality is discovered. Then there is access to the fountain from which creativity flows.

The minds of men must be prepared, and many universal forces and factors must be in harmony for specific kinds of knowledge to be available to the intellect of man. When the time and circumstances are appropriate, then the concepts are received by those minds capable of receiving them. This is why in science sometimes several researchers independently make the same discovery at the same time. They are in harmony with the music of the Timeless Player.

CHAPTER 11
INTELLIGENCE

What is intelligence? The experts cannot agree on a definition, although they theorize extensively. Two main themes consistently reappear in discussions of the nature of intelligence. One is that intelligence is the capacity to learn from experience, and the second is that intelligence is adaptation to one's environment. Most theories assume intelligence is based on our thinking processes and thinking is assumed to be a function of the mind, which is assumed to reside in the brain.

However defined, psychologists have been trying to test intelligence for almost a century. A Frenchman, Binet, who wanted to predict which children would be able to function adequately in school, developed the first individual intelligence test. World War I brought the Army General Intelligence Test, a group test which predicted how well men could function as soldiers. Wechsler Intelligence Scales, individual tests for children and for adults, were later developed, as were assorted group tests of intelligence. These tests were constructed so that the average score or mean for any age would be 100. Scores 30 points or more above or below the mean were considered significantly higher or lower, so that a person with a score of 130 would be considered bright, and a person with a score of 70 would be considered mentally retarded. The scores came to be called "IQ" (for Intelligence Quotient) scores. Scores were used to admit students to programs for the "gifted," and to place students in classrooms for the mentally retarded. Although very popular for awhile, their use decreased dramatically as a result of a court decision citing their cultural bias. Most primarily tested verbal ability, particularly vocabulary, and reasoning ability—logic or rationality.

American theorists have focused attention on three areas in trying to define and measure intelligence. Learning theorists see intelligence as a build-up of environmental stimulation-reaction (Stimulus-Response or S-R) bonds of various qualities and quantities. The factor approach is based on obtaining estimates of relationship (intercorrelations) between scores on different tests of mental abilities. This yields "factors"—grouping together those elements which are highly correlated with each other. Spearman, who invented factor analysis, assumed there is a single general intelligence ability or factor, which "could best be understood as a kind of 'mental energy.'"[177] and as many sub-factors as there are kinds of tests. Guilford, in contrast, proposed that intelligence comprises 120 elementary abilities, each of which involves the action of some operation upon content to produce a product. It is important to recognize that these concepts depend totally upon what is already measured, for they are based on tests. There could be plenty more, and evidently is, for traditional intelligence tests account for only 10 to 25% of the variance in real-world performance.[178]

Cognitive theories are information processing conceptions of intelligence, which share the idea that people mentally represent and process information. The computer program is a frequently used metaphor. Sternberg, currently the most popular theorist, proposes a three-part theory.[179] Information processing consists of: 1. Metacomponents which are executive decision making processes, 2. Performance components which are the processes used in the task, such as encoding and comparing, and 3. The processes used in learning new information. He emphasizes the importance of context—of environmental aspects. His theory tells us little about how information processing takes place. He asserts that although the content of intelligence varies across cultures, the hardware (physiology) and potential software (cognitive processes, strategies, mental representations) are found in varying degrees in all people in all socio-cultural milieus. All aspects of intelligence are therefore related to context."[180]

Some well known experts are suggesting: "'Perhaps the whole measurement approach is becoming obsolete.' 'Is this 'intelligence' or is the whole concept irrelevant here?' Perhaps the question should be: 'How does this person function?' in various situations."[181]

Howard Gardner proposes that intelligence takes multiple forms, which we all possess to a greater or lesser degree. Each form of intelligence has its unique neurological pattern as well as its own course of development. He describes seven types of intelligence: Linguistic, Musical, Logical-mathematical, Spatial, Bodily-Kinesthetic, Interpersonal, and Intrapersonal.

Most important schools of thought regarding intelligence tend to assume the social nature of its development, yet rarely talk about it. Investigators from other countries focus on it. The famous Russian psychologist, Vygotsky stated:

> Every function in the child's cultural development appears twice: first, on the social level, and later, on the individual level; first between people (interpsychological) and then inside the child (intrapsychological). This applies equally to voluntary attention, to logical memory, and to the formation of concepts. All the higher functions originate as actual relations between human individuals.[182]

In other words, our thought processes, including our intelligence, are a sort of tape recording of interpersonal interactions. Bourdieu in France asserts that social division, as between intellectuals and manual laborers, vests intelligence with considerable social importance. Judgments about intellectual capacity are consequently strongly influenced by social background. "Systems of social interaction influence individual cognitive development while at the same time social interactions in different cultures have common elements influencing the initiation of cognitive development." [183] Hall's work in non-verbal communication supports the notion of the social basis for "intelligence."[184]

The importance of cooperation in intelligence is often emphasized abroad. Piaget stated that only cooperation, which he defined as any interaction in which there is no element of authority or prestige "constitutes a process in which new cognitions may be produced, while autism and social constraint can lead only to the various forms of prelogic." Moise and Dugny describe: "it is not a matter of merely acting on reality—it is rather in the coordination of one's own actions with others that systems of coordination which can later be reproduced autonomously develop. . . interaction enables the individual to master certain abilities which allow him to participate in more complex social interactions which in turn promotes continued cognitive development."[185]

The Russian Alexander Luria showed how important social change such as collectivization and the spread of literacy in agricultural communities gave rise to capacities for abstract thought. The work of Brazilian Paolo Freire, who educated illiterate peasants using a cooperative model, was successful in teaching them reading and also teaching abstract thought. His results were so good they resulted in his exile, for literate, "Thinking" peasants constituted a political threat.

Evidence from other disciplines indicates different aspects of the social nature of intelligence. Biologist Lewis Thomas says: "We do not like the notion that there can be collective societies with the capacity to behave like organisms."[186] Yet they exist, in flocks of birds, hives of bees, and schools of fish. Termites accumulate intelligence as more of them gather together. When they reach a critical mass, the architecture begins. Computer experts have begun programming computers to pool data. Business has discovered a corporate, collective power is far greater than any one individual can exert. "We do not often feel our conjoined intelligence. Perhaps, however, we are linked in circuits for the storage, processing and retrieval of information, since this appears to be the most basic and universal of all human enterprises."[187] Thomas tells us: "We have access to all the information of the biosphere, arriving as elementary units in the stream of solar photons. The circuitry seems to be there, even if the current is not always on." [188]

According to Piaget, from about age eleven on, full cognitive or intellectual development is reached. Some recent theorists propose that development continues beyond that point, on into adulthood. Michael Commons believes that age, education and "working at it" are necessary to reach the peak of adult intelligence—"being engaged in the world and actively confronting problems is a necessary condition for continued mental development. You have to place yourself in situations where you have to face, and deal with, challenges."[189]

Commons and Francis Richards, after nine years of study proposed three additional stages of intellectual development AFTER Piaget's final stage:

* Systematic Reasoning: (Piaget's Logical Reasoning requires you

mentally manipulate variables in a stable system. In systematic, you manipulate the system itself).

* Metasystematic Thinking: Moving beyond systems

* Cross-Paradigmatic Thinking: So rare no way has yet been found to test it—it is creating a new concept by combining old ideas

Jonathan Baron believes that most types of mature intelligence are rational thinking. Since rational thinking can be taught, people can also be taught to be more intelligent. A rational thinker tries to understand all viewpoints, and is prepared to discard opinion if further evidence proves you wrong. It probably does not occur until adulthood—it requires finding answers, critically examining those answers, and questioning your belief in them.

Intelligence is often envisioned as like other capacities: "Use it or lose it." Various methods of sharpening intelligence are proposed:

* Be Open-minded: Re-evaluate your ideas in the face of new evidence. To achieve this, actively practice changing your mind. Deliberately take the opposing viewpoint.

* Confront and Challenge: Take risks, and actively look for problems.

* Learn to Concentrate: Computerized EEG recordings, have found previously unseen electrical patterns, which showed a direct link between ability to concentrate and subsequent performance.

* Meditate: Herbert Benson found that meditation before exams resulted in higher grades.

* Go back to school: In every culture, higher stages of thinking are related to the amount of education people seek. It is, however, not the books, but the questioning environment that appears to improve intelligence.

However intelligence is defined or conceived of, psychologists see intelligence as culture-bound, for what is considered "intelligent" behavior, and what benefits the individual in terms of survival varies markedly from culture to culture. The perception and definition of what is intelligent behavior is different in different cultures. The "intelligent" South Sea Islander knows ocean currents. The "intelligent" Eskimo must be able to perceive many kinds of snow, whose differences are imperceptible to us. Our culture prizes verbal and reasoning ability, so we have honored these forms of the intellect in our school systems. We have also used it as the basis for most intelligence or "IQ" tests, both individual and group. These tests have recently come under severe criticism. A recent

California court decision has effectively prevented their use without substantial additional assessment to determine placement in special educational programs.

SUFISM AND INTELLIGENCE

All of us are familiar with mental processes. They are necessary and useful in helping us function in everyday life. The intelligence perceived by psychology is an attempt at describing and assessing the functioning level of the electro-chemical biocomputer which is our brain. One brain may well function more rapidly or more slowly than others. It may be able to perform more or less functions, depending upon the input of software programs. However, is this intelligence? Or is it simply a matter of input received through the sensory modalities and processed in specific kinds of ways? The computer receives information, stores it, somehow cross-references it, and retrieves it when necessary. In addition, it is programmed to perform various processes with the information. Addition and division are simple examples. No matter how well we perform, we are always functioning on the limited basis of the biocomputer.

In *Wealth of Solouk*, Hazrat Pir discusses how the processes of induction and deduction, valued as "intelligent" behavior, are not based on true knowledge. They are, instead, images and illusions construed in the mind through the interplay of the physical senses and the natural environment. They explain only a limited aspect, value, and dimension of man, which is why, with each variable, different and sometimes contradictory results are obtained. People using these thought processes, the philosophers, theologians, psychologists, sociologists, etc., do not have access to man's central level of stability and identity. Thought and the activities of man's sensory level which are generally a combination of his sensory perceptions, cellular needs, unfulfilled desires, nature and experience, on the one hand, and his cultural heritage, personal and creative aptitudes, on the other, cannot provide the ultimate cognition of the absolute truth of man.[190]

Intelligence in Sufism is considered the Higher Mind—that faculty of the intellect that ensures the appropriate decision is made, action is taken, and a result obtained. It is a process derived not from reasoning but from inspiration. It is a receiving of, and accepting knowledge from the Source of Knowledge. No visible activity of the frontal cortex of the central nervous system bio-computer is required.

In *Al-Rasa'el*, Professor Angha describes the theoretical powers of the human self. The type of reason, of rational thinking considered as intelligence by psychology is only the first of four stages of these theoretical powers. This power of reasoning, as when the intellect is used in the service of worldly affairs, is called natural wisdom. It includes information from the physical senses and has the ability to accept all reflections. The second state is the sensory and intellectual powers used for cognition. It is called hidden wisdom, and is reflected in the more delicate attributes of the self. Development of the "eyes to see and ears to hear" referred to in the Bible and the Quran are necessary. Movement is from the cellular, automatically functioning level of man toward the locus for the development and interrelationship of the magnetic bodies and for mental, sensory and psychic powers. The third stage is the power to receive and be in the reality of spiritual truths, and the ability to realize them at all times. Literally speaking, it is called complete wisdom. The fourth stage is the complete realization of all inherent states of wisdom. This is the mysterious inner level, which is the central point of stability of man's true character and identity. As one progresses through the stages, knowledge of the mind becomes cognition of the heart.

In *Dawn*, Professor Angha describes the experience: "This transcendent state is one where all illusions can be swept away and knowledge—pure intuition—ascends to the center of the being."[191] The cognition of wisdom "is the all-encompassing state of all the states of existence."[192] Cognition of wisdom is cognition of God. It is "witnessing the Magnificence of the Glory of His Divine Countenance; in other words knowing the Exalted Lord God by His Divine Essence and, with certainty of cognition, affirming that everything is at His command."[193]

How can one attain this cognition, this state of wisdom, this absolute intelligence, absolute knowledge? Hazrat Pir tells us: "This kind of cognition is obtained only through loving, obeying and worshipping God by all means, with the self, heart and mind under the supervision of a master who will be introduced inwardly and secretly by God through the seeker's heart."[194] It requires presence in the heart with all inner powers and all mental and spiritual faculties and full commitment to seeking God, so that no thoughts, good or bad, can interfere.

Then one can come to know the special meaning of the word "intellect" in Sufism. Those who are annihilated in love are governed by their power of intellect. For them, astronomical destiny is synonymous with their will. For the lover, the Beloved's wish becomes their desire. Love is a word, or a reality, which is similar to life and God. Love is either intellect or life, or the most influential agent for these two agents, because the effects of love are accompanied by a superior order of life in all researchable fields. As love is a king of motion in the material world, life should be a shining reality and fixed, genuine foundation which is also called love. Gnostics and researchers call the middle axis between the two poles of real and unreal love the intellect. Professor Angha says that in his view, love, in all the three stages, is the very first, second, and third intellect which collectively rules the order to existence.[195]

CHAPTER 12
LANGUAGE

Most research in language is done not by psychologists, but by linguists, although psycholinguistics is becoming a more popular field. It may be that language learning begins while the fetus is still in the womb. The fetus reacts to sound, and studies have shown that infants prefer stories read to them during gestation. The young infant moves its limbs in synchrony with the sound of its mother's voice, so rhythmically that it looks like a dance on slow motion video tapes. The young infant can distinguish, and make, all the sounds of any of the hundreds of languages in the world. But if the sounds are not heard in his environment, the ability to make them is quickly lost—gone before the end of the first year. The acquisition of language is an amazing process, and very rapid. American preschool children are estimated to learn the meanings of some 16,000 words.[196]

There is extensive debate over whether or not we come "pre-wired" for the acquisition of language. Noam Chomsky states there is a biological predisposition to develop language, that we somehow have a "mental organ" that is functionally specialized for language.[197] Bickerton calls it a "language bio-program," which he sees as derived from a genetically coded program, expressed in ways as yet unknown through the structures and modes of operation of the human brain.[198] To support this idea, he produces evidence that grammar is produced in the absence of the generation-to-generation transmission of particular languages. Slobin[199] claims "Basic Child Grammar" is displayed by most children; that structures are consistently used by young children that violate the grammatical rules of their "native" language, but are cross-culturally consistent. An unsolved puzzle from this point of view is that languages have evolved forms inconsistent with the bioprogram.

Charles Ferguson reports mothers also come "pre-wired" to speak "baby-talk," using a high-pitched tone with short sentences, nonsense sounds, and simple phrases, regardless of cultural background.[200] Lenneberg has argued for the existence of a universal grammar. He states: "Social settings may be required as a trigger that sets off a reaction. Perhaps a better metaphor still is the concept of resonance. In a given state of maturation, exposure to adult language behavior has an excitatory effect upon the actualization process much the way a certain frequency may have an excitatory effect upon a specific resonator; the object beings to vibrate in the presence of the sound."[201] He also postulates, as do most, a "critical period" of "language-readiness." If language is not learned during this period, there is permanent impairment in language learning. The information available on supposed "feral"(raised by animals) children and abused children appears to substantiate this point of view.

Some critics of this point of view instead support the idea that language acquisition occurs as rapidly as it does due to the efficiency of processing mechanisms—in other words, the brain, or that it is the result of interaction of input with innate structuring tendencies. "Marler has shown that the innately wired version of some bird species' song emerges only in birds that have been deafened or isolated at birth; all birds reared under normal conditions learn and use the song dialect that happens to be current in their particular area."[202] From a common sense point of view, it is difficult to see how language development could take place as it does without some sort of genetic encoding.

Jerome Bruner has carefully studied how infants learn language. It appears to be initially learned from the mothers, for fathers tend to talk to infants far less. It is so closely interlaced with learning of social behaviors as to be almost inseparable. Language and social behaviors are learned simultaneously, very early in life. When a child is about two years old, he learns to talk to himself. This forms the basis for evaluating actions without performing the action first. Evaluations are likely to be in terms of social consequences. Once the child establishes this inner language, he can pre-evaluate behavioral possibilities. Jerome Kagan believes this sets the stage for performance anxiety and fear of failure. Up to 24 months of age, most infants will happily imitate any adult behaviors. At about that age, signs of distress over "performance" begin to appear, based on using language to rehearse and evaluate behavior before acting. As Luria points out, words codify our experience. They appear first in practical usage, linked to action. Only later do they become independent signs.[203]

Children are able to master the four major dimensions of language. These are the sound system (phonology), the system of meanings (semantics), the rules of word formation (morphology), and the rules of sentence formation (syntax). Animals, despite valiant attempts at teaching primates various types of "languages," simply do not have the linguistic capacity human beings have. Although they may learn variations of language, they cannot master these four dimensions as well as a six year old child can.

Language usage is primarily controlled by the left hemisphere of the brain in right-handed people. Damage to localized areas of this hemisphere produce specific kinds of language difficulties. Severe damage to specific areas in adults may result in the inability to use language. If such damage occurs early in childhood, the other hemisphere of the brain may be able to compensate and the child will learn language. Lesions in the deeper regions of the brain may also result in loss of language, "not because of the disintegration of a language system, but because of a disturbance in a nonlanguage system that influences the control and flow of speech."[204]

Whorf states that language shapes the way we think, for we think in words, and the words we learn, the words we know to use, define how and what we think. Anyone fluent in more than one language can tell you about differences in thinking patterns dependent on the language being used. English is known as a technological language, for example, since it contains innumerable technological terms, reflecting the activity of the culture. Persian is known for its poetry, particularly love poetry. Other languages reflect concerns and/or values of the people who speak them. Jaynes insists, "Language is an organ of perception, not simply a means of communication."[205]

Words can be very powerful tools, as advertisers and propagandists are well aware. Propagandists on every side, for example, frequently repeat terms like "motherland," "fatherland," or "homeland" during wartime. They are powerful not because of their explicit definition, called their denotative meaning, but because of their personal, emotional meaning, called the connotative meaning. The connotative meaning is based on personal experience, and may be highly individualistic. The word love is a clear example. To the normal child, "love" may include hugging, feeling safe and warm and well cared for. To the severely abused child, "love" includes being beaten. To Romeo and Juliet, it meant death. We talk about "loving" chocolate or various kinds of games. Our experience of the word love gives it the connotative, emotional meaning. Osgood has measured the connotative meaning of numerous words using a "Semantic Differential" scale. He found that almost all connotative meanings boil down to 3 dimensions: good-bad, strong-weak, or active-passive.

Since much of the connotative meaning is acquired early in life, interesting consequences ensue. Adults usually operate on the basis of overlearned language rules, and operate virtually automatically. Rarely do adults consciously consider their own speech. Hearing a tape recording of themselves often comes as a surprise. Even then, adults listening to such a tape are preoccupied with how they sound, and do not attend to the meaning of the words they are using. This concept is extremely important, for what it tells us about our behavior is that adults are attempting to communicate with words on the basis of what they learned connotatively as very young children, without ever attempting any rational, conscious consideration or weighing of the symbolic communication they are using. They are, so to speak, running on an "automatic pilot" programmed years previously in very different circumstances. Luria emphasized that even in adulthood, the emotional connections to words from early childhood are preserved.

In Western cultures, particularly in the United States, verbal learning is heavily emphasized. Language is considered of key importance, and much of the lengthy educational process involves learning the linguistic expressions of assorted authorities. Perhaps as a result, almost all the therapies rely on the spoken word, usually heavily. In fact, psychotherapy is often called the "talking cure." Some exceptions, such as the "Expressive Therapies" of music, dance and art, focus more on the non-verbal element, but still utilize conversation. Psychoanalytic, psychodynamic and many cognitive therapies depend almost entirely on the use of words.

SUFISM AND LANGUAGE

In Western society, words are highly valued. We forget that words cannot transfer the meaning. They are only signs or symbols for things, a form of symbolic communication. Like all signs and symbols, they are different from what they stand for, just as a map is different from the territory it portrays. The map and the territory are not the same thing. The map and the territory do not even look alike. For example, have you ever been to a foreign country or a far distant city? If so, did you read about where you were going before you went? Was actually being there different from reading about it?

The old saying, "One picture is worth a thousand words." conveys the inability of words to accurately depict anything. No matter how many words are used to describe even the simplest object, they can never present a total, complete, precise definition which would allow us to accurately envision the object in all its most minute detail. The situation becomes more obvious, and more impossible, when we attempt to describe a person with words.

What if I told you all about the delicious piece of candy I ate yesterday, which was red, with little sparkly crystals on it, and was the sweetest thing I had ever tasted. Would you know how that piece of candy tasted? You could not, you would only be reminded of other sweet things you had eaten. If a man were in the desert, and dying of thirst, with a parched, dry throat and cracked lips, how would he feel if he received a piece of paper with the word "water" printed on it? He needs the real thing, water, to assuage his thirst. You can never satisfy a hungry person by saying the word, "bread." A hungry person will never be filled simply by hearing the word, "bread." The satiation of hunger requires actually consuming what we call "bread," not the word. Words do not contain and cannot transfer the meaning.

The meaning words have for us is based on our past sensory experience. When we think of the color, blue, we think of things we have seen we were told were blue. Actually, we did not see a thing at all, blue or not, for all we see are the reflections of light rays. No two people attach the same meaning to a word, for no two people have quite the same experience. Have you ever loved? The meaning of the word "love" is based on your experience of it. One could read every book ever written on love, but still would not know what love was until love was actually experienced.

What matters most cannot be adequately expressed in words. Words simply cannot convey accurately anything abstract, anything of great import.

Western society teaches us to depend upon language; teaches us that learning is dependent upon written and spoken words. We are required to read dozens, if not hundreds or thousands, of books, and regurgitate their contents. Yet it has been said that what one finds in libraries is not answers, but cross-references. Repeating the words of others will not provide peace nor meaning to our own lives. Repeating all the words ever written by famous men will still not gain us wisdom nor closeness to God. We cannot gain serenity and survival through reading, hearing, nor reciting our own words or the words of others.

John Holt states: "We are in the grip of an astonishing delusion." We think people learn from explanations. "Most of the time, explaining does not increase understanding, and may even lessen it."[206] We have all experienced a teacher trying to explain something we did not understand. A typical example would be understanding how a loom works—we learn best from observing and doing rather than hearing about it. "Words are not only a clumsy and ambiguous means of communication, they are extraordinarily slow."[207] He states we become addicts of symbols, and don't know how to let go of them when they are of no use to us . . .we must be ready to give them up, and use our minds in more appropriate ways.

If we keep ourselves preoccupied with language, with words, if we keep our brains busy playing with the ideas conveyed by language, it is practically a guarantee that we will never be able to attain inner peace nor tranquillity. If our mouth or our brain are preoccupied with words, are busy chattering, we cannot even hear someone else. How, then, could we hear God?

Language is useful for the ordinary activities of daily life. But words deceive us, and lull us into placidly accepting an artificial social consensus for reality. We know that nothing really important we have ever experienced can be adequately described in words, yet we cling to them. Words keep us enmeshed in the boundaries of ordinariness, imprisoned within the confines of societal rigidity, sensory perception and illusionary imaginings of our busy brains. Each word is like a minuscule cord, enswathing us until we are bound, like Gulliver in Lilliput. The frightening possibility is that we may not even recognize we are bound. Entrapped in words, we cannot escape. Einstein and others have told us how words can interfere in the creative process. Professor Angha tells us: "Words are the veil of Truth." Perhaps things were once different. The Revised Standard translation of the Bible (Genesis 11:1-9) tells us: "Now the whole earth had one language and few words." and men were "one people." That was until men came together and tried to build a tower to the heavens. God then "confused the language of all the earth," and scattered them abroad.

What language does God speak? Is language even appropriate as a concept concerning what is called "The Word" of God? The Holy Bible and the Quran both tell of God speaking to man. If God does not speak a language, how does God communicate? In Luke 8:10, Jesus tells us: "Unto you is given to know the mysteries of the kingdom of God, but to others in parables, that seeing they might not see, and hearing they might not understand." Sufism teaches the way to "the mysteries," to cognition, to the knowing beyond language.

Only if we can let words go, release them, and move into the quietness of the essence of our being may we hope for freedom. Only if we can hear beyond the words will we ever be able to cognize God. Sufi Concentration and Meditation techniques help us learn how to attain this goal, enabling us to gradually quiet our mind, and move into heart to heart communication. When we learn silence, when we develop our own inner subtle and delicate faculties, only then may we listen and hear the music of the Timeless Player. Only when our cup is empty will it be filled. Unless we are able to become again as little children, and relinquish our attachment to the spoken word, we cannot attain cognition. The famous Sufi poet, Rumi (Mehlavi) tells us: "When the lips are silent, the heart has a hundred tongues."[208]

CHAPTER 13
THOUGHT

Psychological definitions of thought are as multitudinous as definitions of intelligence. Every theorist seems to come up with their own. What is a thought? And what is it good for?

The word "thought" is Anglo-Saxon; "think" comes from Middle English, which means both are relatively new words. Both refer to forming or having in the mind, of reasoning, of judging in some manner. A typical psychology text definition is: "mental manipulation and combination of images, concepts, words, rules, symbols, and precepts."[209] It includes daydreaming, fantasy, problem solving, and all the things we "say" to ourselves internally, as well as free association. What is and is not a thought obviously depends on one's definition. Imagery is usually considered thought, and includes not only visual imagery, which is like a mental picture, and which 97% of people have, but auditory imagery (92%) and also movement, touch, taste, smell, and pain imagery, which 50% of people have as well.

Some writers speak of units of thought as including: images, language or symbols, concepts (categories), and muscular responses. The last unit surprises some, but some researchers believe we evidently "think" with our entire body. Einstein said his ideas usually came through visions or through his muscles. Thinking can sometimes be hard work because it is often accompanied by muscular tension and muscular micro movement.

Different societies value different ways of thinking. In Western society, we are taught to value logical, analytical thought, and are carefully taught specific methods of reasoning. Traditional psychology emphasizes the importance of such rational thought, which focuses on the use of "knowledge" from outside the self. Jerome Bruner suggests there are two modes of thought: propositional thinking, which is logico-scientific, and abstract, with primarily left brain hemisphere processing, and narrative, which includes descriptions of concrete human and interpersonal relationships, and is primarily processed in the right cerebral hemisphere. He comments on how people make up narratives about their own lives. They "think" their own story. And he tells us the oldest form of moral literature is the parable, and the most common form of informal instruction is the anecdote.

Another division of thought is similar, including the logical-analytical, but the second modality is considered spatial-metaphoric, with much more emphasis on encompassing the internal environment. When these two modes of thought are integrated, then higher thought processes, such as synthesis and creativity, develop. Other writers have described active and receptive modes of thought, with the former responding, and the latter accepting.

Guilford also divided thought into two major categories, calling them Divergent and Convergent Thinking. The convergent thinker is the ordinary person who learns and accepts the social consensus of reality and thinks the same way everyone else does. The divergent thinker thinks differently—his ideas are original, and often creative. As indicated, the highly creative often describe their most creative concepts as somehow "coming" to them, then afterward they "think" about it in the ordinary sense.

Margaret Mead, based on her studies of other cultures, saw thought as simply the conversation of gestures internalized, stating that: "Even before self-awareness of anything that could strictly be called thought appeared, interaction between two individuals provided a base on which symbolic thought could be built." This ideas fits the discovery that infants move in synchrony with their mother's voice, performing what looks like a dance in slow motion. Mead also, when asked where her mind was located, stated that it was "All over her body."

However we think, more and more researchers are coming to accept

Vygotsky's concept of thought as a social product. He sees the developing mind as embedded in society. Thought is developed and maintained through interpersonal experience, and thinking is intimately related to and dependent upon internal and overt speech.[210] This is in line with ethnographic research which suggests "thinking is an interaction between an individual and a physical and social situation."[211] Thinking is situated in contexts of beliefs, assumptions and understandings about knowledge that differ markedly between individuals and social groups. The fundamental characteristics of thinking are determined by these social contexts. "Thinking can be viewed as a skill."[212] Study of "successful thinking" in various specific subject-matter fields indicates that the thinking uses information specific to that particular field.

Current psychological thought sees all forms of thinking as examples of narration, of story-telling. Science has emphasized objectivity, until quantum mechanics proved there is no real objectivity, for every experiment and observer affects the results. Science used to believe it had found true theories, but can no longer intellectually defend this position. Now it knows science is a form of story-telling, telling theoretical stories ever closer to the truth. Logic and rationality are a form of story-telling appropriate in certain circumstances. But if we wish to know the meaning of life, for example, we might prefer narratives from literature, clinical psychology, or religion. Even mathematical thinking is storytelling. Our multiplication procedure is one story, the abacus tells a different tale. In this perspective, several forms of thinking are seen as variations on the central theme of story-telling. Objectivists are now being described as "inventors who think they are discoverers—they do not recognize their own inventions when they come across them."[213] Constructivists acknowledge they play an active role in creating mental images, and thus, in creating reality.

Like Descartes, we tend to think, "I think, therefore I am." But most of what we do in our lives, we do without thinking. If we thought of everything we do, we would not be able to do much. Try thinking about everything you do before you do it. If you start when you awaken, you probably won't even be able to get yourself up and ready to go to work on time. Julian Jaynes insists that human beings learn and solve problems primarily without conscious thought, so he states thinking is not conscious, it is an automatic process following an instruction. There is no conscious thought involved in selecting the heavier of two weights, nor in word association or figure completion. In speech we are not conscious of searching for words or of putting them together, or making sentences. Conscious thought would interfere with playing the piano, or tennis or weaving, or other motor skills.

A wealth of research data indicates problem solving occurs much faster than we can think. Children have intuitive conceptual understanding of many tasks and areas before they can "think" about them.[214] Thinking is actually inefficient. Our "mental processes," like a computer, work much faster than our thoughts can keep up with. One example is that of "subliminal messages," which are presented on TV, video, or film too rapidly to enter our conscious thought process, but nevertheless have a measurable impact. They never become a thought but affect our behavior nevertheless. Advertising is often based on visual messages received in a matter of seconds, but which never enter our conscious mind.[215]

Thought is limiting. When we try and think of "tree, we think of a particular tree. There is no way to think of the concept "tree." There is no way to think of most concepts—we can only think of examples. If we think of childhood, we can only think of a succession of incidents. In classical conditioning, like Pavlov's dog learning to salivate at the sound of a bell, thinking can often interfere with learning.

Once we have learned patterns of thought and a definition of self, we guard it zealously. Greenwald spoke of the "Totalitarian Ego," which protects our mental organization. Our ego determines what we think. It seeks out information which agrees with it, rewrites history if necessary, and does not even see or hear threatening information. This is often obvious to others, but not to ourselves. Research in perception continually adds new evidence that we see and hear what we want or expect to see and hear, not what is there, and then we "think" it. The flash of anger people often feel when they are presented with information conflicting with what they already think is the mind's way of protecting its organization, its basic belief system. Greenwald described people's behavior succinctly: "My mind's made up, don't confuse me with the facts."

Several psychotherapeutic theories emphasize that how we think, particularly about ourselves, dramatically affects our lives. *The Feeling Good Handbook*[216], which deals with overcoming depression, primarily by changing our thinking patterns, is a best-seller. For example, the author discusses how to change what he calls TIC's (Task-Interfering Cognitions), which are typically distortions of thought.

Negative thinking can be stressful and detrimental. Rational Emotive therapy teaches that our life problems stem from irrational assumptions (thoughts) we have about the world. The point is to change the way we think. Examples of erroneous assumptions are the ideas that one has to be loved by everyone all the time, or that one has to be perfect in every way. The basic idea is that it is not what happens to us in life that makes us unhappy, but how we think about what happens to us. They describe catastrophizing, in which a mountain is created from an anthill. A good catastrophizer can escalate the cap being left off the toothpaste tube into a great dramatic scene in which the catastrophizer ends up believing nobody loves her because her spouse left the cap off. How does one change the thought of a catastrophizer so he or she instead sees an event as a godsend? They can learn to minimize the event seen as negative, or learn to "reframe" it—perhaps seeing it as a powerful learning experience—or simply learn to divert their attention, and do something else to keep their mind busy.

Therapists often ask clients to make affirmations about themselves—to make a list of qualities they would like to exhibit more, for example, and then to say them aloud as if they were true, or write them out on a daily basis. For example, "I am courageous." Or "I am joyful." Therapists speak of "self-fulfilling prophecies"—what a person thinks is going to happen tends to happen. So they try and teach clients to think positive thoughts, to have positive expectations. For example, if a client expects people to give him a hard time, he is asked to change his thinking and instead expect people to help him.

Transactional analysis focuses on "life-scripts"—our patterns of behavior learned very young, and how to re-write them more satisfactorily. The "lines" of our scripts are our thoughts, the things we tell ourselves about ourselves and our lives.

SUFISM AND THOUGHT

Thought is a secondary phenomena, a reaction. No matter how much we value it, it is still always a reaction. Thinking often consists of rehashing and rehearsing—that is, going over the past and anticipating the future. How often do you dissect and analyze events that are over and done with? How often are you speculating on what may happen in the future? If one is constantly thinking of what has already happen and/or what will happen, it is impossible to be in the present moment, so that moment is lost. And the present moment is all we really possess. We receive information, and we store it, and storage may give us another idea. The creativity, the logic and reasoning of our mind gradually builds our sensations, our nature, our life. We need to know our own mind, and to know it, we must know the sources of the information and the results of the information it contains.

For example, if you use the word "tea," you refer to past experience. You have taken dried leaves from a box marked "tea," poured boiling water over them, and then drunk the resulting hot liquid. Your mental process goes to this information like a computer. You have the necessary data.

All our experiences can be placed in two major categories: Prior experience, for example, with tea and no prior experience: what we have heard or read or thought. We cannot consider a person wise who refers to what they have not experienced. If we have even a little experience, we can understand "tea." We know it is not a shirt, and we know how to use it. We don't use it for a footbath.

In the second category, that of no prior experience, the mind creates something in order to provide a response. For example, if you have never seen snow you really don't know snow, yet our mind creates something for itself, which changes when you finally encounter snow. Have you an adequate definition for happiness? It is abstract and cannot be defined. We can only give examples, describing situations when it occurs. Millions of words have been written about death, but who has experienced death and can describe it knowledgeably? Most of the problems in people's minds are caused because they think they know what they have never experienced.

Let's use another example—smoking. If you have not done it, could any words accurately describe the experience? The colonists in 1492 saw the Indians smoking. What did they do? They poured water on them because they thought they were on fire. That is what their experience told them. Our mind and our thoughts are under the influence of past experience.

We have all listened to people talk, and have read articles and books about God. What is important is the experience of God. If we have none regarding God himself, whatever we think is like the settlers pouring water on the smoking Indians. What about hell, paradise, angels, heaven, mercy, grace, light? What actual experience do we have of these? We have to learn to surrender what we have already experienced. Then we have to find the real way and the real door. The matter of cognition happens when we are totally free from words. We read words and speak words, but are free from them. Our mind is a liar, inevitably. It lies to us. Consider: If the bank of information in my mind is misinformed, how can I understand that it is misinformed? The mind is not bad, it is very good and very capable, if it is under the influence of the heart.

When our mind is chattering away, with thought upon thought, can we really hear anything else? We need to learn to quiet it, to silence the chattering brain. Those portions of the brain essential to functioning will continue to operate, as they do even when we sleep. But the continual noise of thoughts is not only unnecessary, but actually interferes in functioning well. Hazrat Pir uses the example of riding a horse. We need to learn to ride the horse, to control it, not to let it take us wherever it pleases. We need to be in charge of the horse that is our body, including our brain, which is also physical. When we first try to bridle, saddle, and ride our horse, it tries to buck us off, but slowly, gradually, over time, it settles down and allows us to control it. If we ride it daily, it soon learns to follow our directions, and to move at the directed pace.

Professor Angha's book, *Manifestation of Thoughts*, discusses all aspects of thought. He tells us the naive person mistakes the introductory information learned in formal education and readings for essential truths. Caught in the maze of everyday life, he is "enveloped, engrossed and enamored" of it. His thoughts incorporate the material, and he thinks he knows what there is to know. He repeats, internally and externally, the words and works of others, like a "talking book" from the library, or the TV newscasters. People memorize and write the words of great people and never realize they have done nothing to be proud of. But one who only talks about science is not a scientist. One who reads the Psalms of David in a very fine tone does not have the spiritual privilege of David. This is obvious. What is not so obvious is how we continually repeat ideas garnered from everyday life, from acquaintances and TV, co-workers and newspapers. How often do we repeat early parental dictates? The ordinary person grows obedient and imitative in their thoughts, and their actions follow. The basis of inquiry is silenced. "His thoughts acting like a calculating machine, a mechanical piston, he merely performs blind imitations and rituals, feeding, as it were,on the toil and fruits of other men and nations."[217]

Professor Angha tells us the true scientist reads the necessary background material with a dynamic, questioning mind, understanding that new scientific discoveries constantly change and replace current ideas. Their thought searches and inquires, rather than simply accepts. The true scientist has an open mind, uncluttered by past thoughts. With a quiet mind, one is prepared to hear and receive. In this state, one is prepared to receive the little "lightning bolts" of inspiration and revelation. What is required is a deep connection of the inner self with the essence of Existence and with the meaning of outer sensory perceptions—a harmony between the open, receiving mind of the thinker and the manifestations of the universe, so that thoughts may emerge as water flowing from a pure, clear spring, unpolluted by contaminants.

As we pay attention to the mundane trivia of everyday life, we rarely pause to consider how the forces of nature may be affecting our thought. Yet we are obviously not exempt from the laws of physics. When we gaze at the heavens on a clear night, with planets, satellites and stars shining brightly, we think each is on its own course, independent. Yet from the grain of sand to the entire ocean, the Milky Way to globular clusters and mammoth groups of galaxies, into the infinity of space—at each point, fierce and grand waves are constantly at play, guiding each under precise, knowledgeable and calculable laws. How could the movement of particles and waves not affect our being? Could Nature's influence stop at our bodies, or are we, too, part of the cosmic dance? How could man, dependent upon and vulnerable to nature, despite all attempts to "conquer" it, infinitesimally tiny in the vastness of space, be worthy of possessing free will?

Professor Angha asks if orbital gravitation leads the planets, could not universal mind lead to the spirituality of the planet's inhabitants? When a susceptible mind attains proportionality and balance, the ability to recognize invisible truths under the influence of the physical and metaphysical waves is developed. The proportion of the electromagnetic spectrum which our senses receive and comprehend is tiny. Our senses are capable, under the proper influence and with additional ability and strength, of comprehending more expansively. For this to occur, there must be a true correspondence between the natural reality and man's spirituality, between his or her true character and existential levels. Then the capability of receiving more intricate, fine phenomena can be developed.

Joseph Cenil writes that he perceived the Sixth Sense through the realization of magnetic waves. Like a radio, the proper equipment is needed for receiving from the desired sender. Static, noise and interference must be eliminated, and then the desired channel can be tuned in. The sender and the receiver must be on the same level, and in harmony with existing conditions. When there is harmony and coherence of the physical and spiritual forces with the universal forces and powers, then the mind is ready and capable of tuning into the entire spectrum of waves. For this to occur, control over a specific part of the brain must be achieved. Most miss the broadcasts.

Only the wisest men, like Socrates, know how little science knows of even the physical level of the universe. What we perceive in everyday life is so limited as to interfere with vision and audition of the absolute, for it creates artificial boundaries. Our everyday thoughts cannot encompass nor mind comprehend the true reality. The intuitive scientists, the seers, the thinkers of the East, have told us that if all of our natural powers and faculties—our senses, thoughts, heart and nature, are in unity, and can be concentrated on a precise, sensitive, metaphysical point of existence, then we will be able to cognize natural principles phrased in metaphysical terms. We will then comprehend even the energies beyond waves, as well as our own spirit and divinity in the depths of our soul and mind.

What happens when this occurs? What transpires when the infinite, universal waves contact the neurons of an alert and reflective mind? It is then that the mind can receive and bring into conscious thought the discovery of one of nature's secrets, or bring forth a new theory to develop new frontiers. This is the "lightning bolt" experience of the creative scientist, the "muse" of the poet. This is why it is not unusual for scientists far separated geographically, with no information about each others' work, to make almost simultaneous discoveries. Conditions are ready, and they are ready to receive.

Professor Angha tells us it is the responsibility of a true and noble society to improve science and knowledge, to encourage its scientists and learned men. Each of us has the responsibility, the obligation, the capacity to respond to the higher levels which is necessary for true scientific growth and development, both in ourselves and in others, if we are willing to develop it and use it for the benefit of humanity rather than for personal gain. It is of crucial importance that new scientific and artistic thought be supported and encouraged, particularly by the universities. A university which does not encourage and accept innovative ideas, new realms of thought, is no better than a public library. The university can be visualized as working like the brain of a society, if and only if it is at the center of new developments and discoveries. Otherwise, it is like an empty shell.

Professor Angha, in *The Mystery of Humanity*, tells us how to handle thought:

> The divine vision is the observer of the shadows of life, and like a glistening star, bright and still, shines in your heart without hesitation. Concentrate your thoughts at this point in your heart and calm them; when it becomes steady and undisturbed the truth of your life will be revealed. If your thoughts turn to insignificant matters and blindly become a slave of your senses, your heart will disobey the commandments of God and will fail you along the rough road of life.
>
> Guidance is in the union of thoughts, the heart, the senses and nature; and going astray is disarray and confusion among these four.
>
> Gather all your energies and concentrate them on the source of life in your heart for your findings to become imperishable, so that you will live in balance and tranquillity and know eternity.[218]

CHAPTER 14
HUMAN DEVELOPMENT

The dictionary tells us develop is from the French word meaning to unfold or unwrap, and multiple meanings are given:

1. to cause to grow gradually in some way; 2. to expand; 3.to strengthen; 4. to bring into activity; 5. to unfold gradually; 6. to make more available or extensive; 7. in photography, to put exposed film in chemical solutions to make the picture become visible. Western psychology has a different definition.

The study of human development in Western psychology focuses primarily on description of the physical, mental and social changes which occur over the typical chronological age span. In other words, it is a linear and time-dependent perspective, strongly culture-bound. Some attention is paid to deviancy from the norms, but essentially, developmental psychology describes normal (average) behavior chronologically from before birth to death. However, only selected aspects are covered in most developmental texts. For example, emotional developmental is not always examined, and spiritual development is rarely included. Some cross-cultural studies have been attempted, but they are limited. Most of the research in the field has focused on infancy and early childhood. Texts covering life-span development have essentially described the social situations which occur, and their consequences, for example, divorce.

Philosophers have philosophized about development for centuries, particularly about the state in which the new individual arrives in the world. The Middle Ages gave us the joyful conception of the infant as born with original sin, and therefore an evil being (this view is still held by some today). British philosopher John Locke argues that a baby is born as a "tabula rasa" or blank tablet. Modern theorists can be divided into two groups. Empiricists believe the personality is formed on the basis of the information the person, first the infant, then child, then adult, receives through its various sensory modalities. Note that this is a matter of belief, of faith. Nativists believe that the human infant is born with certain characteristics—that, at the least, we come into this world "pre-wired," so to speak, in some areas. They believe we come with some innate capacities, such as the propensity for language development, mentioned earlier.[219] Rather obviously, what we see is determined by where we look, particularly if we use a microscope or telescope. Developmental theorists have not aimed their "scopes" in the same direction, much less at the same target. Consequently, they see different things.

Arnold Gesell placed most emphasis on the biological approach to development. He and his associates observed and noted the behavior of large numbers of children, and saw development as directed from within, unfolding according to a biological timetable, and believed capabilities appear when children reach the appropriate stage of maturity.[220]

Sigmund Freud's psychosexual theory of personality and development, mentioned earlier, is prominent. He developed his theory from observing and interpreting the behavior of his adult, disturbed and unhappy patients. Freud saw humans as motivated by irrational urges toward pleasure, and considered these urges to be expression of the "libido" the "life force" or "psychic energy" which motivates human behavior. According to Freud, the young child's instincts inevitably conflict with social demands, therefore socialized sensuality is of utmost importance. He named the unconscious impulses toward pleasure the ID. He stated that the EGO begins to develop at about 6 months, using memory, reason, and forming judgments. The role of the ego is as mediator between what one wants, and what one must or must not do. Finally, the SUPEREGO, the conscience, which is an internalization of parental values and standards, develops.

FREUDIAN STAGES

Stage	Age	Focus	Behavior
Oral	0-18 months	mouth, lips	seeks oral stimulation
Anal	18-36 months	rectum	enjoys retaining and ejecting feces
Phallic	3-6 years	genitals	fondles genitals, falls in love with other-sex parent
Latency	6-11 years	self	mastery of developmental skills
Genital :	from puberty	other people	mature sex relationships

Greenspan and his associates developed a theory of ego development based on a clinical study of "multi-risk infants and families and normal infants and families."[3] Two basic assumptions underlay his theory. The first is that the capacity to organize experience is present very early in life and progresses to higher levels as the individual matures. The second is that for each phase of development there are also certain types of experience that occur within the organizational structure. For example, the newborn is first interested in the world, then in forming a human attachment.

Greenspan's Stages of Ego Development

Homeostasis	0-3 months	self-regulation and interest in world
Attachment	2-7 months	forming bond with caregiver
Somatopsycho-logical Differentiation	3-10 months	purposeful, reciprocal communication with caregiver
Behavioral, Organization Initiative and Internalization	9-18 months	development of complex sense of self

Probably the most famous developmentalist is Jean Piaget, who based his theory of cognitive development on observations of his own children, followed by experiments with many normal children. His theory is discussed in the Chapter on Learning and Cognition.

Erik Erikson saw development as resolution of conflicts between individual needs and social demands. He believed personality develops according to steps predetermined by the individual's readiness to react with a widening social world. Each stage has its own characteristic conflict requiring resolution. Erikson is one of the few developmental theorists who covered the entire life span, rather than focusing almost exclu-

Erikson's Psychosocial Theory: Stages

Infancy:	0-18 months	Basic trust vs. mistrust
Early Childhood:	18-36 months	Autonomy vs. shame, doubt
Play Age:	3-6 years	Initiative vs. guilt
School Age:	6-11 years	Industry vs. Inferiority
Adolescence:	puberty to 21	Identity vs. role confusion
Young Adulthood:	20-40	Intimacy vs. isolation
Middle Adulthood:	40-60	Generativity vs stagnation
Old Age:	60 +	Integrity vs. despair

Having a sense of accomplishment in adult life depends on giving loving care to others and regarding your own contributions to society as valuable. The final stage in Erikson's theory should result in a sense of wholeness, of purpose accomplished and a life well lived. People who develop ego integrity see meaning in life, and believe they did the best they could under the circumstances.

The relative importance of heredity and environment in development has been a continual source of major controversy. The studies of identical twins reared separately indicate heredity to be of great importance, for astonishing similarities were found. One set of twins reared apart were found to have wives, sons and dogs each with identical names. However, studies of the impact of the environment also indicate its major importance. Orphanage studies indicate high mortality rates and often retarded development and physical debilitation.[222] The logical conclusion is that both are of crucial importance, and both profoundly affect the individual.

Physiologically, soon after the union of sperm and ovum, cellular reproduction begins in the fetus, and numerous identical cells are formed. At some unknown point in the first fourteen days after union, cell differentiation begins.[223] Cells within the human body vary enormously—brain cells are very different from skin cells or blood or bone cells. Somehow, the pattern for this crucial cell differentiation unfolds smoothly and rhythmically. At twenty-one days after conception, when the fetus is still very tiny, the first rudimentary fetal heartbeat begins. The electrical system is activated. Then the circulatory and central nervous system begin development. By the end of the fourth week, the four chambers of the heart have formed, and blood vessels surface.[224] Other systems develop in a systematic, pre-programmed fashion. Slowly and gradually over the next thirty-five weeks, growth and development progress until birth occurs. During this period of time, the fetus develops everything it will need to function in his life—eyes to see, ears to hear, feet to walk. For all this period, the fetus is totally dependent upon the mother for everything needed for life. All nourishment and all removal of waste materials is provided by the mother. Her bloodstream both feeds the developing fetus and cleanses it. Within her womb, the fetus is protected. The fetus may be strongly and even irreversibly affected by the behavior of the mother, particularly by what she eats, smokes or drinks, but also by her emotional and mental state. The fetus responds measurably to both strong light and sound during the last stages of pregnancy. Some research indicates preferences after birth for songs and stories recited by the mother during gestation. At approximately thirty-eight weeks after conception, development is complete, and the process of birth begins.

Much of our sensory equipment is very well developed at birth. At first, senses other than sight appear to be of prime importance. A newborn infant, who has never even eaten, reacts strongly and obviously to strong odors and strong tastes, making faces at fish oil, and seemingly expressing pleasure at sugar.[225] By one month of age, an infant prefers his or her own mother both on the basis of smell and the sound of her voice.[226] By one month, babies are beginning to see complex, as well as simple, visual patterns. They see color and hear speech. Eight week old infants can learn to kick to move a mobile by a ribbon tied to their ankle, or suck on a pacifier to make a movie clearer. Infants also demonstrated learned helplessness. Voluntary smiling occurs at 4-6 weeks. From month 2-3, babies appear capable of recognizing specific faces, and thereafter, the faces of familiar people. Newborn infants move their arms and legs in synchrony to the rhythms of human speech. Babies are born mimics. At 20 days, they clearly imitate facial expressions of strangers. Negative reactions to strangers typically occur after age 9 months.

The brain and central nervous system are not fully developed at birth, and grow very, very rapidly during the first two years of life. Within the two years, the brain triples in size, reaching 75 to 80% of adult weight and dimension.[227] Positron emission tomography (PET) of the brains of normal infants indicate that the active areas of the brain in the newborn are the sub cortical or "lower" areas. The cortex is simply not being used at first. At eleven weeks, neuronal activity is spreading through the cortex. It is not until after about seven and one-half months that a neuronal brain pattern similar to that of an adults is visible. Sensory and motor experience appear to be important in stimulating maximal growth in corresponding brain areas. Newborn infants have slow responses to sight and sound, which gradually increase with age. The average child is four years old before their brain can respond as quickly as an adults. The activation of the cerebral cortex, and, for all we know, its patterning, is dependent on the input from the external environment, mediated by the sensory modalities—sight, hearing, taste, touch, and smell. Even in infancy, numerous and sometimes great, differences in sensory functioning between individuals have been documented.[228]

In the US, the developing infant is very carefully and systematically taught to differentiate himself from others, to see himself as an individual separate and apart from others, and successful learning of this concept is considered an indication of successful "normal" development. For no clearly discernible reasons, if the family can afford it, the infant is isolated, kept alone in a separate room.

Parents are the primary socializers of the child, for they provide the early environment. Their effect is long-lasting, if not permanent. Children usually internalize their parents' values and standards. Parents' disciplinary styles differ. Induction, which appeals to the child's reason, pride, desire to be grown up, or concern for others, seems to teach the child the ability to display behavior appropriate for the situation better than power-assertive or love-withdrawal disciplines.. Children are treated differently, based on gender, from the moment of birth, and learn society's definition of their role. The number and sex of siblings affects the children. Same sex siblings tend to become more harmonious, mixed-sex pairs tease, threaten and compete more. Confluence theory considers the family like a river. The younger the child, the less the child contributes. As families get larger, the intellectual development of the younger children suffers.

In the US., the "traditional" family is now well in the minority (17-20% of all households). Most mothers work outside the home. Daughters of working mothers tend to be independent high-achievers with high self-esteem. Sons seem better adjusted and hold less traditional gender views. Divorce is so frequent that more than 50% of children today will spend at least part of their childhood in one of the one in four households that is a single parent home, usually that of the mother. This may lead to greater responsibility, self-sufficiency, and maturity. However, most families headed by women fall below the poverty line. Within five years, up to

75% of divorced persons have remarried. Perhaps 35% of today's children will spend part of their lives in a stepfamily. This adjustment is most difficult for children aged nine to fifteen

Child abuse is being reported more and more often. No single combination of factors clearly identifies the abusing family. Parents with low self-esteem appear to become angered at children more easily. The characteristics of the child also contribute to the likelihood of abuse. Just being male increases the risk of serious injury. Abused children tend to be more aggressive, less trusting, more passive, and more friendless.

Peer groups are significant in the US. They teach each other various skills and offer support and acceptance. Children lacking social skills who are rejected by peers suffer in most aspects of their lives. Children tend to conform to groups from about ages five to eleven. Dominance hierarchies exist in the groups.

Teachers reinforce sex and other social roles. They prefer high achievers and the less creative. TV strengthens many stereotypes, and aggressive behavior is associated with watching many violent TV shows. Schools are based on middle-class values and beliefs, which they reinforce. This culture stresses verbal, analytic skills. Assessment devices, such as the so-called "IQ" (intelligence quotient) tests, compare the child's performance with others of the same age. Educational systems have a profound effect on the developing child, either positively or negatively. Children's interpretations of school successes and failures affect their motivation and attitude.

Sexual maturity begins with puberty. Girls tend to mature younger than boys. Reactions depend on personal feelings and experiences. The individual is forming their identity, their sense of self, and examining, if middle-class, possible roles and goals. Adolescents do not necessarily have conflict with parents, nor are they separated by a generation gap. It is not a period of unusual emotional turmoil.[229] There is heavy emphasis on relationships with the opposite sex in the US. "Dating" may begin in junior high school, in groups, and progress through high school, into development of a "permanent love object.." Stress is placed on romantic love in all forms of the media, and many are sexually active. Teen pregnancy is commonplace, and a social problem. Teen AIDS cases are increasing. The majority of adolescents in the US. experiment with some form of drugs. Adolescent suicide is an increasing problem. Eating disorders appear to be increasing due to the social ideal of extreme thinness.

Those with eating disorders tend to be females with low self-esteem.

The middle-class young adult faces establishment of a career, a relationship with a permanent partner, a home, and a family, often all at the same time. Couples in the US. are today tending to marry later. Cohabitation has increased, but may now be decreasing again. Mead dubbed the marital pattern of divorces "serial marriage." Most mothers are now working outside the home, but most are in low-paid, dead-end positions. Parenthood is often delayed. Androgynous young adults tend to become more traditional once they have children. Child care is a problem for many families. Parenthood intensifies both pleasures and dissatisfactions. Adult cognitive development may move beyond the stages Piaget postulated to include acceptance of contradictions and integration of conflicting viewpoints. Information is used in a different way, is applied directly. Three principles of adult intellectual development are theorized: decline in speed and mechanics, failure to use full capacity, and compensation for declining functions by developing expertise.

Middle age people feel younger and happier than their parents and grandparents did at the same age. They are better educated, and the women are more likely to be employed. Midlife crises do develop. Children leave home, and aged parents may have to be cared for, which can create financial difficulties. Most marriages are institutional—satisfactory relationships. Extramarital affairs are common, and divorce rates are climbing. Men tend to re-marry, women do so less often. Grand parenting is an enjoyable experience for most.

Twelve percent of the US population is now over 65, and the percentage is steadily increasing. Physiological changes, particularly decreasing sensory acuities, become more pronounced and troublesome with age. The conduction velocity of nerve fibers drops about 15% between ages of twenty and ninety. Simple reaction time to lights and sounds drops 50% over the same period. One of the consequences of aging is deterioration in hearing ability. Loss is more pronounced at higher frequencies. Most people begin to need reading glasses soon after age forty-five. Scores on measure of fluid intellectual abilities have decreased, but scores on crystallized abilities have increased with age. The rule in all aspects of being—intellect, sexuality, physical agility, etc., seems to be: "Use it or lose it." People are living longer, and most are healthy and vigorous. Women outlive men. Retirement may become a problem, if not planned for, if income is markedly reduced, and if inactivity results. People have to come to terms with death. Choices may have to be made about custodial care, and these are not pleasant. Kubler-Ross proposed five stages of death: denial, anger, bargaining, depression, and acceptance. Developmental psychologists assume everything ends with the death of the physical body.

SUFISM AND DEVELOPMENT

Psychology describes the events during average chronological life-spans, but it does not tell us how to evoke the unfolding, the expansion, the growth, the development of the ideal human being or the ideal society, even though the descriptions indicate such development is crucially needed.

To describe development, Hazrat Pir uses the analogy of a seed. The destiny of a tree is all in the seed. Everything is prepared to be—the trunk, the bark, the roots, the branches, the leaves, the blossoms—all in one small seed. For it to grow, we must put it in the soil and provide water. It does not matter if we keep the seed in a box, or cloth, or a gold coffin, or whatever. If the seed is not cultivated, nothing else matters. If it grows in the soil, it will reproduce. If left, it will eventually rot, and will be ruined without using its knowledge.

We have our own "seed" which we can come to know. It lives within our body, which is like the soil. What is the seed? The seed is the "I," the true identity of man. It has to be found in the heart. Environmental conditions need to be prepared for it. Meditation prepares the ground and provides the proper conditions for the seed. We have only one "I," a seed that needs to be cultivated for growing. When you discover it, it will grow and overwhelm all else. This part, religions call God. Through growing, we see the reality of knowledge in the trunk, leaf, root, seed—everywhere. For every seed, there is a gardener. We must listen to the gardener. Each person has the truth within himself, to be discovered. It is not a matter of thinking, it is a matter of revelation. The "I" never thinks.

If you want a seed to grow well, the soil must have the proper nutrients and the site must have sufficient, but not too much sunlight, with no windbreak needed. The seed and growing plant must be protected from extremes of temperatures. Before planting, the land must be cleared—any large stones.removed What can be done with them? Fences made out of stones removed from the soil last for centuries. Any old trees must be cut down—they can be used for fire wood. Once the trees are cut, digging out the roots is the hard work. They go deep. The brush must be cleared, so the land is open to the sun. Then the soil must be tilled. .The seed should not be planted just any old time. The gardener knows when to plant, and he knows the depth. Different seeds need different depths. Weeding must be selective. Some varieties of plants in certain locations do better with certain kinds of weeds growing around them—weeds that keep away insects and parasites. Watering must be the right amount for the kind of plant you want to grow. Support must be provided if necessary—staking or a trellis may be needed for certain plants. Ultimately, most plants need careful pruning.

The seed sprouts and grows, and ultimately blossoms and bears fruit. The roots draw sustenance from the soil, and the plant ever reaches upward toward the sun, essential for its survival. Different kinds of seeds require different periods of time to reach maturity. An orange tree bears after four years, an apple after three years. Celery bears after two months, but dates only after thirty years. Only when fruit is borne has the plant fulfilled the promise of the seed, and produced the truth of the tree. Different kinds of plants take different lengths of time to mature. And so with the human being. Development is an unfolding of what is already within, the blossoming of our potentialities. It is also a preparation, in the case of the human, for the next life.

Hazrat Pir uses another analogy. The fetus spends nine months in the womb, slowly and gradually developing all the essentials needed for this life. It does not worry nor fret, it simply takes what is given it and grows. It develops feet to walk, hands to handle, ears to hear and eyes to see, all before it is possible to use them. Could the fetus possibly conceive of what life would be like after birth? It has no experience, no basis for conception, so of course it cannot. The environment is so different, there is no way the fetus could imagine it. Yet the fetus grows and develops to prepare for it, from within. The mother's umbilical cord gives it everything it needs—food, water, oxygen, removal of wastes. The entire developmental process is systematic and orderly, pre-programmed.

To the fetus, birth is like a death, for it is the end of the old life. It is death to womb life. After birth into this life, the earth itself provides everything we need for survival—water, oxygen, food. We are totally dependent upon the planet, however much we like to think of ourselves as "conquering" it. Earth provides our sustenance, our life support, and it is sustained by the energy from the sun.

Similarly, this life is a time of development for the next life. Just as the fetus could not conceive of this life, so our limited minds cannot conceive of the next life, for it is as different from this life as life in the womb was. We have no experience, no basis for understanding. We must develop all the capacities necessary for the next life in this life, and we must do so before death. Death to this life on earth is also a birth, and the new child to be born into the new life needs to have fully developed all the necessary capabilities for that life. Whatever we are born into the next life with is what we have in that life. This developmental process is also gradual. It cannot happen overnight.

Many Sufi works refer to the four stages of life: stone, plant, animal and human. These are actual physiological states. At first we are a combination of cells comprised of basic elements—hydrogen, carbon, oxygen, etc.—plus water, energies and the package of knowledge that is our genetic heritage. The elements are referred to as stones, so the first twenty-one days after conception are called the "stone" life. The first movement of life is the rudimentary heartbeat that begins at twenty-one days. Generation of the heart, then brain and nerves, bones and limbs, begins. The form is that of a tree, so this stage is called the plant or botanic life. This continues through birth up to 1 1/2- 2 years. It takes this long to learn how to walk, observe, think, know—to develop capacities beyond that of a tree. If a child dies in the botanic stages, it is like an uncultivated seed. The third stage is the animal stage. All the characteristics common to animals are displayed. The person grows, talks, walks, thinks, eats and multiplies. For the majority, life stops at this point. They will die in the animal state—ordinary activities come to an end. The elements are dispersed without ever showing the abilities and talents and essence. Another state of being, that of the true human, can be developed. Human beings are the fourth stage. This stage can be obtained with determination and knowledge.

For the fetus to develop, the mother received the sperm, signifying she received life. This time, for the human to develop, we must receive spiritually instead of physically. This time we receive in the heart—through love. Our heart and body is a womb for that essence which will be separated from us in the next life. The spiritual child must grow and develop, just as the fetus did. Then our body will die, and we will continue. It is simple.

To pass through the gate to true humanity, one has to leave everything animal behind. There is something within each of us that motivates us to start the way. There is a knowledge, an eagerness, a desire to know that brings us. Once we pass through the gate, we become one with Him. As in the womb, you are then constantly together. The Heavenly Father is then with us, whatever we do, and wherever we go—eating, waking, sleeping. There is no separation from him. If we develop our potentialities and are united with the Beloved, God, then we, too, are infinite and eternal. The truth and the essence of life are eternal and immortal.

In his work, *Peace*, Hazrat Pir tells us: "What a child does when he is born is to develop education which has already been implemented within his own being."[230] It is a blessing Nature has provided. We do not enter the world as blank tablets. Look at your hand and think of what you use this efficient instrument for each muscle, bone and nerve "has been directed and educated by an inherent knowledge." Other examples are the analysis of sound vibrations by our ears, opening or closing the lenses of our eyes to distinguish objects—both are development of the existing systems. We come with all the equipment and education necessary to walk and to talk, and would probably fare better if we did less of the latter and more of the former.

"Each human being is born with different characteristics and abundant aptitudes."[232] Unfortunately children are then subjected to family, social and educational experiences involving people who have neglected to discover the true meaning of education and development, and the incorrect teaching methods result in lack of development of their talents and abilities. The Prophet Muhammad (peace be upon him) says: "Each human being is like a mine—gold, silver, or jewel. Excavate their goodness so that you may have peace."[232] Sufism is the way to evolutionary development, to discovery of the precious treasure within.

CHAPTER 15
PERSONALITY

We see the word "personality" all the time. We tend to think of our personality as who we are; it is our self-identity. There are few words in the English language which have such a fascination for the general public as the term. Magazines have little quizzes about "personality." They even have contests for "Miss Personality." If you were to describe your personality to someone else, what would you say? What is your own "personality?" We usually pride ourselves on at least some aspects of what we consider our "personality," whether others are properly appreciative of our sterling characteristics or not. Yet are we really certain of what we are talking about?

The word is believed to have been derived from the Latin "persona," meaning the mask worn by actors. In psychology, according to *Webster's*, It means: (a) the totality of an individual's characteristics, especially as they concern his relations to other people. (b) an integrated group of emotional trends, interests, behavior tendencies, etc.. Split and multiple personalities are also mentioned.

Is our personality the persona, the social mask, the role of the actor we take in relationship to the social world and to others? If you stop and think about it, how many personalities do you have, really, based on the psychological definition given above? Ego psychology says we all have many, for we play many different roles in this society—child, parent, spouse, student, worker, teacher, friend, sibling, peer, member—the list is lengthy for each of us.

Most popular meanings fall under one of two headings. The first equates the term with social skill and adroitness. It is assessed by how effectively one is able to elicit positive responses from different people under different circumstances. So-called "charm" schools which specialize in glamorizing the American female teach "Personality Training." Teachers may refer a student, stating he has a "personality problem"— often meaning he has trouble getting along with either the teacher or his classmates. The second usage considers the personality to be primarily the most outstanding characteristic or strongest impression which one creates in others. So we say someone has a "passive-aggressive" personality, or a "fearful" one. Evaluation is obvious in both usages. Personalities are usually judged as good or bad.

Gordon Allport studied the definitions of personality used in psychology. He found almost fifty different definitions, which he categorized. One category is that it is the reaction of others to the individual which defines his personality. Another is describing of everything considered of importance about the individual. Another is the idea that personality is the pattern or organization of the various different behaviors of the individual. The adjustment definition says that personality consists of the varied efforts at adjustment carried out. The unique definition describes those characteristics that are distinctive, and set an individual apart.

Hall and Lindzey, authors of a popular personality theory text, state: "No substantive definition of personality can be applied with any generality." This is because theorists all perceive personality differently, based on their own values and ideas. *"Personality is defined by the particular empirical concepts which are a part of the theory of personality employed by the observer."*[233] Personality consists of a set of values or descriptive terms which are used to describe the individual being studied according to the ideas which occupy a central position within the particular theory utilized.

They indicate that theories of personality try to explain the totality of human behavior. They attempt to deal with any behaviors which can be shown to be of importance to the adjustment of the individual. Therefore, as Gordon Allport stated: "All books on the psychology of personality are at the same time books on the philosophy of the person. It could not be otherwise."[234] In other words, personality theories are all philosophies, and are as different as the philosophizing theorists are different. Each examines the person with the lens and boundaries of their own past experiences. The theory is a statement of values held by the theorists, of what they consider to be of importance, for the theory consists of his ideas, his thoughts.

Current theorists usually assume the infant is born neither good nor bad, with the potential for both. Whatever personality is, it is created out of interaction of our physical apparatus with this world. It includes our physical body, and thus includes the genetic inheritance we have received from our ancestors of bygone centuries. As anyone who has carefully observed infants knows, we are born with certain characteristics which are measurably different, even in very young infants, such as activity level. Some babies sleep more than others, some are fussier than others. Some have "colic," while others do not. These characteristics form the basis for, yet do not totally determine, the development of our eventual personality.

The interaction of heredity and environment together create the being we become. Either may become the determining factor, depending upon its strength. For example, studies of infants placed in institutions have definitely demonstrated the necessity for human interaction if the baby is to develop normally, and, in many cases, even to survive. The mortality rate for infants deprived of touching and holding is extremely high. This clearly demonstrates the importance of certain environmental conditions. Another simple example is the need for adequate nutrition. The infant who suffers from malnutrition may be physically impaired, or die. The effect of heredity can often be seen physically, in body shape or hair color, or the inheritance of disorders like hemophilia, the life-threatening inability of the blood to clot. Studies of identical twins reared apart tell us, since identical twins have identical DNA, RNA, and physical characteristics, of the relative importance of heredity, since they were reared in different environments. The studies show remarkable similarities. A Minnesota study indicated twins reared apart often had similar jobs, interests, habits, and we already mentioned the pair whose wives were named Betty, their sons James Alan, and their dogs Toy.[235]

Lets examine the beliefs about personality and how it develops presented in some major theories.

PSYCHOANALYSIS: Freud's theory of psychosexual personality development was discussed in the previous chapter. Freud postulated an internal struggle between what he called Thanatos and Eros, but which are more frequently described as the movement toward Life or toward Death. These two forces often conflict with one another, and movement toward Life is resisted. Horney commented on the internal conflict between two groups of factors with contrasting or competing interests, which she saw as the basis for resistance. The interest of one group is to maintain unchanged the illusions and the seeming safety of the status quo. The interest of the other is to gain inner freedom and strength.[236]

Alfred Adler, a member of Freud's circle, early disagreed with him. Adler saw people as mainly motivated by social interests. They are goal-directed and purposeful, and strive to become successful; they try to fulfill their own unique potential. There is an initial tendency for people to feel inferior, and if they do not overcome it, they develop an inferiority complex. If they over-compensate, they develop a superiority complex. He placed great emphasis on birth order, for the placement of each child within the early family environment strongly affects their personality development. He saw individuals as guided by their own fictions, for they act as if the world were based on their subjective evaluations. In the healthy personality, there is focus on three main tasks: society, work and sexuality, with two other challenges of life: spirituality and coping with the self..[237]

Carl Gustav Jung was also a member of Freud's circle. but Freud could not tolerate his different point of view. Jung saw psychic energy as a manifestation of life energy, which is the energy of the organism as a biological system. Jung believed man's behavior, hence, his personality, is conditioned not only by individual and racial history, but also by his aims and aspirations. He believed man is shaped and molded by the cumulative experiences of past generations extending far back. The foundations of personality are primitive, innate in the unconscious, and universal. Personality consists of the Ego of Conscious mind, the Personal Unconscious, containing repressed, suppressed, forgotten or ignored experiences, and the Collective Unconscious, a deeper, inborn layer, which is hereditary, universal, and identical in all humans. It is the inherited, ancestral foundation of the whole structure of personality. Jung described the Persona as the mask worn in response to the demands of social tradition and convention—the public personality. He also described the Shadow, the animal, "dark," undesirable characteristics of people, which we do not want to see in ourselves, although it is easily visible to others. He saw the self as the central point, as what motivates man and causes him to search for wholeness, especially through the avenue of religion.[238]

HUMANISTIC OR EXISTENTIAL:The self is a central concept. For a healthy self, positive regard, such as love, care, respect and acceptance is needed. Many people receive only conditional regard, which creates conflict. Victor Frankl emphasizes how each person seeks, and is capable of finding, a personal meaning and purpose in life.[239] Carl Rogers considers the human to be "positive, forward-moving, constructive, realistic and trustworthy."[240] and moving toward self-actualization. Fritz Perls, who developed Gestalt Therapy, focused on patterns, and believed that all humans possess inner wisdom and work toward wholeness and completeness.[241] Like Jung, he emphasized that we all contain polarities within, which must be accepted and/or reconciled. People function as total units, and the totality of self is a series of processes learned through constant interaction of the individual with his inner self and his environment.

BEHAVIORAL OR COGNITIVE THEORIES: Cognitive theories all emphasize the importance of what we think and how we believe in personality development. Social learning theory states that human behavior (which is our "personality") is a reciprocal interaction between cognitive, behavioral, and environmental determinants. We learn how to be who we are not only through conditioning, like Pavlov's dog salivating at the sound of a bell, but also through observation and imitation of others. Choice is involved in selection of behaviors from their models. All agree difficulties develop when we learn irrational or distorted assumptions ("wrong thinking") about ourselves and/or the world.

SYSTEMS THEORY: The general systems theory developed by biologist Ludwig Von Bertalanffy has been expanded to include human behavior, with the family seen as a system of which the individual is only a part. Personality development is seen as a function of one's role in the family system. The individual is an interacting component constantly being affected and changed by family members. The family is seen as the primary personality builder. John Bradshaw's books and videos on how the "Dysfunctional Family" creates dysfunctional adults have been best-sellers. This idea could be systematically expanded to also view the family as a subsystem within the various other systems of which it is a part.

EGO PSYCHOLOGY: The child develops patterns of behaviors which are appropriate for different situations through experience. Patterns may also develop through internalization of authority figures, such as parents, or significant others of childhood. In severe trauma, the child may split off a portion of him or herself to handle the trauma. Normal personality structure then, is a collection of segments or patterns, called "ego states," each with their own individual identity. Each of us is a "family of self" internally, which may function well or poorly. Usually one ego-state tends to be predominant, but not in all circumstances. The difference between normal and multiple personalities is in the intensity and the openness of ego state boundaries.

PSYCHOSYNTHESIS: The person is a soul and has a personality, which is unique and complex. The personality is composed of sub-personalities, which are like the instruments in an orchestra. They may be out of tune and in discord, or they may play beautiful music—magnificent symphonies. These develop in early childhood, and are strongly influenced by the culture—the assigned role given each sex is an example. "Each man may be considered as an element or cell of a human group; this group, in its turn, forms associations with vaster and more complex groups and from these to the entire human family between these individuals and groups arise problems and conflicts which are surprisingly similar to those we have found existing within each individual." [242] A spiritual awakening is essential to full development.

TRANSPERSONAL PSYCHOLOGY: Transpersonal psychologists believe a core, true Self exists at birth. From birth, we respond to, judge and learn from the environment, layering the core Self with social conditioning, which is an illusion, a social consensus of reality which is not the true reality. The social "personality" is a state of hypnosis, in which we are entrapped, and from which we must escape to reach the true goal of transcendence or enlightenment. When all the limiting identifications and attachments of ordinary life have been dropped, "awareness experiences no limits to identity and directly experiences itself as that which is beyond limits of time or space, that which humanity has traditionally called God." [243]

William Shakespeare, a brilliant psychologist, long ago described people as actors in this life.

> All the world's a stage,
> And all the men and women merely players:
> They have their exits and entrances;
> And one man in his time plays many parts.[244]

Shakespeare named seven stages, from "mewling and puking" infancy to the second childishness of old age.

In counseling and psychotherapy, Transactional Analysis speaks of our "Life Scripts," of the stories we live out in our lives. These "scripts" are the stories of who we learned we are, and of what the world is, as we grew up. Whatever our childhood experience, it becomes the script for the story of the rest of our lives, endlessly repeated with minor variations. Looked at in this way, the personality is the actor in the drama of our life, constantly performing. The personality as actor repeats memorized lines and portrays emotions on cue, just as he was trained and directed to do. He follows the script provided by the external influences of his environment. In this instance, the outcome is clear—death.

This physical script, dictated by society and social circumstances, is the drama most choose to play out in life. They know the script and all the motions well, and are comfortable with it. There is nothing new to assimilate, it comes easily, effortlessly, requiring no thought nor preparation. The lines are perfectly learned. But it is important to examine carefully the following questions. Who wrote the script? Who directs the action? Who produces the show? Is this the writer you would choose? Do you want this director? Is the producer appropriate? If you are satisfied, fine. If you are dissatisfied, there is another choice.

SUFISM AND PERSONALITY

Robert Briffault tells us: "The whole edifice of human conceptions has been built, ultimately, upon a single concept—that of individuality."[245] Our entire system of thought and our vision of our "self" is based upon an erroneous assumption. It is a deception of the senses, which consistently fool us. Our eyes tell us our bag of fluid is separate from the bags of fluid of others. "You perceive yourself by reflection as a coherent thing persisting amid various settings, delimited from an external world by a surface of skin." Outside the skin is "not-you." But is it? Biologist Lewis Thomas says:" A good case can be made for our nonexistence as entities."[246] Even our very body cells are not our own, they are ecosystems.

Each cell contains mitochondria, which oxidate the cell, little separate creatures with their own DNA and RNA, inherited only from the mother, as well as a good many other obscure and foreign tiny beings, on which we are completely dependent. Our body cannot function without them.

Physics tells us molecules are changeable, depending on circumstances; each atom within our cells contains rapidly moving component parts, microcosms of the macrocosm. Our mass is an exponential function of motion. Boscovitch's theory states that all substances, including our bodies, are composed of systems of points which are centers of forces.

What we call our "self," our personality, was not created out of nothing. It has a history; an endless story, dating back to Adam. The individual life is only one step, one link in the process of life. The thing, the continuous and coherent system, is not the individual, but the entire chain of life. Life develops, what we call the individual develops. But individual is an artificial unit. It is only as a part of the continuous whole that we exist. As is biologically obvious in simpler forms of life, the "individual" organism is merely a semi-detached part of another organism. As John Donne said: "No man is an island, separate from the main."[247] Essentially, we are all One.

The stream of life is a verifiable fact, a form, a configuration of forces. Each of us is a measured portion of energy which can issue into the displacement of weights by our muscles, the composition of poetry, an act of heroism, or into as much heat as will boil a pot of water. The qualitative differences are manifestations and differences in form, in complexity of configuration. That is all. Our dissection of the world into separated and discreet "objects" is a purely utilitarian manipulation of our cognition. It is not real. When its characteristics are enumerated and examined, there is nothing the Earth itself resembles so much as a single cell..[248]

"The atom only exists by virtue of its effects upon every other atom in the universe, and is itself but the result of all the forces in the universe."[249] The atom and the universe are not separable entities; our distinction between one and the other is but an abstractional manipulation. Science texts tell us we breathe in trillions of molecules with every breath, molecules that once were a part of everyone who ever lived on this earth. We actually breathe each other, every time we take a breath. Within each and every one of us are molecules from everyone else who ever lived. We are, literally, physically, all One.[32]

The personality, the "self," of everyday life is our human nature, our mind, emotions, body, which develops through the interaction of the physical senses with the environment. What we think of as "personality" is a product of the memory unit of our electrochemical biocomputer, the brain, which reflects the determined and arranged program it has received. In addition to this aspect, which is what psychologists and the ordinary person think of as "personality," there is within us an aspect of our being which is the reality of the presence of the Source of Life, of God, within us. It is the Divine which is within, but of which we may not be aware. We are all born with this level; it comes with human life. Just as the rudimentary heart of the fetus receives the gift of simple independent beating, so the fetus receives the gift of what we call the "spiritual" self, for lack of a better word in English.

Part of the "charm" of the young child, and the basis of the almost universal human reaction to protect and not harm young children, is the visibility of this higher Self, the presentation of the purity and clarity of the Divine. As Lewis Carroll described what occurs:

In her eyes is the living light
Of a wanderer to earth
From a far celestial height:
Summers five are all the span—-
Summers five since Time began
To veil in mists of human night
A shining angel-birth.[251]

The young child, full of innocence and wonder, is slowly and gradually taught the perception of the world of the environment in which he or she grows up. The innocence disappears, the wonder evaporates, and we may think it lost forever beneath the preoccupation with the trappings of the physical, social world. Jesus told us what is necessary to regain this state, to rediscover the finest of our own Being. " Truly, I say to you, unless you turn and become like children, you will never enter the kingdom of heaven. Whoever humbles himself like this child, he is the greatest in the kingdom of heaven."[252]

The process of the Way of the Prophets is the rediscovery and development of this atom of the Divine. This point is the "I," the essence of our humanity, the source of inspiring wisdom, of healing love, and our basic will to Life rather than death. We are all aware of the presence within of something greater, grander than our everyday selves. We have each caught glimpses, if only for moments. It can be known through our most noble acts, our greatest peace, our highest aspirations, our tenderest moments, our best insights, and our greatest creativity.. Through the practice of Concentration and Meditation we learn to move beyond the social personality level and regain contact with the Essence within us.

However, any movement toward liberty from social bondage, from the social personality toward the Divine, is resisted. And "The intellect is an opportunist, at the service of whatever interest carries the greatest weight at the time."[253] Therefore, we cannot depend upon our mind, for it will betray us at the slightest change in the balance of weight. In this sense, our mind is our enemy, for it is likely to be hard at work trying to maintain the status quo and resisting our progress toward freedom and toward union with the Beloved, God.

One of the aspects of Concentration and Meditation is to begin to behave like the person who rejoices because his glass is half full rather than lamenting because his glass is half empty. How can hope and joy grow if we besiege ourselves with intense discouragement and constant guilt? Pessimism and negativity is destructive, while the positive is nourishing and constructive. One cannot see upward while continually trying to fill a hole. Constant self-critical thinking is disturbing, motivating us to defend our innermost self, while positive thinking allows us to accept what is good and healing into the most central portion of our innermost being. So we must practice, again and again, our ability to see what is valuable, right, beautiful, good, healing, true, essential, refreshing, revitalizing and strengthening, and to incorporate these into our own being. "The delighted souls and the eyes that can see are in love with beauty and rejoice in it, and do not erect dumps or live in the deep corners of sorrow."[254]

In order to do so, we must quiet the mind, which constantly calls us to occupy ourselves with the external, physical world. For many of us, the mind does not simply call us. It is quite likely to chatter incessantly, nag, scream and yell, demand, throw temper tantrums or dramatic "Poor Me" fits, or use whatever devious tactic is most effective in regaining our attention and devotion. Unless we find the way to 'move beyond the everyday limitations, our personality will remain trapped within the boundaries of physical, sensory experience, preoccupied totally with the past and the future, with feelings, thoughts, physical needs and petty desires. For most people, this is enough. They do not care to look further.

It may seem satisfying much of the time, but it is incomplete, just as a fruit tree which bears no fruit is barren. For many, a recognition of the inadequacy of the "personality" comes only at times of great personal distress, such as at the loss of a close family member or during severe ill-health, or after experiencing marked trauma of some kind. Then only is the pain deep enough to cut through the outer layers of the social self and reach into the heart of our being. Otherwise, as Susanne Langer puts it: "We live in a web of ideas, a fabric of our own making...,"[255] a fabric which is the shroud covering the light of the Divine within us.

The practice of Sufi Concentration enables us to establish contact with this aspect of our being, to rediscover this essential element. In so doing, we rediscover the healing, love, wisdom and joy accessible to us. As we become more and more responsive, and begin to think and act on these wavelengths, we gradually become attuned to greater measures of healing, love, wisdom and joy. This is the purpose of Concentration; to help us establish the contact, to reconnect with the Source of Life, to develop the eyes to see and the ears to hear told us by both the Bible and the Quran.

We can then turn from the script of man to the Word of God, and allow Him to become the writer, the director, the producer of the drama. We can allow that element of the Divine within us to take charge, rather than endlessly replaying the childhood social dramas. We can let go of the old play, and let the new play occupy center stage. This involves a conscious, rational choice; a decision to act rather than to react. Allowing this to occur provides both healing, whether it be mental, physical, emotional or spiritual, and enrichment—and expansion beyond the capacity of the unenlightened mind to imagine. The "personality," the physical self, remains the actor upon the stage, for it is our vehicle for expression, for living upon this earth. We may choose it to be the vehicle for continued expression of prior social circumstances, or to be the vehicle for the expression of the wisdom, talent, love, creativity and potential of the most spiritual essence of our being.

The higher, spiritual, level is characterized by delicacy and subtlety. It is tender, like the tender heart of a nut encased within a hard shell. We must treat it with care. Like a young tulip, it must be protected from storm and wind and scorching heat until it can grow strong and sturdy. But first, Spring must come, and the tulip must once again break through the earth to bloom in the sun.

The true self, the "I," is constant and unchangeable, regardless of time or place. Finding the "I," complete cognition of the true self, is an experience incapable of description through words. It is a "banquet of joy."[256] an intoxication of rapture from the wine of the Divine Cup-Bearer. Hazrat Pir speaks of "That safeguarded fervent ecstasy that absorbs and revives, that radiant magnificent star, as a shooting star that descends and penetrates, that pure distilled frenzy of love."[257] It provides "That child-like joyfulness, the fervor which nourishes the inner self."[258] It comes from "The fount of the sun hidden behind the darkness of a hundred veils, that quivering and glittering dew of life, that water drop, flowering to bloom the gardens of paradise, that rejoicing bud which is the nightingale's heart."[259]

CHAPTER 16
SELF-ACTUALIZATION

C linical psychologists have primarily focused their attention on the problems or illnesses people had, on what was wrong with them. This was natural, since they wanted to be of assistance. The field was called Abnormal Psychology, or Psychopathology. Often theories about human behavior were developed on the basis of clinical experience with troubled people. New psychiatrists and psychologists gradually turned their attention to the other end of the spectrum, toward those who were healthiest, who were functioning extremely well. The question then became one of defining health. For example, a Scottish psychiatrist studied Britons and Americans who considered themselves "eccentrics."[260] He found they see a physician only once every ten to fifteen years, on the average, while other people see one every six months to two years. The eccentrics are creative and expressive, with a childlike innocence and wisdom, and simply do not care what other people think. They follow their own dreams in preference to social norms. Are eccentrics the model for health?

Abraham Maslow is the best known of this group. He studied people he called "Self-Actualized," whom he considered the healthiest specimens. These were people whose needs had been met that he considered lower level, including the physical, the need for safety and security, the need for love and belonging, and the need for competence and esteem. He studied Americans, with a few rare exceptions, who seemed to be making full use of their talents and potentials and who would fit Carl Rogers' description of "fully functioning."[261] He began with the great, then expanded his studies. People whose lives he examined included Albert Einstein, Ruth Benedict, Eleanor Roosevelt, William James, Abraham Lincoln, John Muir, and Walt Whitman.

He found that self-actualizers from all areas of life shared certain characteristics. These included:

1. Efficient perception of reality: They judged situations accurately and honestly and noticed the fake and dishonest.

2. Acceptance: of self, others, and nature. They accepted their own shortcomings as well as those of others and the contradictions of life.

3. Spontaneity: They were uninhibited, not concerned with what others thought, alive and engaged.

4. Goal Orientation: They had a mission, task, goal or problem outside of themselves to pursue.

5. Autonomy: They were relatively culture-free, resourceful, and not dependent on others or on external authority.

6. Freshness of Appreciation: They had the innocence of vision of a young child, constantly renewing appreciation of life's gifts.

7. Fellowship with humanity: They identified deeply with the human condition, and with others in general.

8. Deep Interpersonal relationships: They had deep, loving bonds with a select few people.

9. Unhostile sense of humor: They could laugh at themselves, and life's amusing events.

10. Peak (mystic or oceanic) Experiences: These occurred frequently.[262]

Maslow had instructed people to think of the most wonderful experiences of their lives, ecstatic moments, moments of rapture, etc. Most people have had at least one or more such experiences. Their responses characterized what he called "peak experiences"—which occurred often for self-actualizers, and which were described as including:

1. Perception of the whole of being

2. Total attention, fascination and absorption

3. Perception of the world unclouded by relationship to the individual or individuals.

4. Richness of perception

5. Ego-transcending, self-forgetful, egoless, detached perception

6. Great value, revelation, self-validating and justifying
7. Loss of time and space
8. Good, desirable, awesome, wondrous, amazing experience
9. Absoluteness—as if perceiving a reality independent of man and persisting beyond human life
10. Passive and receptive awareness
11. Emotional reaction of awe, reverence, humility and surrender
12. Whole of world seen as unity
13. Dichotomies, polarities and conflicts are resolved or transcended
14. Complete, loving, uncondemning, compassionate and perhaps amused acceptance of the world and of the person
15. Complete loss of fear, anxiety, inhibition, defense and control.[263]

The results of peak experiences have included permanent loss of neurotic symptoms, healthy changes in view of self, others and the world, greater spontaneity and creativity, and increased valuing of life.

Maslow saw the fully human person as possessing what he named "B" or "Being" values; These included Truth, Goodness, Beauty, Wholeness, Transcendence of Opposites, Aliveness, Uniqueness, Perfection, Necessity, Completion, Justice, Order, Simplicity, Richness, Effortlessness, Playfulness, and Self-Sufficiency. These are in contrast to "D" or "Deficiency" values, which are experienced by most people. In "Deficiency" values, the organism acts to satisfy deficits in order to avoid illness. In "B," most of the organism's needs have been met, and the organism acts to produce positive health. For example, the love need is a deficit need involving selfish love for those who did not receive it in childhood. It is a void to be filled. For the healthy person, love is unneeding, unselfish, and non-possessive. "D" perception is colored by our wishes and desires. Others are perceived in terms of what they can give or supply us. "B" perception is clear, uninvolved, and desireless.

Later, Maslow differentiated between two degrees of self-actualizing people, those who were clearly healthy but without transcendent experiences, and those for whom transcendent experiencing was important. Maslow gave the following description of transcenders:

1. Peak and plateau experiences are the most important and precious aspect of life.
2. They speak the language of poets, mystics, seers, and better understand art, music, paradox, parables, etc.
3. They perceive the sacredness in all things and also see them at the practical, everyday level.

4. They somehow recognize each other, and develop rapid intimacy and mutual understanding.

5. They are more responsive to beauty, and beautify.

6. They are holistic, beyond cultural, geographic differences.

7. They are synergistic — what they do benefits themselves and others.

8. They are lovable, awe-inspiring, saintly, easily revered.

9. They are apt to be innovators and discoverers.

10. They perceive the sacredness of every living thing.

11. They retain a strong sense of awe and mystery.

12. They are more apt to be reconciled with evil, understanding its inevitability and necessity.

13. They tend to regard themselves as carriers or instruments.

14. It is easier for them to transcend the ego, to be selfless.

At the very end of his life, in an interview, Maslow stated that his theory needed revision, for he had observed that, particularly in young people, all the lower level needs could be met, and yet the persons were not self-actualizing. The higher level needs had not arisen as predicted. Some were depressed, unhappy, and despairing, even though all the basic needs had been fulfilled.

The concept of persons functioning at a different and higher level than that of the ordinary person is an old one, but most writers on the topic come from backgrounds other than psychology. The idea is presented in Buddhism, Hinduism, Judaism, Christianity and Islam, for example. Other contemporary figures associated with psychology have also begun describing their vision of the healthiest, most highly developed human. Roberto Assagioli, the Italian developer of the therapeutic techniques of Psychosynthesis, envisioned the development of "Supernormal Man."[264] Alan Watts, after years of study of Buddhism and then Hinduism, spoke of the "Taboo against knowing who you are," and described the ultimate state as that of the "liberated man."[265] R. D. Laing wrote of the "true sanity" of the person who rises above the functional level of the ordinary person in everyday life.[266] Gurdjieff, known to most from the movie "Meetings with Remarkable Men," spoke of the "fully developed" person, the conscious, non-mechanical person who is human in the full sense of the word.[267]

SUFISM AND SELF-ACTUALIZATION

As in other aspects, Western psychology has described characteristics, in this case of those who appear to function better than others in Western societies. However, it has been unable to demonstrate how to assist people to attain these higher levels of functioning. Transpersonal psychologists discuss what techniques should be helpful, but have not been able to demonstrate any definitive positive results. There is no literature documenting the success of any psychological methodology in attaining "self-actualization." Psychology just does not know how to attain this goal, nor does it know how to help people reach the even higher levels described in the literature of Sufism, for such development is spiritual, metaphysical.

Maslow's theory is incomplete and incorrect because, although intensely interested, he never fully perceived the essential centrality of the spiritual realm. He based his theory on a physical, rather than metaphysical foundation. Current therapists come closer to the truth in using the analogy of an onion with the soul or God at the center. He did not include those humans who have functioned at the highest possible level, the prophets, in his descriptions. This is a curious omission. If Maslow and others had extended their investigations and discovered the vast body of Sufi literature, they would have found a level of human development far beyond that of even the transcending self-actualizers. The writings of fourteen hundred years of experience continuously document examples. This realm of development is not just an historical artifact. It is a reality which can be achieved by the contemporary student, if the student is truly motivated by the desire to know and not by greed, lust or desire for power. And, at every level, even taking a beginning Concentration and Meditation class, the teachings of Sufism are of practical benefit in everyday life. Students can improve the quality of their lives in every aspect.

Hazrat Pir teaches that each of us has the potentiality for perfection, within us. He states: "You are perfect. All you have to do is discover it." Those who truly want to find peace, to find Truth, to know God, may do so, God willing. As the *salik* learns and progresses, he gradually acquires the values and aspects described as those of the transcending self-actualizer. He also develops additional aspects of his being, more advanced characteristics. At each stage, Sufism benefits us at every level, including all aspects of everyday life. The progressive salik could be described as "Superhealthy" in current psychological jargon.

CHARACTERISTICS OF THE SUPERHEALTHY

Physical
No addictive behaviors
Excellent condition, limber and flexible
Extraordinary physical control
Need little sleep
Need little food
Rapid healing of any physical problem
Truly relaxed

Social
Exceptional interpersonal relationships
Quiet assertiveness
Independent of others and of "experts"
Independent of cultural norms or
expectations, culture-free
Experience oneness with humanity
Possess humor
Giving, generous

Emotional
Free of fear
Tranquil and serene
Enjoy life
Inner Contentment
Self-Accepting
Focused beyond personal ego
Balanced, stable
Harmonious
Experience Ecstasy

Spiritual
Kindness
Love
Genuine Humility
Healing
Submission to a Higher Power
Cognition of God
Selflessness
Ultimately: Union with the Divine

Mental
Highly Creative
Efficient perception of reality (They
know the emperor wears no clothes)
Focused concentration
Great productivity
Spontaneous, active, alive, engaged
Resourceful
Freshness of appreciation, like the
wonder & innocence of a young child
Intelligence beyond intelligence tests

Rather obviously, the Superhealthy have some extraordinary characteristics, in realms previous researchers did not investigate. However, even these characteristics are limited unless the ultimate goal of Sufism, of Union with the Beloved, of Annihilation in God, is reached. Then, and only then, is true actualization of the Self, true self-fulfillment, true transcendence attained. Words become woefully inadequate for description, for it is different from, and beyond, all prior experience. A new level of meaning is necessitated. Professor Angha describes:

> When the *salik* has fully adhered to the aforementioned, he shall have reached his rank at the summit of devotion and servitude; his words and actions shall be strengthened by the Divine Light and he shall be blessed. As the Almighty has promised: *God is the protector of those who have faith: from the depths of darkness He will lead them forth into Light* (The Quran 2:257). In his state of purity, the streams of knowledge shall flow from his heart to his lips, and he shall see what eye has not seen, nor ear heard, nor the heart of any human being witnessed, and he shall know ever clearly the reality of the manifestation of attributes. Whenever God desires the welfare of His servant, He shall open the eye of his heart, and in solouk (journey through truth), He shall fulfill His commandment and enfold him in the Blessings of His Grace, and by His Magnanimity sustain and guide him.

The true Sufi, the *Arif,* the Pir, has attained the highest level, has achieved perfection. He is the Man of Our Time. This concept is difficult for the Western mind to fathom, as we have usually been taught perfection is not possible, and we have a very limited concept of advanced spiritual levels. Yet we have also learned of at least some of the Prophets, of Moses or Jesus or Buddha or Muhammad (peace be upon them), and recognize them as far advanced in comparison to the ordinary person. The resulting mental state is often cognitive dissonance for the Western reader, which includes a tendency to immediately reject a notion which appears to conflict with prior beliefs. Instead of immediately fighting the idea, or thinking the old concept has to be given up, try letting it into the front hall of your consciousness for a little while. You don't have to let it into the living room or bedroom if you do not wish to do so, but just let it into the front hall for awhile. Perhaps the old ideas and new concept can be reconciled. Consider that perfection is possible, in aspects requiring a new level of knowing. We must move beyond everyday thinking, beyond the boundaries of ordinary language, in order to fathom that which can be understood only through heart to heart communication. It seems a different world, although there is only one world.

Consider the descriptions written by an *Arif*, Professor Angha:

The journey of the salik is at first in the world, whose actions are the garments of appearance and as he passes through this state the Eagle King of the Soul shall take him on his journey to malakut (the heavenly realm) witnessing the realm of meaning. And, enlightened by the blessings of the Exalted Lord, he shall journey with ceaseless effort and perseverance to be crowned with the Divine Attributes in jabarut (the sphere of Divine power) and shall receive the luminous lights as a single ray and in this spiritual state he shall be elevated to the rank of Angha of Mount Eternity in the realm of lahut (the luminous kingdom) in the presence of the Absolute Essence, and shall reach the state of annihilation which is man's most exalted state of existence.... In witnessing the Glorious One he shall be united with the Kingdom of His Radiance. He shall be flawless and the concealed secrets shall be fully revealed to him.[269]

In order to attain perfection, the *salik* must know the seven lights or mounts of the heart, one after the other. "The seven mounts of the heart correspond to the hidden lights of the sky of the heart that by divine inspiration and absorption in the rapture of love, the heart is illumined and freed on its flight to its Origin."[270] In speaking of attaining the sixth of the seven goals, Professor Angha states:

At this time, for the esteemed and the chosen, the soul's cup is filled solely with the clearest, purifying, divine wine, the eternal wine of His glorious Presence, blessed by the touch of His Magnificent Countenance, the ever eternal wine of blissful Light for the circle of those yearning for the Face and Eyes of the Bearer of wine.[271]

Its superior manifestation is the perfect man, Adam, whose physical body represents the whole nature; his soul indicates the universal soul and his wisdom represents the Omniscient, and he is the mirror for divine deeds, qualities and essence."[272]

To be able to reach this point of perfection, where the seeker sees nothing but God, there are seven stages through which he must pass. These trials and seekings are known as *sayr-va-solouk*.

THE STATE OF NATURAL STRENGTH AND PLEASURE

Natural strength and pleasure refer to eating, drinking, sleeping, etc.

The seeker must pass this stage and separate his human characteristics from behaviors which are recognizable in all animals and living plants. The seeker must discipline himself to partake of the minimum amount of food and other natural instincts and pleasures.

THE STATE OF SELF

In this stage the seeker should sever all dependence and start a quiet and solitary life. He must begin with the designated prayers, obey religious laws, and through repentance, endeavor and purification, reach the point where he can step outside this illusive world.

THE STATE OF HEART

The word "heart" is used here to signify the return, or revolution and change, that occurs in the seeker's internal behavior. The heart is the place where the door to the hidden world will open up to the sincere seeker.

THE STATE OF SOUL

At this stage the seeker has already passed the state of heart which, in a way, is the path of connection between soul and self. The seeker is free form earthly attachments and sentiments, and reaches the stage of absolute spirituality.

THE STATE OF SECRET

At this stage the seeker reaches the point of cognition and from then on, everywhere he looks he sees nothing but God. Where hearts are glorified by the light of cognition, everyway they turn, they first see God.

THE STATE OF HIDDEN

The seeker, at this stage, will see and hear God only. He will see himself dissolved (he will become lost) in God. In this condition the veil will be lifted and the truth about existence will appear.

THE STATE OF MORE HIDDEN

The difference between this stage and the previous one (in which the seeker sees himself dissolving in God) is that, at this stage, the seeker is not aware of his dissolution. This is the stage at which he reaches the state of supreme being. Sufism is the last state of sayr-va-solouk and the perfect stage of cognition.[273]

As indicated previously, there are thousands of volumes written by and about the Sufi Pirs or 'urafa, those who have achieved the state of perfection, of annihilation in God. Through the centuries, they have been continuous beacons—teaching, healing, and illuminating the way for all who sought God. Since words are totally inadequate to describe their goodness, helpfulness, kindness, purity, wisdom, and love, the metaphor and allegory of lyric love poetry was often used as a vehicle for expression of respect and admiration.

In the 13th century, the famous Sufi mystical poet, Molana Jalaluddin Molavi Balkhi Rumi, in a state of revelation wrote the following about Molana Salaheddin Ali Nader Shah Angha, the current Pir, Oveyssi:

Fragrance of that Garden, glories of flowers in spring is he,
  Rapture of the Beloved, Life of Creation, Bestower of blessings is he
.
This Sun that shines has illumined all faces as radiant suns,
  The lustrous moon's envy is this Sun that shines.

Ever since Yussef, awake time reposed to see his beauteous Face,
  What greatness! What praise! Awe of angels is he.

What Khidr is this? Bearer of wine from the Fountain of Life is he.
  The mysterious qaf and most precious and **Nader Angha** is he

Inflamed of quest are both the East and West,
  This Light of sight is Molana's Life of life.

What hiddest thee? Herald the truth, hide not the seen,
  The might of God and king of ours, His arms is he.

Peace of both spheres, Protector of both worlds is he,
  Bearer of woes, Guardian of tomorrows is he.

In whirls of awe now turns, this world inflamed,
  O God! What love is this? What grace is this?

What song is this that beckons all hearts?
  I tell ye then, the Jewel of that Sea is he.[274]

Sufism presents the living model of perfection in the person of the Pir. He has attained the goal all seek. He is called "Light of the Path," because he has made the complete journey; he knows the way and can therefore enlighten and guide others.

Chapter 17

Consciousness

What is consciousness? Both the words conscious and conscience are derived from the Latin word meaning to know. We tend to think of it as thoughts, awarenesses. "Stream of Consciousness" literature is a flow of words. "Modern (Western) concepts of consciousness tend to emphasize self-consciousness, a self-referencing or self-reflective process that focuses on an inner sense of self."[275]

The classical philosophers had no word for consciousness. John Dewey tells us that: "In both the Greek and medieval periods, the rule was to regard the individual as a channel through which a universal and divine intelligence operated. The individual was in no true sense the knower; the knower was the 'Reason' which operated through him."[276] Julian Jaynes points out the lack of consciousness in *The Iliad*, one of the oldest classic pieces of Western literature, and in other ancient works. He thought "volition came as a voice that was in the nature of a neurological command, in which the command and the action were not separated, in which to hear was to obey."[277] Even the poem itself was "heard" by the bard and recited. "The presence of voices which had to be obeyed were the absolute prerequisite to the conscious state of mind in which it is the self that is responsible and can debate within itself, can order and direct, and that the creation of such a self is the product of culture. In a sense, we have become our own gods."[278]

Ornstein sees our consciousness as constructed, as Piaget suggested, in order to help us manipulate objects, be aware of threats and separate ourselves from others. It helps biological survival. He suggests we first select the sensory modalities to be used, by a multilevel process of filtration, mostly sorting our stimuli perceived as survival-related. We then construct a stable consciousness from the filtered input. Consciousness is something we create. William James likened it to the sculptor carving a statue out of marble. We may all sculpt, but each sculptor's statue is unique. "We see that the mind is at every stage a theatre of simultaneous possibilities."[279] Consciousness compares, selects, and suppresses, primarily through attention. Consciousness then is mental—our thoughts and images, consisting of words and/or of visions.

Jung declared: "Western consciousness is by no means consciousness in general, but rather a historically conditioned and geographically limited factor, representative of only one part of humanity."[280] Other cultures look at consciousness very differently. The fundamental premise of the ancient medical tradition of India, Ayurveda, is that consciousness is primary and matter is secondary.[281] Guenon emphasized the limitations of consciousness, making it clear that: "knowledge, understood absolutely and in all its universality, is in no way synonymous with or equivalent to consciousness."[282] Knowledge is absolute and unlimited while consciousness is constricted, bounded. William James was keenly aware of other potentialities: "Our normal waking consciousness, rational consciousness as we call it, is but one special type of consciousness, whilst all about it, parted from it by the filmiest of screens, there lie potential forms of consciousness entirely different. We may go through life without suspecting their existence."[283]

Assorted different types or levels of consciousness have been advanced. For example, Freud spoke of the conscious and the unconscious. What does he and others mean when they speak of the "unconscious"? How is it different from consciousness? Essentially, they seem to mean that of which we have no but which motivates our behavior. Jung described another level, that of the collective unconscious, which he saw as universal to all men, containing the symbols of all nations, and the ancestral memory and entire spiritual heritage. He tells us: "Individual consciousness is only the flower and the fruit of a season."[284] Later Jungians elaborated on this concept, proposing multi-levels of unconsciousness, including the individual, then the familial and other group levels, the level of large social, cultural, or national units, and finally, universal archetypal structures.[285]

Very different kinds of experiences are all considered to be "Altered States of Consciousness" (ASC's), simply because they vary from our conception and experience of ordinary, everyday consciousness. These include sleep, mystical states, meditation, comas, amnesia, trance states and hypnosis, as well as certain states caused by organic diseases, psychosis and the results of drug use. Some of these states are considered beneficial and "adaptive," others are obviously unpleasant and maladaptive. It is clear that in spite of scientific speculations not much is known about ASC's because language is inadequate to describe them, and the authenticity of reported experience is difficult to assess."[286]

> It has been estimated by Bourguigon that almost 90% of the world's 4,000 societies have institutionalized at least one set of procedures for systematic cultivation of specific kinds of altered states. ASC's produced under these conditions are regarded almost universally as providing access to a sacred world of spiritual realities underlying or interpenetrating the everyday profane worlds. The great value placed upon such states by many societies is clearly reflected in the extremity of the psychological and physiological measures which they are willing to employ to produce them.[287]

The majority of ASC rituals were primarily social events, in which group participation helped shape the emergent physiological, psychological and symbolic drama of the ASC individually and collectively.

Mind-altering drugs are frequently used to attempt to produce altered states of consciousness. Such drug usage is not necessarily connected with "spiritual" rituals, as, for example, the consumption of alcohol at cocktail parties in Western cultures. Various hallucinogens, particularly LSD, have been "touted" by users for their adaptive and beneficial effects. However, they are also known to sometimes have unpleasant and maladaptive consequences, as when the user relives a traumatic experience, or hallucinates in fear and terror.

Prominent drug researchers have equated hallucinogenic drug-induced states with states of mystical ecstasy. Some psychiatrists have suggested psychosis, particularly schizophrenia, and mystical ecstasy are essentially the same, but research refutes both these views. In some cultures, epileptic seizures have been considered a visitation from God, and therefore seen as similar to mystical ecstasy. Thapa and Murthy investigated the experiences of groups of psychotic patients, epileptic patients, and advanced meditators, and found the psychotic and epileptic experiences to be maladaptive and non-integrative, and the meditative experience to be adaptive and integrative.[288] A Dartmouth analysis found that the subjective experiences of schizophrenia, hallucinogenic drug-induced states, and mystical ecstasy are more different from one another than alike. All are undoubtedly Altered States of Consciousness, but different altered states, producing sometimes markedly different results.[289]

Since the number of research studies done has been limited, many aspects of ASC'S remain to be investigated. Studies have demonstrated that body posture significantly affects the state of consciousness.[290] Fasting has been documented as affecting consciousness, and undoubtedly such everyday activities as diet and exercise must also affect it.

Hypnosis, a state characterized by narrowly focused attention in which the person is extremely suggestible, is usually considered an ASC. Some consider it a special form of trance, if trance is described as states of mind characterized by the relative unawareness and non functioning of the generalized reality orientation. The levels of trance in hypnosis, and the resultant responses, vary in depth. Most of us have seen hypnotists entertain audiences. A number of articles attest to the value of hypnosis in psychotherapy. People who were punished severely and frequently in childhood tend to be most susceptible to hypnosis. Hypnotic age regression, used in therapy to help clients remember early childhood experiences, when "checked out" has been found to be not only woefully inaccurate, but often fabricated. Some experts believe there is no such thing as hypnosis, only suggestibility, willingness to conform to the commands of an authority.

SLEEP AND DREAMS

Science is still uncertain as to what sleep is or the functions it serves. We spend about 25 years of our life sleeping, and we cannot function without it. After about 72 hours without sleep, most people become psychotic. Most of us need 7 1/2 to 8 hours sleep, but there are some people who exist on only 15 minutes of deep sleep per night. When we fall asleep our metabolism and temperature are lowered. Sleep is divided into stages measured by Electroencephalograms (EEG's), which trace the electrical brain waves. Stage 1 sleep shows small, irregular waves. Stage 2 shows sleep spindles—short bursts of activity. Slow delta waves occur in Stage 3. Stage 4 is deep sleep.

There are two states of sleep. Rapid Eye Movement (REM) sleep and Non-REM sleep. During REM sleep, all other muscles become completely quiet, while the heart and respiratory rate increase. Blood pressure, brain temperature, and blood flow increase. REM and non-REM sleep stages alternate in about 90 minute cycles during the night. The delta waves that characterize stages 3 and 4 occur early in the night, and REM sleep is more prevalent at the end.[291] Both sleep states are considered altered states of consciousness.

Our mind is not quiet during sleep. Mental activity is evidently ongoing. People awakened during non-rapid eye movement (non-REM) sleep describe experiencing brief, non-detailed "pictures" very much like everyday thinking. People awakened during REM sleep describe ongoing processes, with detailed recall of content, which is usually quite different from everyday thinking. The dream is obtained 80-85% of the time in REM period awakenings, but only 7% of the time during non-REM awakenings.[292] Dreams are usually spaced about 90 minutes apart. The first dream of the night is usually only about 10 minutes long, while the last dream averages 30 minutes, and may go up to 50 minutes. Most adults spend 20% of their sleep time with REM, so there is ample opportunity for dreaming. REM sleep increases when people are subjected to added stress.

Newborn infants go directly into REM sleep. At birth, about half of each hour-long sleep cycle is in REM sleep, then the proportion gradually drops. Infants sleep 16-17 hours a day, usually sleeping about four hours, then awakening for one half hour. By about six months, the typical infant sleeps through the night. In the vast majority of human cultures, babies sleep with their parents, and they interact physiologically. The peculiar American custom of isolating babies is thought to increase the probability of Sudden Infant Death Syndrome.[293]

The relationship between regular sleep, the "sleep" of anesthesia, and a coma is not clear. They think that general anesthesia produces its effect by deactivating the neurons of the reticular activating system, which controls sleep. Cutting this area produces a coma. A person in a coma appears to temporarily lose the use of those portions of the forebrain required for responding to or interacting with the outside world. However, the brainstem and limbic system keep right on maintaining and regulating vital bodily functions.[294] Research on persons undergoing surgery shows that some patients "remember," and can repeat what was said during the surgery, even though they had general anesthesia.

Dreams are often difficult to recall. Most (61%) are in color. Dream content, including with children, is ordinary, commonplace, and dominated by references to current concerns. Some 2 year olds dream. Young children's (3 1/2 - 5) reports of their dreams are short—"impoverished" in comparison to older children's. Dreaming is measurably affected by several influences, the most obvious being disruption of the sleep-dream cycle, such as occurs in sleep deprivation or repeatedly awakening the sleeper. Social isolation increases dream time. Alcohol, barbiturates and amphetamines decrease dream time.[295] External stimuli, like ringing phones, are often incorporated into dreams.

Jung emphasized how in all times and races the dream has been regarded as a truth-telling oracle. Various psychotherapeutic theories, particularly psychoanalysis, have placed great emphasis on the interpretation of dreams. Freud believed that every dream represents the fulfillment of a repressed wish. He saw the dream as a sort of facade, hiding something. Jung also interpreted dreams, but considered context important, and saw dreams as a sequence, as part of a pattern. He believed dreams mirror exactly the underground processes, revealing "the unknown inner facts of the psyche and of what those facts consist."[296] The Gestalt Therapist, Fritz Perls, believed dreams were special messages about what is missing in our lives. He asked clients to "speak for" each person and object in their dreams.

It is not unusual for solutions to scientific problems to come in dreams. Kekule had long attempted to determine the molecular structure of benzene. He was awakened by a dream of a snake eating its tail, and realized the structure was a ring. The Nobel Prize winner, Loevi, dreamed of an experiment for three nights. The first two nights, he made notes, but could not later decipher them. The third night, he got up and did the experiment, and made his discovery.

Analysis of dreams is one of the bases of the Senoi society of Malaysia. Dreams are used to teach social co-operation, beginning in childhood. Every morning, all the children's dreams are analyzed, so the child receives social recognition and attention even for presenting anxious or aggressive content. Dream reorganization is then guided carefully. The child is taught he must refuse to settle with the denizens of the dream world unless they make a socially meaningful and constructive contribution.

> ...the authority tells the child that every dream force and character is real and important, and in essence permanent, that it can and must be faced, subdued, and forced to make a socially meaningful contribution, the wisdom of the body operating in sleep seems in fact to reorganize the accumulating experience of the child in such a way that the natural tendency of the higher nervous system to perpetuate unpleasant experiences is first neutralized and then reversed.[297]

Dream analysis is also social. If a child dreams he is attacked by a friend, he is advised by his father to inform his friend. The friend's father then tells his child that it is possible he has offended the dreamer without wishing to do so, and allowed a malignant character to use his image as a disguise in the dream. Therefore, he should give a present to the dreamer and go out of his way to be friendly to him.

The Senoi sleep in "long houses" and claim there have been no violent crime or intercommunity conflicts for more than 200 years. They use dreams to solve difficult social situations, and often creative and inventive solutions, using poems, songs, dances and music emerge. Using the Senoi as a model, Western psychologists have discovered they can influence the outcome of dreams, making them more positive, by discussion before sleeping.

PARANORMAL EXPERIENCES

Paranormal or parapsychological experiences are those which cannot be explained on the basis of the physical senses. Such phenomena have been reported in almost all societies throughout all of human history. "Parapsychic phenomena were often part of religious ceremonies and beliefs; they were considered miraculous interventions by God or supernatural beings into natural processes."[298] Most people, if you ask them, can tell you of events in their lives that are simply not "scientifically" explainable. Often these events involve people close to them or crisis situations.

There are two major problems in studying paranormal phenomena. The first is how to adequately set up experiments. Attempts to prove the existence of Extra Sensory Perception (ESP) in "scientific," very carefully controlled circumstances has been limited, often to boring tasks of little intrinsic interest, like "discerning" what playing cards someone else was looking at. Most research has been questioned. Trickery has been sometimes established and often suspected. Criticism is commonplace. One cannot help but be reminded of animal research, in which it was belatedly discovered that the behaviors being studied so diligently in captivity were often completely different from the behaviors of the same species of animals in the wild. The kinds of laboratory situations used so far simply do not duplicate the kinds of behaviors occurring in everyday life.

One of the better research designs used 1,188 kindergarten children and their 29 teachers. When the teacher looked at pictures of objects the children had copies of, the children could indicate which picture she was looking at. The probability was less than one in ten million that this result could have occurred by chance. If a stranger visualized, the children could do no better than chance.

In the US, the leading researcher has been Dr. J.B. Rhine, who was Director for decades of the Parapsychology Laboratory at Duke University. The research done has uncovered two groups of people. Those dubbed "sheep" believe in ESP, and do significantly better than chance in experiments. Those they call "goats" do not believe in ESP, and they do significantly worse than chance. This means they have ESP, or they would not be able to do significantly worse.

The second problem is the number of charlatans. At the end of the last century, seances were very popular, in which a "medium" supposedly communicated with some deceased relative. This was a very lucrative business, but no medium was ever able to win the substantial sum Science offered for a demonstration in which the effects could not be achieved by trickery. The modern version is the enormous financial success of "channeling," in which someone dead supposedly speaks through a live person, often with great dramatics.

In a Science magazine article entitled "Science and the Supernatural," chemist George Price stated: "No intelligent man can read the evidence for the existence of extrasensory perception and doubt that it exists, *but*, since we *know* it is impossible, we must conclude that all this evidence is due to error and fraud." He goes on: "they know a priori that there are no such phenomena, therefore they never bother to read any evidence which might indicate there was, and then say they have never seen any evidence to contradict their belief."[299]

The primary areas of investigation include telepathy, clairvoyance, and precognition, which are all forms of extra-sensory perception (ESP), as well as out-of-body experiences and psychokinesis. Many instances of ESP involve loved ones. Clairvoyance is envisioning objective events, people or places, regardless of distance. One might "see" an earthquake or an ill relative in a city thousands of miles away. It may suggest the perception of finer energy elements. Telepathy is the perception of the mental state of another person. It is direct mind to mind communication. It may be occurring when people state: "That's just what I was going to say!" or "That's just what I had in mind." Precognition is prediction of the future when it cannot be inferred from known physical events. Someone may suddenly suspect a relative is coming to visit. Psychokinesis involves the direct influence of the mind on matter, for example, moving an object without touching it.

In "out of body" experiences, consciousness is experienced as being outside of the body. More and more cases are being documented of such experiences occurring when patients are under anesthesia in the operating room. It is not unusual for children to experience such phenomena. When having an "out of body" experience, the individual can sometimes look down and see his own body, and has the subjective experience of leaving it. The Dutch professor, W.R.C. Tenhaeff, argues that ESP preceded sensory perception, and suggests we regard telepathy as an "archaic" contact between people.

Most spiritual traditions warn of the dangers of becoming focused on paranormal experiences. They consider it a form of entertainment, of playing games. Psychic attainments are considered obstacles in the way of attainment of self-realization. Humphreys warns: "Any attempt to work for power or the development of psychic powers is extremely dangerous, nor is the development of abnormal powers any evidence of spiritual development."[300]

SUFISM AND CONSCIOUSNESS

We act as if our own personal consciousness is the way the world is, that an objective reality is perfectly seen in our consciousness. Most people never even realize there is any other possibility. But our consciousness is constantly being affected—by our own body functioning, our pains, thoughts, movement, etc.,—by the behavior of others—by environmental forces like radio waves, radiation, light, gravity, air pressure, etc. Our personal consciousness is not capable of representing more than a small portion of all this. Our senses cannot even detect many energy forms. As we indicated earlier, consciousness is dependent on language, and also on needs and desires. As the 13th century Persian Sufi Poet Rumi wrote: "What a piece of bread looks like depends on whether you are hungry or not." Poor children see coins as bigger than richer children. Would the sight of a beautiful green garden be entirely different to a child, to a poet, to a condemned man, to a lover?

In *Manifestation of Thoughts*, Professor Angha speaks of how people grow obedient and imitative. They mistake introductions for essential truths, acting like a first-grader loudly and proudly reciting the alphabet to show off his superior knowledge. Or like a child, who, after having just read his first basic science book, inquires if you know butterflies come from caterpillars in such a manner as to indicate his advanced and superior expertise. We smile with amusement, rarely recognizing adults, perhaps even we ourselves, do the same thing. The child never dreams that studying the introduction is just the beginning of discipline. After learning a little about various topics, this child will treat some, if not all, of the information he has gleaned as fixed and unchangeable laws. These become his consciousness.

Many people memorize or learn and paraphrase the words and works of great men, then present them as if they had done something important. Our academic institutions teach us to do this. But this is nothing to be proud of. Our memory is no more valuable than a library. We read books and see plays and videos and movies, but none can acquaint us with the reality and actuality of any character. All are the perceptions of the writer. Every actor plays Hamlet differently. Plato's description of Socrates is not an accurate portrayal of Socrates. It is Plato's perception of Socrates. Such concepts fill our ordinary consciousness, but they are neither truth nor knowledge, but an illusion, based on sensory input.

Socrates, defending himself at his trial, described how, at the Temple of Delphi, Apollo had responded to Chearephon's question as to whether or not there was anyone more learned than Socrates by saying there was no one more learned than Socrates. Socrates, when he heard the story, knew he did not know much, but also knew God did not lie, and so he pondered on the meaning behind the words of God, examined himself, and talked to scholars and saints. He finally concluded that since God is the only one who is truly wise and knowledgeable, the voice must have meant that the most learned man was the one who was willing to confess his own lack of knowledge.

Professor Angha tells us that true consciousness cannot be attained through the sensory modalities, which are the source of what we think of as knowledge. "Its virtually impossible that the ultimate reality penetrates his consciousness freely and purely; for his animal self presents Him— through his sensual perception—with crippled, impaired images, screened through the lenses of his current inner state."[301] He tells us we are always deceived by the conclusions we draw based on appearances. "The real is what we can't see."[302] He tells us we are like hand tools, with the power of the Almighty as the doer. Buckminster Fuller tells us: "Common to all.'human' mechanisms—and without which they are imbecile contraptions—is their guidance by a phantom captain."[303]

Sleep is essential, a favor from God. It is a temporary separation of the self from the body. In deep sleep we leave the physical body and do something else, whether we are dreaming or not. The distance traveled depends upon the lightness and purity of the one who is sleeping; the purer, the more expansion occurs. Five minutes of correct, deep meditation is equal to twenty-four hours of sleep.

Many traditions speak of a higher state of consciousness. In English, it has been called the Ultraconscious or Expanded Consciousness or Cosmic Consciousness. In Buddhism, it is called nirvana; in Zen, satori; in yoga, samadhi. Richard Bucke gives the following characteristics of "Cosmic Consciousness":

1. Intense light: The mind is filled with light, rare, inexpressible light. Dante describes the light powerfully in *Il Paradiso* of *The Divine Comedy*.

2. Ecstasy, filled with the emotions of supreme joy, rapture, triumph, assurance .

3. Intuitive, intellectual illumination of awareness of all meaning, of the universe; an identification and merging with Creation, with infinity.

4. Transcendental love and compassion.

5. Physical and mental suffering vanishes. Fear of death disappears.

6. Realization of the unimportance of material things and the importance of the spiritual .

7. Enhancement of mental and physical vitality and activity, an uncovering of latent genius and creativity.

8. A sense of mission—the revelation cannot be contained.

9. A new radiance, a charging with divinely inspired power, a magnetic force that attracts and inspires others; a transfiguration of being.[304]

Are you conscious of the senses or conscious of the soul? Professor Angha tells us that the human being is actually not a very material organization. It is not in the brain's biocomputer but in the electromagnetic fields and centers of our being, and in our receptive capacities that consciousness of reality lies. The electromagnetic elements and connections are those aspects of being traditionally perceived as spiritual. "The personal magnetics of man are constantly in connection with the universal electrics, and the nervous system and magnetic particles create a combination which govern human life in a way that every man's life has possessed."[305]

He states:

> When revelation and spiritual inspiration alight the heart, the gray area of the brain simultaneously becomes vibrant from its power, and the result of this wave of life is its vast relation with the heavenly spheres and the recipient of the universe and what lies beyond it. The result of this immense unity is the sensitivity of the brain, body and heart in uniting in harmony all the senses in the discovery of truth. The descent of the heavenly waves into the heart shall cause the limbs to tremble and this is the Divine Light that enlightens the sky of the heart.[306]

When this occurs, "when a human being succeeds in overcoming the speed of light he will be informed about the life manifestations of all the past and future." "Discovering future events and keeping past incidents in sight depends on being an observer in the present." This subject in Sufism is called breaking the limited boundaries through the infinite. Through the loss of the boundaries of time and space, all the capacities which are called paranormal are available. Communication with the spiritual personalities of others is possible. It is this communication that allows more spiritual beings to immediately recognize each other. This can only occur for those persons who wish knowledge without any desire whatsoever for any personal gain.

Hazrat Pir, in his exquisitely beautiful poems, "The Secret Word" and "The Approaching Promise," speaks of the lack or loss of this state, of the imprisoning boundedness of attachment.

That safeguarded fervent ecstasy that absorbs and revives,
That radiant magnificent star, as a shooting star
    that descends and penetrates,
That pure distilled frenzy of love —-
    that creator of Names,
What happened to That? What became of it?[307]

Professor Angha, in *The Mystery of Humanity*, tells us how to reach the highest spiritual level, which is beyond all the levels described, and is the level of true consciousness. It is the goal of Nirvan, in the allegory by that name. At this level, one has moved beyond emotion, an idea which bothers the Western mind, addicted to emotional stimulation to feel alive. He tells us: "Search for truth in your heavenly double, at a third point in the heart, the point of union of the two worlds, one delicate and one harsh, between sleep and wakefulness."[308] "Graft the sapling of your heart to the *source of life* so that it shall be nourished, until the blessed tree of justice bears fruit and permeates your being."[309]

CHAPTER 18
RELIGION

E instein said you could analyze one of Beethoven's symphonies in scientific terms, precisely describing the characteristics of the sound waves. To do so would, of course, make it lose all meaning. This is the sort of thing which tends to happen when psychology examines religion, with a few notable exceptions. The classic text is still William James' *The Varieties of Religious Experience*, published in 1902, before psychology lost its soul. Jung rediscovered the psychological value of the spiritual realm in the 1930s, and published *Psychology and Religion* in 1938. Gordon Allport, who published his book in 1960, says psychology has a "tenderness tabu," and that "it is still rare to find a therapist who sees health-giving significance in the concept of 'love of God'."[310]

The word "religion" comes from the Latin *religare*, meaning to bind together (*ligare*) again (*re*). The dictionary lists divergent definitions, defining it as belief in a divine power, expression of this belief, any specific system of belief (sacred or profane), a way of life expressing love for and trust in God, and so forth. Psychologists admit they cannot adequately define religion, and have difficulty differentiating between *religion* and *religious institutions*. Like most people, they tend to consider the institution, and institutional rules and beliefs to be the religion.

171

James summarized what he considered "the characteristics of the religious life," including these beliefs:

1. That the visible world is part of a more spiritual universe from which it draws its chief significance;

2. That union or harmonious relation with that higher universe is our true end;

3. That prayer or inner communion with the spirit thereof—be that spirit "God" or "law"—is a process wherein work is really done, and spiritual energy flows in and produces effects psychological or material, within the phenomenal world. Religion includes also the following psychological characteristics:

4. A new zest which adds itself like a gift to life, and takes the form either of lyrical enchantment or of appeal to earnestness and heroism.

5. An assurance of safety and a temper of peace and, in relation to others, a preponderance of loving affections.

Psychology does not usually ask: "Who or what is God?" nor "How can God be found?" Psychology does speculate upon the motivational basis for religion. Early psychologists spoke of religion as natural, innate, unlearned and instinctual—stemming from a primal source. Later views included the idea it is defensive and protective; human feelings of weakness and inadequacy create the need for religion. Psychological research data has usually been obtained from questionnaires. Most of the data psychology has accumulated about religion is based on what college students say they think about religion, or what they say they do in regard to religion.

Young children take words concretely and literally, so they often have interesting concepts of who or what God might be—perhaps the tall stature in the square, or Santa Claus. They ask questions like: "If God was there before the world was made, what did he walk on?"[3113] The more "religious" (usually measured in terms like frequency of attending services) the parents, the more "religious" the children tend to be. Allport states about two-thirds of US children somehow react against parental and cultural religious teaching —even if it is simply a change of church membership. In the U.S. the average age of conversion is sixteen—mid-adolescence.

US college students today, though 70% consider themselves actually or potentially religious, are very ignorant about religious viewpoints. "Even more certainly are students ignorant of the reasoned doctrines of

Hinduism, Islam and all the other great faiths."[312] Yet more than 40% of the students who say they feel the need for a religious orientation find the system in which they were reared unsatisfactory for their needs. The early and middle twenties are the least religious period of life. Women are more interested in religion than are men.

Most psychologists who consider religion do agree there are two different types of "religious" orientations. One is extrinsic, or externally focused, and provides status and security. The second is intrinsic, internalized, integrated, and an end in itself. Allport states that "in probably no region of personality do we find so many residues of childhood as in the religious attitudes of adults."[313], and differentiates between the religion of the immature and mature religion. Fromm considers the immature to be authoritarian—ridden by a sense of obedience, self-sacrifice, duty and resignation. Allport reports that subjects who accept religion unreflectively and uncritically seem uniformly immature in all areas. "They are found usually to have repressed conflicts hostility, anxiety, prejudice."[314]

> Jung describes the extrinsic:" What is usually and generally called 'religion' is to such an amazing degree a substitute that I ask myself seriously whether this kind of 'religion', which I prefer to call a creed, has not an important function in human society. The substitution has the obvious purpose of replacing immediate experience by a choice of suitable symbols invested in a solidly organized dogma and ritual. The Catholic church maintains them by her indisputable authority, the Protestant church (if this term is still applicable) by insistence upon faith and the evangelical message. As long as these two principles work, people are effectively defended and shielded against immediate religious experience."[315]

In contrast, mature religion is functionally autonomous. "It behaves no longer like an iron filing twisting to follow the magnet of self-centered motives; it behaves rather as a master-motive, a magnet in its own right by which other cravings are bidden to order their course."[316] "Advanced religious thinking makes a prominent place for mystical states and invites their occurrence, sometimes regarding them as the highest attainment of religious striving."[317] Moberg tells us extrinsic religion decreases in old age, while intrinsic increases.[318] The intrinsically motivated are less fearful of death. There is no fanaticism in mature religion. Jung depicts fanaticism as hiding secret doubts. The terms exoteric and esoteric are also used to describe religious orientations.[319] The exoteric level is concerned primarily with form, ritual, ceremony, etc., while the esoteric level is concerned with the knowing of the Creator, oneness with God.

Psychologists who write on the topic usually write as if religion were something capable of achievement through the mind and the process or thought. For example, Allport calls the great faiths "reasoned doctrines...the solutions reached by great minds in the past."[320] Allport contends that for religious freedom, a person must understand clearly:

> ...the forces of culture and conformity that invite him to be content with a merely second-hand religion. It is equally essential to his freedom of choice that he understand the pressures of scorn and intimidation that tend to discourage his religious quest altogether. Such pressures emanate from narrowly conceived science and from some teachers and writers who, in the face of the bigger issues of life, are as ignorant and helpless as any other seeker.[321]

Others point out the pervasive and perennial interconnections between politics and religious institutions. Spilka, Hood and Gorsuch, speak of "civil religion" in the US, stating it "provides a kind of divine stamp of approval of the social order as it now exists."[322]

Psychotherapists have traditionally, except Jung, avoided dealing with religion, and have found it troublesome, beginning with Freud. Recently however, there is renewed interest, and the line between "pastoral counseling" and psychotherapy is becoming more blurred. Scott Peck therapeutically popularized the perennial interest in evil; Lewis Andrews speaks of "Ethical Therapy," and John Bradshaw focuses on the central and saving role of spirituality. Since their inception, "Self-help" groups, like Alcoholics Anonymous (AA) and Narcotics Anonymous (NA), which have a higher recovery rate from addictions than any therapies, have insisted on the necessity of surrendering to a "Higher Power," and in using prayer and meditation to do so. Jung stated that of his thousands of patients over thirty-five, "all have been people whose problem in the last resort was that of finding a religious outlook on life." These therapeutic orientations have revived the importance of concepts like conscience and responsibility (which AA has always included) in achieving a state of psychological well-being. In doing so, they are partially following a well-known dictum: "What is demanded by the great religions is self-abnegation, discipline, surrender. To find one's life, one must lose it."[323]

Jung and Allport have commented in a similar perspective on the Deity. Jung says: "What one could almost call a systematic blindness is simply the effect of the prejudice that the Deity is *outside* man.," and speaks of "*the God within.*"[324] Allport states: "The theory that the individual mind is merely a fragment of a universal mind seems to be present in nearly every religion. ...It provides a possible channel for the inrush of divine consciousness into the individual mind."[325] Johnson uses the principles of induction and conduction as an example. Conduction is direct contact with a source of energy—like putting your finger into a light socket. Induction is being close enough to a source of energy to be warmed or energized or quickened by it, but the energy does not flow directly in. All transformers work on the principle of induction. Electricity of the proper voltage goes through a coil and back out. The coils close by get a charge of energy excited by induction. "In this way we can stand close to God or to the collective unconscious and be safe. When 100,000 volts of unconscious energy flows on its way, 110 volt household current is generated in our human lives, and we are enlightened by it."[326]

Johnson also bemoans "the loss of spiritual ecstasy in Western society which has left a void people fill in the only way they know how: with danger and excitement."[327] A recognition of the importance of the ecstatic, mystical experience is repeatedly found. Many feel modern Western religious institutions may fail to provide meaningful forums for mystical experience. Yet research indicates 30 to 40% of people in the US and Britain have experienced mystical type phenomena.[328] Research has also found that personal religious commitment is more related to mystical experience than it is to church commitment. Mysticism and psychological well-being are closely related. The mystic is psychologically healthy.

SUFISM AND RELIGION

People often think of religion as a relic, as something ancient. The ideas are old, but true religion is always new for each breathing person.

The tides move the seas, and the sun shines today just as it did 5,000 years ago, and so does the reality of religion. Hazrat Ali (peace be upon him) tells us: "The Truth is always the same."[329]

Professor Angha describes the origin of religion in *Dawn*. People must have felt helpless before the great forces of nature—fire, flood, earthquakes, the sun and moon, seas and sky, night and day, thunder and lightning, even the behavior of other people. To try and protect themselves from calamities and to attain what they wanted, they inevitably were inclined to worship these forces, to make them into gods. They created idols and gods as symbolic forms of these forces, built temples in which to house them, developed special ceremonies and made sacrifices, hoping they would then be protected and their needs would be met. They asked the gods for what they wanted. From the most primitive wood carvings to the sophisticated gods and goddesses of the Greeks and Romans, they are still gods of fear and desire.

This continued through the centuries until the appearance of the prophets. The essence of the message of the prophets is that the gods were limited, unchangeable, and inconstant. They taught there is only one God, who is all-powerful, all-knowing, and supreme. Their message is that they know God, are in communication with God, and whatever they tell us are His words. The prophets—such as the Gautama Buddha, Moses, Jesus, and Muhammad—were pure and sound in their words and deeds, and were true and well-founded in their beliefs.

Eventually, but not without extensive conflict, people accepted the words of the prophets and got rid of their idols. Most people, however, accepted God merely out of obedience or because of anticipated benefits. They did not know God, nor have any communication with Him. They thought they could attain what the prophets were telling them though their own reasoning ability and thought processes. Consequently, different schools of thought gradually appeared. People had destroyed the idols in the temples, but they replaced them with even stronger idols in their own mind and thoughts, and then worshipped the new idols in pagodas, synagogues, churches and mosques. They still do so today.

The philosophies that developed can be placed into two major categories: spiritualists and materialists. If the arguments of both groups are examined carefully, they are basically more similar than different. Materialists say the physical senses portray the truth, found in our cells and outside matter. Spiritualists say truth is found through our mind (which is the product of our brain cells). When asked what causes the movement that indicates the existence of life, the materialists say the power of motion comes from Nature, the spiritualists call it God. Both see it as coming from without.

Participation in today's religious institutions are usually based on people's:

1. Fear of punishment
2. Promise of rewards for good deeds
3. Notion that it is somehow good for people.

People also attend various services for the music and/or social life, and occasionally, for intellectual stimulation. But this is not religion.

In a radio interview Hazrat Pir tells us:

> We have a wrong idea about Sufism. We indicate it is a new religion. Sufism is the reality of religion. For some reason, we have a tendency to separate and divide things; not only Sufism. But what Sufism already exists in most societies actually does not provide and present what Sufism might be, just so many ceremonies and things they have picked up from different groups. Sufism is the reality of religion, a state of awareness and cognition.[330]

There is a story of a road with many people on it. There is a fork in the road. On the right fork is a sign that says: "God." On the left fork is a sign that says: "Lecture on God." Everyone is taking the left fork. Sufism is the right fork.

Professor Angha tells us religion is in our heart, and we have to find it. The presence of God is necessary for one's religion. If there is no presence, there is only thought, and religion is not thinking. The teachings of Sufism guide people to come to this point, to the point in the heart which is the source of life—the contact with infinity. Sufism is the reality of religion. The word Sufism literally means discernment or cognition, specifically, cognition of God. It means submission to God, knowing God, experiencing His Presence, and ultimately uniting with God, the Divine Beloved. Sufism is not a philosophy, for it is not the result of mental processes. Sufism can only be realized through the heart and soul. God must be seen. If God is not seen, not experienced, there is no certainty of sight, and acceptance of religion without certainty of sight is the worship of an idol, for it is worship of an illusionary god—a god we ourselves have formed either through the words of others or through our own imagination.

Those who study Sufism only philosophically, that is, through mental processes, do not know the reality of Sufism. They may be very good at "talking the talk," but do not know how to "walk the walk." There are always many such about, who are often esteemed academics who have perhaps read voluminously, and the ordinary person is attracted to them. People today are often misled about Sufism, based on a somehow learned reaction to writers on religious topics..

Let's suppose a talented writer researches well and publishes a book on the lives of great commanders of a certain epoch. No one mistakes the writer for one of the commanders. No one mistakes the biographer of prime ministers of a great era for one of the ministers. Yet in religious studies, particularly in Sufism, this misunderstanding often occurs. Readers tend to assume the writer is an *Arif*, but this is not correct. Sometimes their intentions are questionable. An *Arif* may research and write about Sufism, but someone who does research on Sufism is not necessarily an *Arif*.

There are different groups of researchers. One group tends to be as objective as possible in studying a subject and recording the historical data. They have no personal experience, no ulterior motives, and try not to present a personal point of view. Another group consists of those who study the subject and also have extensive and complete personal experience of the subject they write about. This group includes, for example, Rumi (Mehlavi) and Attar, author of *The Conference of the Birds*, as well as the works of Professor Angha and Hazrat Pir, since they are *Arif*s as well as researchers in Sufism. Obviously, the works of the latter group will be more valuable than those of the first group. There is another group as well. Today people often depend on booksellers to select books for them in areas where they have little background. Unfortunately, doing so may result in receiving misinformation if the topic is Sufism, for people with ulterior aims and motives have deliberately published books on Sufism which distort the true meaning.

Hazrat Pir uses another light analogy, that of a candle, to explain the reality of religion; to clarify the true meaning of submission to God. People like candles, but they have forgotten the real, symbolic meaning. A candle is a model of what a human being should be, for the candle has the same purpose as the final purpose of the human being— to give light to the world. The candle has two major parts, the wax and the wick. Our physical body is analogous to the wax, but instead of being compact, like the wax, our desires, tendencies, thoughts and imaginings pull us in several directions, so we are scattered. Just look at how difficult most people find it to quiet their chattering brain, which is a part of our body.

The process of concentration and meditation of Sufism is to rebuild us, to reconstruct us, to make us onto two major parts only, like the candle, so that then we can be lit, like the candle. If we examine the outside coating, the candle wax, we discover it has been purified. The consistency is uniform, smooth, and no adulterants are present. It is perfectly clean. In Sufism, our body is purified. The central portion, the wick, is different from the wax. It is made of cotton fiber, the covering of the seed of the cotton plant. It, too, must be cleaned and purified, then twisted, so that the fibers are tight together. The wick is in the middle of the candle; we can call it the heart of the physical body. The wick and the wax are completely different, yet each is necessary in order to have light. The wax will not burn without a wick. If the wick is lighted without the wax, it burns up quickly. It takes the wax to hold the wick to make a candle that can be lit and will give light and heat.

The teachings of the prophets are delineated in the three stages in Sufism. The first is called SHARIAT, and is the obligations and purification necessary for the physical body, namely, fasting and prayer. This is as the wax, and is concerned with all communication and behaviors toward the world outside ourselves. The second is TARIQAT, the wick, and is the inner part of the human, which must be united and concentrated. The third part is HAQIQAT, which is achieving and receiving the truth of the light.

SHARIAT: WAX
TARIQAT: WICK
HAQIQAT: LIGHT

In stage one, the wax is purified by teachings, exercises, fasting and prayers, and the particular way of praying, which means the purification is internal as well as external. In stage two, everything, including our thoughts, emotions, and tendencies, should come together as the fibers are twisted tightly to make the wick. Then we are ready for stage three, the final goal, which is the unification, and receiving the light. For this level to be gained, all thoughts, all behaviors, everything, must be focused in one direction, for one purpose. The human must attain complete concentration, the unique form, to attain spirit. Before, when all is scattered, there is no spirit. The purified, spiritual person is like the candle. The pure person is lit, and gives light. The person who attains this level is the *Arif*. The final goal is lighting the candle. Before that occurs, there is only concentration. Meditation comes from God. It is the receiving and keeping of the light.

Can candles light themselves? Candles cannot get or create light. The light has to come to them. When we are purified and ready, then He will proceed to give us the light, but not before. The quality of light comes to the candle, and the candle keeps it. Human beings cannot give the light to each other. It can come only from God, and is His gift. All the prophets and masters have taught people to purify themselves, to make themselves ready. None have ever taught that man could light himself. None. Only unlit candles make such statements. Perhaps they hope they can someday light themselves, but they cannot. The light is a gift from God. The prophets have taught that the truth of the human being is the same, regardless of physical characteristics such as race or gender. All, everyone, has the ability to be purified and concentrated and to attain the final goal.

In this example of the candle, where is the truth? It is in the middle, in the heart. The qualities of the human being in the light of God are always the same. Does he look at degrees, at wealth, or power? He looks only at the heart.

Light enables us to see, it lights our way. If we want to walk an unknown path, we need a light. Light shows us the safe way, it allows us to avoid dangers. The lit candle is "in His hand," under His protection. When you are ready, God will blow the light into your heart. This lit light is Adam, the true human. We must prepare ourselves. First it is necessary to find and follow the teacher.

We are all members of a tribe— Christian, Muslim, Jew—we live in a community. And people are afraid to leave their tribe. They are held to it out of fear. But if you are connected to God, you will be there, wherever He is, and your light will shine. When we receive the light then we fulfill the function for which we were created. When used for their proper function, candles give both light and heat. "What is your religion?" is a mistaken question. Religion is personal and confidential for everyone, for it is the truth within our own heart. It is the lit candle.

Many misunderstandings center about the holy books, The Bible and the Quran. Many religious groups have mistaken the Holy Book as a treasure rather than as a way to the treasure of God.

$E = mc^2$. Do you understand this? Is it English? The words are English, but the concept is not English. We understand, we have to know the meaning of the words in English, and then we have to know the field. In this case, we have to know physics, quantum physics. Do you understand the words of The Bible or the Quran? People think they do, but they do not. God's word is different from the language. It is the same as the example. The words are there, but they are symbolic. Both holy books tell us the teachings are for those "who have eyes to see and ears to hear." To understand, we have to know the field. In this case, we must know, we must actually experience, metaphysics. In considering the holy books, the difference between translation and relation must be understood. No translation can tell us the contents of the Bible. Jesus can teach us. To learn, we need a relation with him. No translation can tell us the contents of the Quran. Muhammad can teach us. We need a relation with him

The stories in the holy books are more than just history. Each story has a personal meaning, which has to found within, through revelation. The holy Books contain the story of our own life. Try to read the holy book as if you were the only person alive on this earth, and this book had been given to you for guidance. Read it as if it is the story of your inner life—your own inner conflicts, inner discoveries, inner journey. For example, we all must be led out of slavery to the Promised Land. As with all aspects of religion, people have interpreted the holy Books in ways which benefited them personally or as a member of a group. These selfish interpretations should not be accepted. This is easy to see in some aspects, such as the many supposedly religious wars which were really about power and control. In other aspects, it is a little more subtle.

Symbolically, in religious teaching, man has been used to symbolize the essence of being, and woman has symbolized the manifestation of being on this earth—the physical being. In Genesis we read that God created male and female—why do we also read Eve was created from Adam? The Source of Life of every being is the producer and generator of the body. Man and woman come from the same source, from the essence known symbolically as Adam. Every physical manifestation, man and woman, male and female, are Eves, created from the essence. It was the physical manifestation, the cellular life of both men and women, symbolized by Eve, which was deceived by the serpent. Both men and women are Marys who receive the Divine Seed from the Creator, and from whom is born the child of God. The physical beings of both men and women are to be respected, for both have the same quality and capability to produce the knowledge and experience it.

In our physical body, as in electricity, there are negative and positive. Both are essential. The body is negative, the inside is positive. Unification and harmony of both negative and positive provides the continuation of life. Separately, they will die. For men and women, reaching centrality—harmony and unity—is the crucially important point. Submission lies in obedience and submission of the negative side to the positive side. Then we are under the command of the Center, whether we are men or women. In Sufism, equality of rights is therefore a basic foundation.

Hazrat Pir asks students: "If the prophets—Buddha, Moses, Jesus, and Muhammad (peace be upon them) were in one room, would they fight?" The answer if obvious—of course not, for they all taught essentially the same thing. The many conflicts fought in the name of religion are not about religion at all, but about power and possession—about riches and territory and control. It is only when human desires and human ego enter in that conflict ensues. The basis of real religion is always love. There are no "religions." There is only one religion—the relationship of the human heart to the Creator. Religion is not confined by boundaries and limitations; it transcends manmade adversities and the prejudices of societies and cultures. Sufism is the reality of religion. It is the way of the Prophets.

CHAPTER 19
TRUTH

In everyday life, we tend to think of "truth" very simply, as the opposite of "lie." Something is true, or it is not true. Truth is defined as conformity to fact—a judgment or belief of being in accord with what is, has been, or must be. Note that truth is defined as a belief. The ordinary person considers books and experts to be the sources of "truth." When looking for truth, he or she turns to a book or someone who is considered knowledgeable. The result is that society is filled with people who think they know the truth. Actually, they are often convinced they know the truth. They personify the title of an article: "My Mind's Made Up, Don't Confuse Me with the Facts." The classic example of this type is Archie Bunker of TV fame.

What does it take to be dubbed an "expert?" Most people assume it takes special knowledge. Two graduate students, hired by a publishing firm to quickly write a book on a "hot" topic, were appalled to find themselves considered experts on the basis of what they considered the equivalent of a course research paper. All it takes to be an expert is an audience. The danger of reliance on experts to define the truth is clearly portrayed in any history of science, which is also a history of mistaken notions. *The Experts Speak*,[331] a book filled with examples of authoritative misinformation, illustrates the point. Academics themselves fall victim to the "expert" myth. An actor who was hired to speak at a professional conference, alternating jokes with meaningless but "high-sounding" sentences, received excellent ratings from the audience. The professionals thought he had said something important.[332].

Psychology reflects the social definitions of truth. When you open an Introductory Psychology text, the Table of Contents you see is a mirror of social belief about what is important in human behavior. Even using the physical methods, what is seen is, of course, dependent on where we look. In science in general, and in psychology in particular, the search for truth has therefore become limited to those specific bits of information which researchers have wanted to know about and been able to figure out a way to investigate. The "truth" of psychology then is bounded by the minds, by the interests, wishes and desires of those who have performed the experiments or who wish to propound their ideas. It is also often further bounded by the need for money to pay the costs of experiments. Obviously, whoever provides the funding exerts an extensive amount of control over not only the topic of research, but over research methods as well. Scientists used to hope for the patronage of royalty. Today the major source of research funding in many countries is the government. The reality is that the support necessary to pay the costs of research determine, in large measure, what is presented as "truth.." This is so obvious we often forget to notice it. Even the most benevolent society defines truth according to the wishes and the purposes of those who hold the power within the system. Cultures define truth to serve the ends of those in power, however good or bad they may be.

Many scientists, including psychologists, complain that additional funds are not forthcoming if research results are not in accord with the desires of the funding source. Psychologists who move too far beyond the social bounds (and bonds) may be, and often are, not only criticized by their colleagues, but their sources of funding and even their job may suddenly disappear. Robert Becker, a prominent researcher, lost funding for his work on the effects of electromagnetic fields after he criticized government plans for installation of huge ELF (low-frequency electromagnetic field) facilities.[333] Key lost his professorship for refusing to stop researching and publishing data on the covert messages in printed advertising.[334]

In other words, what is defined as truth is controlled. Are we not taught to think of education, particularly higher education, as the light of truth? Yet sociologist Jules Henry tells us: "the function of education has never been to free the mind and spirit of man, but to bind them; and to the end that the mind and spirit of his children should never escape, homo sapiens have employed praise, ridicule, admonition, accusation, mutilation, and even torture to chain them to the cultural pattern." [335]

In addition, truth always has had and always will have, its enemies, those who wish to define everything to suit their own selfish ends, to serve their own purposes. Both history and literature are replete with examples. From Machiavelli's *The Prince*[336] to Orwell's *1984*,[337] the definition of truth is seen as dependent on whomever holds the power. People are consequently afraid to speak the truth, as evidenced by the popular story of *The Emperor Who Wore No Clothes*. Only a little child, who did not yet know that telling the truth was not the thing to do, would point out that the emperor was wearing no clothes.

To remove the blinders of one's own culture is not an easy task, yet it is essential to finding truth. The social definition of truth, of what reality is and who and what we are imprison us within the cell of social tyranny, preventing us from discovering Truth. Yet most people do not question the social definition of truth. They simply accept what they are given, and do not investigate further, despite the fact that a careful observer cannot help but note discrepancies between the social definition and their own existence. Paulo Freire describes the ordinary person as "crushed, diminished, converted into a spectator, maneuvered by myths which powerful social forces have created."[120] Gatto describes our society as one of mass dumbness, filled with the non thought of secondhand ideas.[121]

SUFISM AND TRUTH

The Western world accepts a very narrow, limited definition of the term "truth" as reality. Psychology mirrors the limited definition. People think about truth, and read about truth. The dictionary tells us there are not only several definitions of truth, but four main types of truth, and even several theories of truth. One dictionary definition most people are unaware of is that truth is true religion or spiritual reality. Thinking and reading and talking about truth is philosophy—it is only ideas, imagination, not reality.

If the social consensus of reality is not the truth, where is truth? How does one find truth?[338] We know that if we are thirsty, thinking about a glass of water will not quench our thirst. We need the real thing—we need the water itself. If we want to know truth, will thinking about truth provide it? Again, no. We need to experience the truth itself. If we are thirsty, what should we do? Obviously, we should find and go to the source of water. If we thirst after truth, what should we do? We should do the same thing—find and go to the source of truth.

People say they want to know the truth, but do you know anyone who is asking: "How can I find Truth?" Most people think they know, so they do not ask. Do *you* know Truth? Do you *want* to know Truth? Are you asking: "How can I find the truth? What is the way to Truth?"

A respected Sufi instructor from another country came to visit a class. The students were excited about his coming, and eagerly anticipated learning from him. When he arrived, he sat down and asked if there were any questions. The students sat attentively and quietly waiting, and no questions were proffered. He asked again if anyone had any questions. There was no response. He then stated that if they had no questions, evidently they already knew everything. He then got up and left.

The prophets, the messengers of God, know and present the Truth: Moses, Buddha, Jesus, Muhammad. They tell us: I have found the Truth. They ask us: Do you want to know Truth? Yet only a very few people have listened to the words spoken by the messengers and asked: "How can I find the Truth?" The messengers told them what to do, and they did it. We must ask if we wish to find the truth. And we must do as the Prophets have indicated to do. Jesus taught: "Seek and you shall find. Ask, and you shall receive. Knock, and the door will be opened unto you."

Forms of the physical world are transient, impermanent, constantly changing. Our cells die, and regenerate; our bodies change. We have a new face every season, an entire new physical body every thirteen years. Truth is different. Professor Angha tells us: "Whatever exists and is constant and unchangeable is truth. Whatever exists but is changeable and not constant, is not truth... The human body exists, but it changes."[341] Seasons change the appearance of nature. Love can change into hate. Even stars will be extinguished. All that we see and much we do not see exists, but is not constant "until the words of God are realized, and everything is annihilated except that everlasting, divine, and tender being that everyone calls "I," the true self." "I" is constant and does not change through time, circumstances, or place. Each of us knows "I" at least briefly in witnessing the manifestations of "I." The "I" is the constant and unchangeable unit that all people have within themselves. The commandments of "I" in all cases are precise, unconditional and without mistake. "As this genuine identity is not bound to a shape or figure, so it is not perceived by observers. Its tangible manifestations have been mistakenly perceived as the genuine identity."

The word, "*solouk*," describing the journey of the *salik*, may be translated as "The Attainment of Truth.." Freedom, which is absolutely essential to the discovery of truth, cannot be attained without purification, without continual struggle against wants and desires, and without disregarding worldly attachments. "For this reason, truth seekers are few, and obstinate adherents are many."[342]

What does one use to discover truth? If one wants to discover anything, the proper instruments must be used. We do not study bacteria with a telescope. We do not use our toes to analyze food, nor our ears to ascertain the temperature of our tea. Our hand tells us about heat and cold, and our nose and tongue tell us about food. But our five senses only know, and are limited to, the physical. It is impossible to find truth through the five senses and the brain. They are not suitable. We have other instruments, which must be developed and used. If we want to know truth, we must forget all the experiences of the five senses.

Stop reading for a moment, and focus your attention on something in the room with you. To really see whatever you are looking at, you have to ignore everything else. The same is true for seeking truth. To find truth, one has to placed in truth, like the fetus within the womb of the mother. We have to do the same thing to receive the vital, precious truth of the Creator. If you wish to find Truth, you, too, must ask. And you, too, must do as the Prophets have indicated to do.

The capacity to hear the messenger must be developed. Like a radio, we must learn to clear all the static and interference, and tune out other stations, and tune in clearly to the station we wish to receive. And so we learn to quiet our chattering brain, to calm our waves of emotions, to physically ready ourselves to receive. That is the goal of Sufi concentration and meditation. All the exercises and experiences are aimed toward the goal of finding Truth.

In *Hidden Angles of Life*,[343] Professor Angha tells us that for all beings there is an intellectual personality in the world, as a guide who encourages and protects them. The Rational soul is the center for all the senses, the spiritual and intellectual powers, and is the protector of the body as well as governor of inner functioning. Lesser forces within govern the various bodily parts and organs, like provinces of a country, but the rational soul reigns over all.

The incorporeal essence which is the guide and teacher for the rational soul of man, has been called the essence by Zoroaster, the Platonic ideas by Platonists, Old Adam by Jewish Sufism, Perfected Man in Islamic Sufism, Gabriel and Soul in Islam, Holy Spirit in Christianity, Atma and Prosha in theosophy and Brahman in Hinduism. Until the advent of modern quantum physics, such ideas seemed contradictory to the laws of Newtonian science, and so there seemed no possibility of a scientific explanation. Today, more and more scientists, particularly physicists, are describing the similarities between the "mystical" teachings and the basic phenomena of quantum mechanics.

Professor Angha tells us that the rational soul may become acquainted with the realities through:

1. The organs of the physical body
2. The five senses (some suggest there are 10 or more) to perceive the lower stages of the celestial world on earth.
3. Inward powers or wisdom to perceive the superior stages of the celestial world
4. Spiritual power and divine forces, with which extremely holy souls can perceive the celestial kingdom and the spiritual world.

The tender, rational soul needs a means of travel beyond the harsh physical body to reach the spiritual worlds. Just as means for travel by air or water necessitates that the vehicle become lighter than air or water when in operation, so the rational soul needs lighter more tender, delicate bodies for spiritual travel. "The Gnostics can see and perceive by their heart's eye, which others cannot do, and know whatever they desire."

Diverse traditions have spoken repeatedly of vital centers, of energy, power, or magnetic centers within the human body. These traditions, ranging from ancient Egyptian to Theosophy[344] have taught of the human as possessing not just one, but several "bodies." They speak of the physical body, and four additional bodies. These "bodies" can be seen by those with the talent to do so. The term aura is today used by those who have the capacity for this vision. They describe seeing a colored halo or halos surrounding the body. The color of the aura varies from individual to individual, and changes depending upon the thoughts and emotions of the individual. Traditionally, painters portrayed the prophets and saints with golden halos. Some painted them around their heads, others as surrounding the entire body. The latter were more correct.

Moving outward from the physical body, the bodies are considered to become finer and more delicate, with extremely rapid waves in the highest body. This is easier to conceptualize when we consider that our physical body is composed of atoms which are mostly large expanses of empty space containing an incredibly minute nucleus surrounded by a cloud of moving electrons. It is through these bodies that ascension to the spiritual level can occur. It is not obtainable for most, for "It needs a fervent love, which is God's astrolabe."

In *Al-Rasa'el*, Professor Angha states very clearly: "The discovery of truth is not the task for the immature mind, nor does it consist of the common comparisons and transient inputs of the senses to the brain. However, cognition of truth is possible by the light of faith and heart discovery."[345] "Words are the veil of truth."[346]

In Maktab Tariqat Oveyssi Shahmaghsoudi, the School of Sufism, the spiritual leaders for 1400 years have unceasingly taught the way to Truth. If you want to know Truth, you must ask the way, genuinely and honestly, and you must prepare yourself so that you will be able to receive the answer, heart to heart. Professor Angha tells us: "The lights of truth shine through to the heart. The source of life in the heart is the light of knowledge and certainty, and the very knowledge itself."[347]

Professor Angha instructs us: "Add to the tenderness of your soul for the truth to reveal itself and rejoice your soul. The lights of truth shine through to the hearts, but hearts are too beset with transient temptations and desires."[130] "The divine message— the message that comes from the depths of the heavens guides the lost seekers to the house of truth, and the hand that heals with the power of God, and the soul that establishes and calms the surrendered hearts for them to live on is vouchsafed by the Almighty God."[348]

CHAPTER 20
LOVE

From birth on, we all seek love. We long for love. Poetry, music, art, are all filled with the symbolism of love. Whence comes this yearning? What is the basis for this search?

Psychology usually simply ignores love as a topic. Love is not considered in most psychology texts, and is not a category in reviewing psychological literature. Maslow called the failure of psychologists to deal with love, ludicrous. Academic psychologists tend to define love as an internal state or process and see it as, at least in part, a response to a living or inanimate object.[350] They tend to divide love into relationship categories, such as parent-child. They then study the behavioral patterns involved.

The most quoted research is that of the Harlows on monkeys. They constructed several types of surrogate mothers for newborn monkeys. Contact comfort, meaning terry cloth rather than wire, and warmth, seemed to be of crucial importance for the surrogate to be accepted and useful for the infant monkey. Once the infant became attached to the mother or surrogate, it was almost impossible to break the attachment. They created several "monster" mothers, which shook, blew compressed air at, or flung away the babies, who nevertheless, came right back. The only kind of surrogate mother, including wire, the infant monkeys would not attach themselves to was one that literally, had ice water in her veins.

Harlow then listed five kinds of love: the love of an infant for its mother or her surrogate, peer love, heterosexual love, mother love, and paternal love, which only occurs under the "right conditions." Is this indeed love?

Eibl-Eibesfeldt emphasizes that the basic bond between mother and infant is based on a desire for contact, not on need for food. He describes the various types of "bond-establishing rites" and behaviors used in greetings. Touching, particularly using the lips, is the most common and almost all-pervasive method of attempting to establish bonds.[351] He also argues that we are pre-programmed, that the disposition to cooperation and mutual aid is innate, as are many specific behavior patterns of friendly contact. In other words, we come "pre-wired" to love.

Spitz describes how infants who were separated from their mothers at ages 6 to 12 months became dejected, passive, refused food, lost weight, and became more susceptible to illnesses. Infants raised in orphanages with little human contact often died, and those who survived displayed all sorts of developmental difficulties. Almost all human infants show attachment, although many mothers and fathers do not. A new psychiatric diagnosis, that of "attachment disorder" is now applied to children (usually badly abused) who have developed no bonds with anyone.

Psychologists try and study love using questionnaires. They have developed scales for describing liking and love. People state that love, meaning romantic love, involves more closeness, dependency, selflessness, absorption and exclusiveness than friendship. They also tend to rate it as less stable than liking. Dorothy Tennov has differentiated between love and "limerance," the latter being romantic passion with an acute longing for reciprocation. Her case histories document the extreme behavior exhibited by people (using her term) "in limerance"[352] They are those who inspire others to call romantic love "temporary insanity," for they obsessively think of the object of their passion, and are characterized by anguish and helplessness regarding it.

Psychotherapists have had to pay attention to love, for many client complaints are centered around love. The psychoanalyst Erich Fromm, in *The Art of Loving*, states: "No objective observer of our Western life can doubt that love—-brotherly love, motherly love, and erotic love—is a relatively rare phenomenon, and that its place is taken by a number of forms of pseudo-love which are in reality so many forms of the disintegration of [353] A commonplace form of pseudo-love is the transference of feelings, expectations, and fears one once had toward father or mother to the "loved" person in adult life. The aim then is often to be loved, to obtain love, not to love. Another form, frequently portrayed in film and video as the "great love," is idolatrous love. It demonstrates the hunger and despair of the idolater, and disappointment inevitably occurs when the idol's "feet of clay" finally become visible. The most common form is probably sentimental love, in which love is experienced only in the fantasies of consumers of love songs, movies, videos, magazine love stories and romance novels. Love is a daydream.

Fromm sees people as starved for love, and yet believing falsehoods about love, thinking they "know" about love, and hence never attaining it. Most people see the problem of love primarily as that of being loved, rather than in loving, in developing one's own capacity to love. They therefore try to make themselves lovable. In this culture what people think of as "lovable" is a cross between being popular and having sex appeal. They are concerned with the object, rather than with the faculty. A common confusion is mistaking the often powerful experience of "falling" in love with being in love. Of course, the "fall" does not last. Many see love as a pleasant sensation, as something that just happens to one if we are lucky, so nothing is easier than to love, rather than recognizing that love requires knowledge, devotion and effort.

Fromm states: "The awareness of human separation, without reunion by love—is the source of shame. It is at the same time the source of guilt and anxiety. The deepest need of man, then, is the need to overcome his separateness, to leave the prison of his aloneness. Man—of all ages and cultures—is confronted with the solution of one and the same question: the question of how to overcome separateness, how to achieve union, how to transcend one's own individual life and find at-onement."[354] The answers found are in the records of human history across time and geographical borders.

One way of trying to achieve this is through "orgiastic" states, which may be achieved with or without the help of drugs or rituals. This method is intense, affects mind and body, and is transitory, so repetition is necessary. Another attempted method is through conformity. "Most people are not even aware of their need to conform. They live under the illusion that they follow their own ideas and inclinations, it just happens that their ideas are the same as that of the majority."[355] Consensus proves their "rightness." The anxiety of separateness is not pacified by conformity, however. One has only to look at the various addictions running rampant in Western society to realize this. A third method is through creative activity. In this instance, man unites himself with the world in the process of creation. Modern society is reducing and discouraging creativity.

Fromm sees certain elements as basic in all forms of real love. They include care, responsibility, respect and knowledge. Fromm sees respect as possible only for the individual who does not need to dominate, control or exploit anyone else. He quotes an old French song which states that love is the child of liberty. Obviously, one cannot love what one does not know. Love is also the fulfillment of the desire for the union of polarities, represented symbolically by union of the masculine and feminine elements, not just without, but within each of us. It is the fusion of the polarities of night and day, heaven and earth, of all life. He points out that: "Erotic love, if it is love, has one premise. That I love from the essence of my being—and experience the other person in the essence of his or her being. In essence, all human beings are identical. We are all part of One; we are One."[356]

The popular view is that it is sinful to love oneself, for it is selfish. However, if it is a virtue to love one's neighbor as a human being, how can it not be a virtue to love oneself as a human being? Fromm states that love of others and love of ourselves are not alternatives. Those who are capable of loving others will also hold a loving attitude toward themselves. "The affirmation of one's own life, happiness, growth, freedom is rooted in one's capacity to love , i.e., in care, respect, responsibility and knowledge. If an individual is able to love productively, he loves himself too; if he can love only others, he cannot love at all." To Fromm, self-love and selfishness are opposites, not identical. Leo Buscaglia has presented the "pop" version of love.[357] He states: "The perfect love would be one that gives all and expects nothing.""If one expects nothing and asks nothing, he can never be deceived or disappointed." He describes how love lives for the moment, not in yesterdays nor tomorrows. He amplifies Fromm's view in a chapter titled: "To Love Others You Must First Love Yourself.," stating: "Love and the self are one and the discovery of either is the realization of both."[358]

Theodor Reik described the many behaviors popularly connected with the ordinary definition of love, seeing love as an attempt to quiet inner tension, and eliminate inner discord, substituting the love object for the ideal ego. The lover loves the ideal of themselves in the other one. The source of love is the feeling of ego deficiency and the need for ego-completion or ego-improvement.[359]

Sorokin and Hanson cite many instances in which what they consider the "power of love" has overcome or dispelled incredibly strong negative forces.[360] They see love as curing and revitalizing, as being the decisive factor in vital, mental, moral and social well-being and growth of an individual. They also comment on how the healing that occurs in psychotherapy is the result of the love of the therapist, love in the meaning of being deeply understood and deeply accepted. Rogers called this "unconditional positive regard.." They see love as the driving force toward the highest values of human life, to the power of truth, knowledge, beauty, freedom, goodness and happiness. "Each of these end-values has its own power that tangibly affects, enriches, and ennobles the life of individuals, groups, and the course of human history."[361] They quote Dostoevski: "'Love all God's creation, the whole and every grain of sand in it. Love every leaf, every ray of God's light. If you love everything, you will perceive the divine mystery in things.'"

The psychiatrist, Jampolsky, in a book of the same title, states: *Love is Letting Go of Fear*.[362] Using Transactional Analysis terminology, Tanner has described loneliness to be the posture of the fearful "NOT OK" child within us, and results in our wanting love, but running from it at the same time. "It is a kind of death."[363] Because of this fear of love we then may unhappily come to settle for being with people in a physical sense, rather than risk advancing toward genuine love.

Rollo May[364] cites the four kinds of love in the Western tradition, stemming from the Greeks. The first is sex—lust, libido. The second is eros—the drive of love to create; the urge toward higher forms of being and relationship. The third is brotherly love or philia. The last is agape, or selfless giving, the prototype being the love of God for man. He unfortunately focuses almost exclusively on sex and eros, seeing the latter, both within us and in the universe itself, as drawing us toward the ideal forms, thus eliciting the capacity to reach out, to let ourselves be grasped, to mold the future.

Interestingly, most social scientists known for their writing about love have "discovered," and quote, the exquisite love poetry of the famous 13th century Sufi poet, Mahlevi, known as Rumi in the West. Since words can never contain the meaning of such an incredibly awesome and unfathomable gift from Divinity, such poets have, for millennia, used the facade of what the unknowing call "love poetry," to disguise the supreme serenity, joy and contentment experienced by the lover of God.

William James, nearly a century ago, is almost the only prominent psychologist who seriously considered and discussed the love of God as a psychological phenomenon. In his book, he quoted extensively from what he called the "religious literature"[365] "'there seemed to be a constant flowing and reflowing of heavenly love, and I appeared to myself to float or swim, in these bright, sweet beams, like the motes swimming in the beams of the sun, or the streams of his light which come in at the window.'" [366] He also made very clear what few psychologists mention: "Yet the unseen region is not merely ideal, for it produces effects in this world. When we commune with it, work is actually done upon our finite personality, for we are turned into new men, and consequences in the way of conduct follow in the natural world upon our regenerative change."[367]

If psychologists have ignored the task of dealing with love, writers in other fields have sought it out. Romantic love is big time economically in the US. Untold billions are spent upon advertising to make us more attractive as lovers, romance novels sell hundreds of thousands of copies, and the TV screen depicts romance 24 hours a day. A prominent researcher considers romantic love to be 90% sexual desire, and it is clearly sexual desire that the advertisers are selling as "love."[368] Adolescents are particular targets in this culture for the sellers of sexual passion as the answer to all human needs. The air waves are filled with the sound of passionate, often unrequited "love" or the sadness of its loss. Romantic love is often considered to involve a number of emotions, including fear, anger, sexual desire, excitement, joy, and jealousy. In these cases, love can usually be equated with "want" or "need." In the U.S. romantic love is considered to be the main reason we get married. George Bernard Shaw stated his view of the consequences: "When two people are under the influence of the most violent, most insane, and most transient of passions, they are required to swear that they will remain in that excited, abnormal, and exhausting condition continually until death do them part."

John Ciardi states: "Love is the word used to label the sexual excitement of the young, the habituation of the middle-aged, and the mental dependence of the old."[369] Ashley Montague insists the word love has been used in so many senses, and has become so debased that the bad meanings of the word have driven out the good.[370] He also believes that what we today encounter is not the expression of love as much as the expression of the frustration of love. In the Western world, lack of love is seen as the source of all Evil—love is the way to happiness—few persons have been loved enough or are able to love anyone else to their own satisfaction. Montague sees hatred as love frustrated. The child is born with the "emotion" of love, and "when that love is consistently and strongly enough frustrated, it turns into hatred or aggressiveness.."[371] The aggression is an attempt to compel love, which, of course, does not work. The result is frightening.

Montague states that love really is interdependence, the state of depending upon each other, and without which no living group of organisms could survive. He sees the source of love, at its most primitive level, as the tendency of all matter to cohere, to stay together, as in the "cooperation" of the particles of the nucleus of the atom and in the joining of atoms into molecules. There is a physics of interdependence in atoms and molecules which can be observed and verified. Moving to the level of the organism, an organism can itself be defined as an organized system of interdependencies.[372] Love has its origin "in the organization of matter, in the integrative, essentially cooperative relations of the particles constituting matter."[373] And love is the most significant ingredient in the structure of human nature. "To inhibit or prevent the expression of love is to do violence to the needs, to the structure, and to the functioning of the organism." [374]

SUFISM: THE WAY OF LOVE

It is the love of God which has historically stimulated the greatest artistic creations, the greatest paintings, sculptures, and music. It is the love of God which is epitomized in those who are the models for all of mankind, the Prophets. It is the love of God which has historically moved and shaped man into a creature of nobility. How can one seriously consider the behavior of man without addressing the love of God?

Love is the essence of Sufism. The goal is union of the lover with the Divine Beloved. The love of God for man, and the reciprocal love of God by man, has ever been the foundation of religion, repeatedly presented by the Prophets, and explicitly expressed in the holy Books, The Bible and the Quran. In Matthew 22:37, Jesus states:

You shall love the Lord your God with all your heart, and with all your soul, and with all your mind. This is the great and the first commandment. And a second is like unto it, You shall love your neighbor as yourself. On these two commandments depend all the law and the prophets.

The Prophets themselves are considered to be perfect examples of love. The great love story of all time is not the tale of a relationship between two pieces of flesh, bound to decay and return to the elements. The epitome of love is when the soul has forsaken love of the world and has united with the Heavenly Beloved, and thereby reached the most exalted state of Existence.

Professor Angha tells us that the Persian word for love, Ishq, is originally an Arabic word, derived from the word meaning bindweed. This is a dense, twining plant, which tends to intertwine and interlace extensively with plants among which it grows, so they become as one. He considers this a very suitable name for this vital, genuine essence.

Professor Angha describes love as synonymous with the most delicate and spiritual levels of life. Love is the power which binds together the particles of matter, which sculpts the manifestations of Existence into its multitudinous shapes and forms, and whose very function is creation. Love is the very glue of Existence. There are three levels of love—ordinary, spiritual and divine. The ordinary level is the level of everyday life, of sexuality, of friendships, of attractions. It includes our likings, the material attachments of everyday life, and even such biological behaviors as the binding together of chromosomes. Hazrat Mir Ghotbeddin described how people today mistake sexual passion, sensual sexuality, for the real and ultimate form of love, when, in actuality, it is the lowest form, based on carnal desire and a worldly veil masking the reality of the soul of love. These people glimpse only the smoke of the burning fire of love. In their preoccupation with physical sexuality, they have failed to discern the divine qualities, and have also failed to recognize that the very existence of the particles of matter is dependent on the attraction of love.

The spiritual level is that which exists between spiritual teachers and pupils, between masters and followers. Jesus tells us in John 14: "If a man loves me, he will keep my word, and my Father will love him, and we will come to him and make our home with him." The divine, or highest level, is that of the holy prophets in relation to the infinite, either positive

Existence or the Almighty. Each manifestation has its own reality. And so with love. The higher levels are hidden, covered by the veils of the lower levels. The masking veils of the everyday, the ordinary, must be removed in order to see the higher levels. In *Love and Destiny*, Professor Angha defined ordinary love as the penetrating electromagnetic power which joins all the particles of the infinite together. For ordinary love, hatred is its reflection, as are evil and goodness, ugliness and beauty, suffering and pleasure. We have all seen love turn into hate. The sensation of ordinary love to a certain extent precedes the experience of everlasting loves, and apparently also the behavior of particles which are restricted within three dimensions. One must be an earthly lover before one can be a heavenly lover. Professor Angha tells us that the effects of love are accompanied by a superior order of life in all researchable fields.

All existence is originated by the power of love. All existence IS love, which has its own manifest on the basic characteristics of every manifestation. Let us take as an model, the human brain. Within the brain, a single neuron, by itself, is insensitive to the electric, magnetic, sonic, and electromagnetic fields emitted by another cell. Two cells interacting in such a manner as to mutually increase their individual sensitivities are more sensitive together. Known electrical processes provide the calculation that such mutual positive feedback would procure a sensitivity which is approximately the square of the sensitivity of the single neurons. Three mutually interacting neurons would have more than the cube of the sensitivity of the three single cells. Four would be to the fourth power, and so forth.

The origin, for the effects and impressions of ordinary loves and desires, is the magnetic source below the sternum, the solar plexus. The second love, spiritual love, happens when complete unification occurs between the two magnetic sources of the solar plexus and the brain. The higher level divine loves of the prophets are of connection and unification of the three magnetic sources of the heart, the solar plexus and the brain together.

The goal of the salik is to remove the veils, to come to know and to cognize God, for one cannot love what one does not know. Hazrat Pir tells us: "This kind of cognition is obtained only through loving, obeying and worshipping God by all means, with the self, heart and mind under the supervision of a master who will be introduced inwardly and secretly by God through the seeker's heart." Ultimately, the goal is to be annihilated in love, to lose oneself completely in the Beloved. For those who are governed by the power of spiritual love, that is, who are annihilated in love, the destiny of heaven lies within. Love behaves accordingly. For the lover, the Beloved's wish becomes their desire. There is no self, there is only the eternal and infinite Presence of the Beloved.

"The *salik* must find the Master of Love and in the permanence of the Eternal Spring without self-existence, reach for life in its abundance and light."[375] He must give up dependence upon his mental processes, for "the mind knows not how this wondrous work is done."[376] Hazrat Pir tells us, "Hasten, and renounce hence they pretentious mind, Thy soul's ablutions with they heart's love perform."[377] Cleansing of the soul occurs through the love within the heart, and the heart is the gateway to the Divine Beloved. "He who calls to God from the depths of his heart, Will find his abode in the clear skies of love."[378] The way to love can only be through the heart and the heart must be fully submitted to the hands of love. This is the submission which is the meaning of Islam.

The love must be pure, without expectation or desire, not dependent upon the granting of any gain. Baghli tells us: "The lover is he who loves God for God, and should a misfortune befall him, his affection shall increase, but if he loves God for His favors, if a misfortune befalls him, his affection shall diminish."[379] The myriad temptations of the physical world which draw one away from the Beloved must be overcome, for no heart can have two loves, there may be only one. "Real lovers are not diverted by the colors of the world; they are judged according to their patience."[380] "Everything eagerly awaits he who eagerly awaits God."[381]Waiting is sweet for the lover.

The star that shines within our heart is the means of travel to the skies of Love. Professor Angha tells us: "The light in my heart is like a steady star in the deep clear sky whose image is reflected at the bottom of a well, bright and radiant, and like Venus, the bride of the sky, calls gracefully to itself my entire being." We must concentrate our thoughts upon this star, at this point in our heart and calm them;[382] we must gather together all our energies and concentrate them on this star, which is the Source of Life. To successfully do so liberates us from the bonds and boundaries of the physical world.

Egotism and selfishness, as well as individuation, must dissolve. The drop of water must lose its boundaries in the ocean of Love on the way to

God. "Lost of self is the man of Love, Lost in self remain the rest."[383] Al-Junayd described what occurs as "the entering in of the qualities of the Beloved in place of the qualities of the lover."[384] Shibli said "it is called love, because it obliterates from the heart all save the Beloved" and "Love is a fire in the heart consuming all save the Will of the Beloved." One is annihilated in the Beloved.

No words can convey the depth or splendor of such love—our experience of the lower levels of love provides only a glimpse of the beauty of this exquisite, sublime love. Professor Angha describes how "at the peak of love I lose myself in His radiance."[385] The power of love is depicted in the poetry of Hazrat Pir. He asks: "Enflame my essence with Thy flame of love,"[386] and describes: "That incendiary sigh that harvests with fire a hundred enraptured suns of love's frenzy."[387] This beauteous and absolute love is invisible through this world. Freedom from the attachments to this world is essential for the ascension of the soul to the heights of love. Professor Angha tells us: "..he endures the hardship of sanctification with pleasure and delight, until gradually, by the pure soul's help, his heart's knots will be untied, and attain the real dignity of freedom;."

There are seven mounts of the heart in the journey of love to God.[388]

The First Mount of the Heart
Is God's opening of the heart to Islam, to submission, .". so that he follows a light from his Lord."

The Second Mount of the Heart
"The center for shining the light of wisdom and belief." The mind is exiled, for it cannot compete with the power of love.

The Third Mount of the Heart
"The place for the light of love." This state knows not words, for the state of lovers needs another ear and another voice. The revealed truths are kept secret in the sanctuary of his heart.

The Fourth Mount of the Heart
The place for seeing; the manifestation of the Friend. "Deaf to the tunes of the world is he."

The Fifth Mount of the Heart

The center for the manifestation of love of God; unity of heart. The drop has become one with the sea.

The Sixth Mount of the Heart

The heart's core; the light of God's knowledge. Annihilation in God; the servant is united by the Divine Breath.

The Seventh Mount of the Heart

"The secret, the center for the manifestation of lights and secrets of God, the place of eternal peace." Flawlessness, with the concealed secrets fully revealed. No sign nor name remains.

There are also seven lights of the heart. At each stage, the *salik* is blessed with the Light of the Divine blessing "according to the measure of his cup."[389] Each light is inwardly manifested, and has a truth, "which is the result of his pure actions and praiseworthy character, and is the means of travel for the enlightened of heart."[390]

The First Light of the Heart

"As moon doth shine." The Light of guidance from the light of Life.

The Second Light of the Heart

Is the saffron House of the Sun.

The Third Light of the Heart

Is the henna Elixir of Love.

The Fourth Light of the Heart

Is blossoms of yellow.

The Fifth Light of the Heart

Is emeralds of green, leaving the world in union with Him.

The Sixth Light of the Heart

The gold of perfection of the *salik*'s heart.

The Seventh Light of the Heart
The black light of the House of God, beyond which light does not travel.

The symbolism of the Divine Wine of Love from the Heavenly Cup is frequently used to describe the elixir of love. The Quran promises: "And their Lord will give to them to drink of a wine pure and holy."[391] Hazrat Pir tells us: "Thy heart is for the Beloved's cup to fill. . . Each wine drop from that cup for the soul is joy, Glory's the splendor for the drunkmen of yore."[392] The cup of love may be received from the Perfect Hand of Love only in moments of freedom from the self. Professor Angha describes: "At this time, for the esteemed and the chosen, the soul's cup is filled solely with the clearest, purifying, divine wine, the eternal wine of His glorious Presence, blessed by the touch of His Magnificent Countenance, the ever eternal wine of blissful Light for the circle of those yearning for the Face and Eyes of the Bearer of Wine."[393]

The perfect example is the *Arif*:
The *Arif* is freed from the bonds of the self,
His heart's entrusted to the Beloved's love.
As dust he now sits at the feet of his God.
Love's pure wine sparkles through his selfless clear cup.[394]

FIGURE 5: COMPARATIVE SUMMARY

PSYCHOLOGY	**SUFISM**
IN PRESENT FORM: Less Than 100 Years	1400 Years
GOALS: Prediction and Control of Human Behavior	Self-knowledge Knowledge of the Creator
METHODS: Quantitative Impersonal	Qualitative Personal

PSYCHOTHERAPY	**SUFISM**
DEFINITION OF PROBLEM: Mental Illness	Sickness of the Soul
GOALS: Mental Health	Healing the Soul Union with the Beloved
PRIMARY METHOD: Conversation	Experience
CHANGES RESULTING: Minor, appearances Adjustment	Deep, permanent Transformation
LOCUS: MAN	GOD

CHAPTER 21
LIGHT

L et us return once more to the original analogy of the lamp.
Psychology describes the various characteristics of the lamp and
psychotherapy makes changes in physical aspects of the lamp,
while Sufism provides the connection to the Source of Power which
enables the lamp to provide light.

Figure 5 briefly summarizes the differences between Western psychology and Sufism, and psychotherapy and Sufism. Psychology has
existed in its present form only during the last century, while Sufism is as
old as humanity, and is more than 1400 years old in its present form. The
goal of psychology is the description, prediction and control of human
behavior. The goal of Sufism is Self-Knowledge, and through Self-
Knowledge, knowledge of the Creator. Psychology is quantitative and
essentially impersonal, concerned with measurable "average" behavior.
Sufism is qualitative and personal. Psychology focuses on the physical.
Sufism accepts the physical, but concentrates on the metaphysical. The
outcome of the study of psychology is ideas and accumulated descriptive
information about human behavior. The outcome of the study of Sufism
is Divine Light.

While psychotherapy is concerned about mental health, Sufism is
concerned with healing the soul, with achieving union with the Beloved.
Psychotherapy uses conversation as the primary method of improving
one's troubled life. Sufism uses inner, heart cognition guided by the spir-

itual master, the Pir. The changes resulting from psychotherapy are usually minor, and involve appearances and "adjustment." The Way of Sufism is a deep, permanent transformative experience. In psychology and psychotherapy, the primary focus is on man. In Sufism, the focus is on God.

Western psychology, while providing useful information, in limiting its inquiry to descriptions of measurable physical phenomena ignores the very essence of its own original meaning—the form expressing the principle of the soul or spirit. Western psychotherapy, focusing on the physical level, and, more specifically, on words, has no means for attaining access to the higher levels of capabilities and potentialities, nor of providing the "healing of the soul" which is its original meaning.

In contrast, Sufism is the way to healing of the soul and to attaining the highest level of human capabilities and potentialities with which we are all blessed at birth. Sufism is psychotherapy in the original meaning of the term.

Sufism answers the key questions which psychology cannot answer: how to develop the perfect human, and how to develop the perfect society. It answers the eternal human questions of identity and purpose in life, and provides the way to the tranquillity and survival we all seek. The Pir lights the path to the connection with the Source of Power which will allow us to fulfill the function for which we are intended, to provide light.

The essential study of Sufism is not through word nor thought, which veil the truth. In the journey to the Light, "truthful words, a pure heart, sincere intention, honest livelihood, firmness of step and true devotion are necessary."[395] Only by the grace of God may the delicate Divine truths be inwardly revealed to the seeker without question or doubt. The guidance of the Pir is necessary to overcome the obstacles of the journey, for: "The one who goes on this journey on his own will drown in the mirage of the self." [396]

Professor Angha tells us:

> Seek the world of mysteries and the truth of your reality in the eternal realm of the heart in total humility and in awareness you shall find the light of God, and in the Light of Divine guidance your life shall fade in the splendor of His Presence, so that the tranquillity you have been seeking shall be yours. Know that what lies without you is not real, and what is within you is your truth.[397]

Hazrat Pir tells us:

This source of brightness by God's grace is bestowed,

'Tis man's own dignity that this Light bestows.[398]

When the Divine Light envelops the realm of the heart of the *salik*, the heart is "enlightened with the light of the guiding stars and he shall know the seven lights of the heart one after the other . . .the world of transition shall succumb to the state of devotion. He shall drink the cup of annihilation and shall manifest the Splendor of God..."[399], for annihilation is the disappearance of impurities from the heart and their replacement with the Divine manifestations.

Professor Angha describes how: "..the seven mounts of the heart correspond to the hidden lights of the sky of the heart that by divine inspiration and absorption in the rapture of love, the heart is illumined and freed on its flight to its Origin."[400] The *salik* is..."blessed in the Light of the Divine blessing at each stage according to the measure of his cup. Each meaning and light inwardly manifested to the salik has a truth, which is the result of his pure actions and praiseworthy character and is the means of travel for the enlightened of heart."[401] The hiddens are revealed in the seven lights of the heart.

The Divine Light illuminates the soul of the salik. The veil between the earth and heaven is lifted, freedom is confirmed, and the "limited self shall break its boundaries and unite with the infinite existence of God and in that moment of union, the delicate is intertwined with the delicate, and the trusted Gabriel shall be the bearer of revelation from the breath of the Absolute Essence."[402] The *salik* "shall be united with the Kingdom of His Radiance. He shall be flawless and the concealed secrets shall be fully revealed to him."[403]

God is the light
Of the heavens and of the earth.
The parable of His light
Is as if there were a niche,
And within it a lamp,
The lamp enclosed in glass,
The glass as it were, a brilliant star,
Lit from a blessed tree,
An olive, neither of the East nor of the West,
Whose oil is well nigh luminous,
Though fire scarce touched it.
Light upon light!
God doth guide whom he will to His light.
God doth set forth parables for men, and
God doth know all things.
The Quran, Sura 24

GLOSSARY

Angha:	The name of the Pir, which means "phoenix."
Arif:	One who is annihilated in God, the perfect human
Haqiqat:	Concentration of all aspects
Hazrat:	His Holiness
Irfan:	Sufism
Islam:	Submission, surrender (to God)
Jabarut:	The Sphere of Divine Power
Lahut:	The luminous kingdom
Malakut:	The Heavenly realm
Molana-al-Moazam	Great Teacher
Pir:	Spiritual Leader, "light of the path"
Salik:	Seeker of truth who is trained under the guidance of the Spiritual Teacher.
Shariat:	Purification, internal and external
Solouk:	Journey to truth
Sura:	Chapter
Tariqat:	Unification, annihilation in God

NOTES

CHAPTER I
INTRODUCTION
1   Angha, Molana Hazrat Salaheddin Ali Nader Shah. (1987). *Peace.*
Verdugo City, CA: MTO Publications.

CHAPTER 2
HISTORY
2   Lecture, Sacramento, CA. March, 1989.
3   Murray, Sir James A. H. (1933). *The Oxford English Dictionary.*
Oxford: Clarendon Press.
4   English, Horace B & Ava C. (1976). *A Comprehensive Dictionary of
Psychological and Psychoanalytical Terms.* NY: David McKay.
5   Wundt, Wilhelm. (1912/1973) *An Introduction to Psychology.* NY:
Arno Press.
6   Murray, David J. (1988). *A History of Western Psychology.* Englewood
Cliffs, NJ: Prentice Hall.
7   Lawry, John D. (1981). Guide to the History of Psychology. Totowa,
NJ: Littlefield, Adams.
8   See Bowne, Borden P. (1886) *Introduction to Psychological Theory.*
NY: American Book Co.; James, William . (1892). Psychology: Briefer Course.
NY: Henry Holt & Co.; Ladd, George T. (1901). Primer of Psychology. NY:
Charles Scribner's Sons.
9   Bowne, Borden P. (1886). *Introduction to Psychological Theory.* NY:
American Book Company.
10   James, William (1890) The scope of psychology. In *The Principles of
Psychology, I,* 1-8. Reprinted in Bornstein, Robert E. (ed.) (1973). *The Nature of
Human Consciousness.* San Francisco: W. H. Freeman.
11   Rogers, Carl. (1951). *Client-Centered Therapy.* Boston: Houghton-
Mifflin.
12   Maslow, A. H. (1968). *Toward a Psychology of Being* (2nd ed). NY: Van
Nostrand Reinhold. See also (1973) *The Further Reaches of Human Nature.* NY:
Viking\Esalen.
13   Hujwiri, Ali, B. Uthman Al-Jullabi. (1911-1976). *Kashf Al-Mahjub of Al
Hujwiri.* London: E.J.W. Gibb Memorial.
14   See Underhill, Evelyn. (1910-1974). *Mysticism.* NY: New American
Library. or Schimmel, Annemarie. (1986). *Mystical Dimensions of Islam.* Chapel
Hill, NC: University of North Carolina Press.
15   Quoted in the preface to Al-Muqaddisi, Shaykh Izzidin. (1980).
Revelation of the Secrets of the Birds and Flowers. London: Octagon Press.

16 Schimmel, Annemarie. (1985). *And Muhammad is His Messenger.* Chapel Hill: The University of North Carolina Press. p. 22.

17 *Mystical Dimensions of Islam.*

18 Smith, Margaret. *Rabi'a the Mystic and Her Fellow-Saints in Islam.* Cambridge University Press, 1984.

19 *Mystical Dimensions of Islam.*

20 Attar, Farid Ud-din. (1990). *Muslim Saints and Mystics.* London: Arkana.

21 al-Ghazali. (1980). *The Alchemy of Happiness.* see also Shah, Idries. (1977). *The Sufis.* both London: Octagon.

22 *Mystical Dimensions of Islam.*

23 Nizami. (1976) *The Story of the Seven Princesses.* London: Bruno Cassirer.

24 Attar, Farid Ud-din. (1984) *The Conference of the Birds.* NY: Penguin.

25 Ibn Tufail, Abu Bakr Muhammad. (1982) *The Journey of the Soul.* London: Octagon Press.

26 Rumi, Jalalu'd-din. (1926-1982). *The Mathnawi of Jalalu'd-din Rumi.* London: E.J.W. Gibb Memorial Trust.

27 *Mystical Dimensions of Islam.*

28 Ibid.

29 Ibid.

30 *Peace.*

CHAPTER 3
GOALS

31 Ehrenfeld, David W. (1975). *The Arrogance of Humanism.* NY: Oxford University Press.

32 Ardrey, Robert. (1970). *The Social Contract.* NY: Aatheneum.

33 See Brown, P. (1973). *Radical Psychology.* NY: Harper & Row.

34 Horney, Karen. *Self-Analysis.* NY: W.W. Norton, 1941.

35 In *Peace.* pp. 57-58.

CHAPTER 4
METHODS

36 Angha, Molana-al-Moazam Hazrat Shah Maghsoud Sadegh. (1975). *Hidden Angles of Life.* Pomona,CA: Multidisciplinary Publications, p. 27.

37 Angha, Molana-al-Moazam Hazrat Shah Maghsoud Sadegh. (1986). *Al Rasa'el.* Lanham, MD: University Press of America. p. 79.

38 Angha, Molana Hazrat Salaheddin Ali Nader Shah. (1988). *The Secret Word.* Los Angeles: Pacifica Radio Archives.

39 Angha, Molana Hazrat Salaheddin Ali Nader Shah. (1992). *Wealth of Solouk.* Unpublished English translation.

40   *The Secret Word* (radio).

CHAPTER 5
THE CENTRAL NERVOUS SYSTEM

41   Ornstein, Robert & Thompson, Richard F. (1984). *The Amazing Brain.* Boston: Houghton Mifflin.

42   Ibid, p. 38.

43   Descriptions are primarily from Tortora, Gerard J. (1983) *Principles of Human Anatomy* (3rd ed.). NY: Harper & Row.

44   Scheibel, Arnold B. Anatomical and Physiological Substrates of Arousal. in Hobson, J. Allen & Brazier, Mary A.B. (1980). *The Reticular Formation Revisited: Specifying Function for a Nonspecific System.* NY: Raven Press.

45   O'Keefe, John & Nadel, Lynn. (1978). *The Hippocampus as a Cognitive Map.* Oxford: Clarendon Press.

46   Klein, David C. (1978). The Pineal Gland: A Model of Neuroendocrine Regulation. in Reichlin, S. Baldessarini, R.J., & Martin, J.B. (Eds.) *The Hypothalamus.* NY: Raven Press. pp. 303-327.

47   Romijn, Herms J. Minireview: The Pineal, a Tranquilizing Organ? *Life Sciences*, 23, 2257-2274.

48   *The Amazing Brain.* p. 37.

49   Ibid, p. 159.

50   Diamond, Marian C. Paper given at The Human Brain Conference, San Rafael, CA: 1985.

51   See Hammer, Signe (1984). The Mind as Healer. *Science Digest.* 92, 47-49. or Wechsler, Rob. (1987). A New Prescription: Mind Over Malady. *Discover*, Feb., 51-61. for articles written for the layperson.

52   A New Prescription: Mind Over Malady. p. 58.

53   See, for example, Locke, Steven & Colligan, Douglas. (1986). *The Healer Within.* NY: New American Library or Pearsall, Paul. (1987). Super Immunity. NY: Fawcett.

54   See Byrd, Randolph C. (1981). Positive Therapeutic Effects of Intercessory Prayer in a Coronary Care Unit. *Southern Medical Journal.* 7, 826-829. Benson, Herbert. (1984). *Beyond the Relaxation Response.* NY: Times Books; and Simonton, O.C., Simonton, S., & Creighton, J. (1978). *GettingWell Again.* Los Angles: Tarcher.

55   Laughlin, Charles D. & d'Aquili, Eugene G. (1974) *Biogenetic Structuralism.* NY: Columbia University Press.

56   Ibid, p. 83.

57   Ibid, p. 150.

58   *Al Rasa'el*, p. 79.

59   Ibid, p. 79.

60   Ibid, p. 80.
61   Ibid, p. 97.
62   The Secret Word.
63   Luce, Gay. (1973) Biological Rhythms. In Ornstein, R. (Ed.) *The Nature of Human Consciousness*. NY: Viking. 421-444.
64   Breithaupt, Helmut. (1979) Biological Rhythms and Communication. In Popp, Fritz Albert (Ed.). *Electromagnetic Bio Information*. Munchen: Urban & Schwarzenberg. 1-23.
65   *Hidden Angles of Life*.
66   Ibid, p. 63.
67   *The Mystery of Humanity*, p. 41.

CHAPTER 6
SENSATION AND PERCEPTION

68   McConnell, James V. (1983) *Understanding Human Behavior*. (4th Ed.) NY: CBS College Publishing.
69   Leukel, F. (1972). *Introduction to Physiological Psychology*. St. Louis: C.V. Mosby.
70   Tortora, Gerard J. (1983). *Principles of Human Anatomy* (3rd ed.). NY: Harper & Row.
71   *Introduction to Physiological Psychology*.
72   *Principles of Human Anatomy*.
73   *Introduction to Physiological Psychology*.
74   Perceptual Development. in Bornstein, Marc H. & Lamb, Michael E. (Eds.) *Developmental Psychology*. Hillsdale, NJ: Lawrence Erlbaum Associates.
75   *Principles of Human Anatomy*, p. 487.
76   Barbe, Walter B. & MIlone, Michael N. Jr. (1981) What we know about modality strengths. *Educational Leadership*, 38, 378-380.
77   Coon, Dennis. (1983). *Introduction to Psychology* (3rd ed.). St. Paul, MN: West Publishing.
78   *Understanding Human Behavior*. p. 208.
79   Quoted in Oyle, Irvin. (1979). *The New American Medicine Show*. Santa Cruz, CA: Unity Press. p. 67.
80   Capra, Fritjof. (1980). *The Tao of Physics*. NY: Bantam.
81   Angha, Molana-al-Moazam Hazrat Shah Maghsoud. (1988). *Manifestations of Thought*. Denham, MD: University Press of America.
82   *Al Rasa' el*.
83   *Manifestations of Thought*.
84   *The Mystery of Humanity*, p. 40.
85   *Al Rasa' el*. p. 81.
86   *The Amazing Brain*. p. 138.

CHAPTER 7
MEMORY

87   For a typical approach, see Lynch, Gary & Baudry, Michel. (1984). The Biochemistry of Memory: A new and specific hypothesis. *Science, 224,* 1057-1063.

88   Alba, Joseph W. & Hasher, Lynn. Is Memory Schematic? *Psychological Bulletin, 93*:2, 203-231.

89   Ibid, p. 203.

90   Roediger, Henry L. (1990). Implicit memory: Retention without remembering. American *Psychologist,45,* 1043-1056.

91   Horton, David L. & Mills, Carol B. (1984). Human Learning and Memory. *Annual Review of Psychology 35,* 361-394.

92   Eich, Eric. (1984). Memory for unattended events: Remembering with and without awareness. *Memory & Cognition, 12,* 105-111.

93   quoted in Isaacson, R.L.& Spear, N.E. (Eds.) (1982). *The Expression of Knowledge.* NY: PLenum Press.

94   Pratkanis, Anthony R. & Greenwald, Anthony G. (1985) How shall the self be conceived? *Journal for the Theory of Social Behavior. 15*:3, 310-329, p. 317.

95   Ibid, p. 317.

96   Pribram, Karl. Holographic Memory. Interview in *Psychology Today.* 1979, Feb., pp. 71-84.

97   *Hidden Angles of Life.* p. 71.

98   Small, Melinda Y. (1990). *Cognitive Development.* NY: Harcourt, Brace, Jovanovich. p.1.

99   Ibid.

CHAPTER 8
LEARNING AND COGNITION

100 Piaget, Jean & Inholder, Barbel. (1969) *The Psychology of the Child.* NY: Basic Books. p. 6.

101 Ibid, p. 28.

102 Ibid, p. 44.

103 Ibid, p. 58.

104 Bronson, David. (1977) "Towards a Communication Theory". *Teachers College Record.* p. 453.

105 Kelly, George A. (1963). *A Theory of Personality.* NY: W.W. Norton, p. 17.

106 See Benjamin, Ludy T. Jr. (1988). *A History of Psychology.* NY: McGraw-Hill.; Murray, D.J. (1988). *A History of Western Psychology* (2nd ed.) Englewood Cliffs, NJ: Prentice-Hall.; and Wertheimer, M.A. (1972). *A Brief History of Psychology.* NY: Holt.

107 *Understanding Human Behavior.*

108 Bruner, Jerome. (1963). *The Process of Education.* NY: Vintage.

109 Holt, John. (1969). *How Children Learn.* NY:Pitman. pp.184-185.

110 Hart, Leslie A. (1983). *The Human Brain and Human Learning.* NY: Longman.

111 discussed in Wittrock, M.C. (1978). *The Cognitive Movement in Instruction.* Educational Psychologist,13, 15-29.

112 *Al Rasa'el.* p. 80.

113 Ibid, p. 80.

114 Zukav, Gary. (1979). *The Dancing Wu Li Masters.* NY: Bantam. p.71.

115 Ibid, p. 200.

116 Ibid, p. 72.

117 *Wealth of Solouk.* p. 7.

118 Ibid, p. 8.

119 *Al Rasa'el.* p. 86.

CHAPTER 9
MOTIVATION AND EMOTION

120 Madsen, K.B.(1968) *Theories of Motivation.* (4th ed). Kent State University Press.

121 Hamilton, Vernon. (1984). *The Cognitive Structures and Processes of Human Motivation and Personality.* Chichester: John Wiley & Sons.

122 Weiner, Bernard. (1972) *Theories of Motivation.* Chicago: Markham Publishing Co.

123 *The Cognitive Structures and Processes of Human Motivation and Personality.*

124 Samuels, Frederick. (1984). *Human Needs & Behavior.* Cambridge, MA: Schenkman.

125 Hoyenga, Katharine B. & Kermit T. (1984). *Motivational Explanations of Behavior.* Monterey, CA: Brooks/Cole.

126 See Hesse, Katherine A. & Campion, Edward W. (1983) Motivating the geriatric patient for rehabilitation. *Journal of the American Geriatric Society 31* (10), 586-589.

127 *Toward a Psychology of Being.*

128 Marken, Richard. (1983). "Mind Reading": A Look at Changing Intentions. *Psychological Reports, 53*, 267-270.

129 *Human Needs and Behavior.* p. 38.

130 *Motivational Explanations of Behavior.*

131 Lazarus, Richard S. (1991). Progress on a Cognitive-Motivational-Relational Theory of Emotion. *American Psychologist, 46*, 819-834.

132 Wundt, Wilhelm. (1973). *An Introduction to Psychology.* NY: Arno Press.

133 Ibid, p. 864.
134 Ibid, p. 865.
135 *Introduction to Psychology.*
136 Wundt, Wilhelm. (1902). *Outlines of Psychology* (2nd Ed.). Leipzig: Wilhelm Engelmann.
137 From papers presented by Dr. Lynda Powell at the American Heart Association Meeting in Dallas, Texas, November, 1990. *Merced Sun Star,* November 11, 1990, p. 3.
138 Schacter, S. & Singer, J.E. (1962) Cognitive, social and physiological determinants of emotional states. *Psychological Review, 69,* 379-399.
139 Ibid.
140 Angha, Molana-al-Moazam Hazrat Shah Maghsoud Sadegh Angha. (1991). *Dawn.* Verdugo City, CA: M.T.O. Shahmaghsoudi Publications. p. 24.
141 Ibid. p. 24.
142 The Holy Quran 17:36.
143 Ali, Molana-al-Moazam Hazrat Amir Al-Mu'minun. (1980). *Nahj Al-Balaghah.* Tehran: World Organization for Islamic Services. Khutba 136.
144 *Dawn.* p. 25.
145 *Biological Rhythms and Communication.*
146 Burr, H.S. (1972). *The Fields of Life.* NY: Ballantine, 1972.
147 Cohen, David. (1975). Magnetic Fields of the Human Body. *Physics Today.* pp. 34-43.

CHAPTER 10
CREATIVITY

148 Kunkel, F. & Dickerson, R. (1947). *How Character Develops.* NY: Scribners. Quoted in Taylor, Irving A. (1976). Psychological Sources of Creativity. *The Journal of Creative Behavior. 10,* 193-202.
149 Jung, Carl Gustav. (1962). *Modern Man in Search of A Soul.* NY: Harcourt Brace & World, p. 218.
150 *Psychological Sources of Creativity.* p. 198.
151 Torrance, Paul. (1974). *Torrance Tests of Creative Thinking.* Princeton, NJ: Personnel Press/Ginn.
152 Koestler, Arthur. *The Act of Creation.* NY: Dell. 1964. p. 177.
153 Ibid, p. 86.
154 Ibid. p. 26.
155 Gowan, John C. (1978). The Facilitation of Creativity through Meditational Procedures. *The Journal of Creative Behavior.* 12, pp. 156-160.
156 Edwards, Betty. (1979). *Drawing on the Right Side of the Brain.* Los Angeles: J.P. Tarcher, 1979. p. 4.
157 Hill, Edward. The Language of Drawing. In *Drawing on the Right Side of the Brain.*

158 In *The Act of Creation*, p. 26.
159 Arieti, Silvano. (1976). *Creativity*. NY: Basic Books. p. 293.
160 Hirsch, D.M.N. (1931). *Genius and Creative Intelligence*. Cambridge: Sci-Art Publishers. pp. 291-292.
161 Peavy, R. Vance. (1979). Therapy and Creativity: A Dialogue. *The Journal of Creative Behavior. 13*,1. 60-72.
162 Kubie, L. *Neurotic Distortion of the Creative Process*. Lawrence, KS: University of Kansas Press, 1958.
163 Ghiselin, Brewster. (1952). *The Creative Process*. NY: Mentor. p. 85.
164 Ibid, p. 69.
165 Ibid, p. 81.
166 Ibid, p. 43.
167 Ibid, p. 203.
168 Ibid, p. 41.
169 Ibid, p. 36.
170 Ibid, p. 82.
171 *Modern Man in Search of a Soul*. p. 218.
172 *The Creative Process*. p. 202.
173 Ibid, p. 192.
174 *Modern Man in Search of A Soul*. p. 223.
175 *The Creative Process*. p. 46.
176 Langer, Suzanne K. (1957). *Problems of Art*. NY: Charles Scribner's Sons.
176a *The Creative Process*, p. 110.

CHAPTER 11
INTELLIGENCE

177 Sternberg, Robert J. & Kaye, Daniel B. (1982). Intelligence. *The Encyclopedia of Educational Research*. (5th Ed., Vol. 2). NY: Free Press. p. 925.
178 Ibid, p. 304.
179 Sternberg, Robert J. (1984). *Toward a Triarchic Theory of Human Intelligence*. The Behavioral and Brain Sciences 7, 269-315.
180 Tyler, Leona E. (1984). Some possible implications of Sternberg's tri-archic theory of intelligence. *The Behavioral and Brain Sciences 7*, 401-402.
181 Ibid, p. 302.
182 In Luria, Alexander. (1982). *Language and Cognition*. NY: John Wiley & Sons. p. 57.
183 Ibid, p. 5.
184 See Hall, Edward T. (1959). *The Silent Language.*; (1969) *The Hidden Dimension*; (1976) *Beyond Culture*. All Garden City, NY: Doubleday.
185 Ibid, p. 23.
186 Thomas, Lewis. (1974). *The Lives of a Cell*. NY: Viking Press.

187 Ibid, p. 14.
188 Ibid, p. 15.
189 Toal, Jeanne. (1991). *The Seven Flavors of Intelligence.* American Health, VI, 62-67.
190 *Wealth of Solouk.* p. 6.
191 *Dawn.* p. 4.
192 *Al Rasa'el.* p.13.
193 Ibid, p. 13.
194 *Introduction to The Mystery of Humanity.* p. 4.
195 *Hidden Angles of Life.* p. 61.

CHAPTER 12
LANGUAGE

196 Rice, Mabel. (1989). *Children's Language Acquisition.* American Psychologist, 44:149-156.
197 Chomsky, Noam. (1980). Rules and Representations. *Behavioral and Brain Sciences.* 3:1-61.
198 Bickerton, Derek. (1984). The Language Bioprogram Hypothesis. *Behavioral and Brain Sciences*, 7:173-188.
199 Slobin, D.I. (1973) Cognitive prerequisites for the development of grammar. In: Ferguson, C.A. and Slobin, D. I., (Eds.). *Studies of Child Language Development.* NY: Holt, Rinehart & Winston.
200 *Understanding Human Behavior.*
201 Ibid, p. 161.
202 Marler, P. (1977) Sensory templates, visual perception and development: a comparative view. In: Lewis, M. & Rosenblum, L.A. (Eds.). *Intention, Conversaton and the Development of Language.* NY: Wiley. p. 218.
203 *Language and Cognition.*
204 Ibid, p. 230.
205 Jaynes, Julian. (1976). *The Origin of Consciousness in the Breakdown of the Bicameral Mind.* Boston:Houghton Mifflin.
206 *How Children Learn.* p. 178-179.
207 Ibid, p. 188.
208 Rumi, Jalalu'd-din. (1926-1982). *The Mathnawi of Jalalu'd-din Rumi.* London: E.J.W. Gibb Memorial Trust.

CHAPTER 13
THOUGHT

209 *Introduction to Psychology.*
210 Belmont, John M. (1989). Cognitive Strategies and Strategic Learning. *American Psychologist. 44*: 2. 142-148.
211 Greeno, James G. A Perspective on Thinking. (1989). *American*

Psychologist. 44 (2), 134-141. p. 135.
212 Ibid, p. 134.
213 Irfan, Lukens and Lukens, quoted in Howard, George S. (1991). Culture Tales. *American Psychologist, 46* (3), 187-197. p. 187.
214 *A Perspective on Thinking.*
215 See Key, Wilson Brian. (1972) *Subliminal Seduction.* (1976) *Media Sexploitation.* (1980) *The Clam Plate Orgy.* NY: Signet.
216 Burns, David D. (1989). NY: Plume.
217 *Manifestations of Thought.* p. 12.
218 *The Mystery of Humanity.* p. 41.

CHAPTER 14
HUMAN DEVELOPMENT
219 *Introduction to Psychology.*
220 Hoffman, et al. (1988). *Developmental Psychology Today* (5th ed.). NY: Random House.
221 Greenspan, Stanley I. (1989). *The Development of the Ego.* Madison, CN: International Universities Press.
222 Bowlby, J.M. (1959). *Attachment and Loss.* NY: Basic Books.
223 *Developmental Psychology Today.*
224 Santrock, J.W. (1989). *Life-Span Development.* (3rd Ed.). Dubuque, IA: Wm. C. Brown.
225 Ibid.
226 Bornstein, M.H. & Lamb, M.E. (1984). *Developmental Psychology: An Advanced Textbook.* Hillsdale, NJ: Lawrence Erlbaum Associates.
227 *Developmental Psychology Today.*
228 *The Development of the Ego.*
229 *Developmental Psychology Today.*
230 *Peac*e. p. 65.
231 Ibid, p. 66.
232 Ibid, p. 67.

CHAPTER 15
PERSONALITY
233 Hall, Calvin C. & Lindzey, Gardner. (1957). *Theories of Personality.* NY: John Wiley & Sons. p. 9.
234 Quoted in Sahakian, William S. (Ed.) (1965). *Psychology of Personality: Readings in Theory.* Chicago: Rand McNally.
235 *Developmental Psychology Today.*
236 See Hall, Calvin S. (1954). *A Primer of Freudian Psychology.* NY: World Publishing.
237 *Theories of Personality.*

238 See Jung, Carl G. (1971). *The Portable Jung*. NY: Viking Press.
239 See Frankl, Victor. (1969). *The Will to Meaning*. NY: Plume.
240 *Client-Centered Therapy*.
241 Perls, Fritz. (1969). *Gestalt Therapy Verbatim*. Lafayette, CA: Real People Press.
242 Assagioli, Roberto. (1965). *Psychosynthesis*. NY: Viking Press. p. 21.
243 Walsh, Roger N. & Vaughan, Frances. (1980) What Is a Person? In *Beyond Ego*. Los Angeles: J.P. Tarcher. p. 60.
244 Shakespeare, William. (1963). *As You Like It*. Act II, Scene vii, line 139. London: Rex.
245 Briffault, Robert. (1921). *Psyche's Lamp*. NY: Macmillan.
246 *The Lives of a Cell*.
247 Donne, John. (1951). *The Selected Prose and Poetry of John Donne*. NY: Modern Library.
248 *The Lives of a Cell*.
249 *Hidden Angles of Life*.
250 Hewitt, Paul G. (1981). *Conceptual Physics*. (4th ed.) Boston: Little, Brown and Co.
251 Carroll, Lewis. (1965). Beatrice. *The Works of Lewis Carroll*. London: Paul Hamlyn.
252 Matthew 18:3-4. (1973). *The New Oxford Annotated Bible, Revised Standard Version*. N.Y.: Oxford University Press.
253 Horney, Karen. (1942). *Self Analysis*. NY: W.W. Norton.
254 *The Mystery of Humanity*.
255 Langer, Susanne K. (1951). *Philosophy in a New Key*. Cambridge, MA: Harvard University Press.
256 Hafiz, Shams-ud-Din. (1986). *Book of the Winebringer*. Paul Smith translation. Melbourne: New Humanity Books.
257 *The Secret Word*.
258 Ibid, p. 6.
259 Ibid, p. 6.

CHAPTER 16
SELF-ACTUALIZATION

260 Rodale, Maria. (1988). *For Long Life and Happiness*. Regeneration., 1.
261 *Client-Centered Therapy*.
262 Maslow, Abraham. (1968). *Toward a Psychology of Being*. (2nd ed.) NY: Van Nordstrand Reinhold. See also (1973). *The Further Reaches of Human Nature*. NY: Viking/Esalen.
263 Ibid.
264 Assagioli, Roberto. (1965). *Psychosynthesis*. NY: Viking Press.
265 Watts, Alan. (1972). *The Book*. NY: Vintage.

266 Laing, R.D. (1967). *The Politics of Experience*. NY: Ballantine.
267 Gurdjieff, G.I. *Meetings with Remarkable Men*. NY: Dutton, 1974.
268 *Al Rasa'el*. p. 110-111.
269 Ibid, p. 109.
270 Ibid, p. 105.
271 Ibid, p. 18.
272 Ibid, p. 112.
273 Angha, Molana Hazrat Salaheddin Ali Nader Shah. *Introduction to The Mystery of Humanity*.
274 Rumi, Molana Jalaluddin Molavi Balkhi. *Divan Shams Tabriz*. p. 241. Translated in Angha, Molana Hazrat Salaleddin Ali Nader Shah. (1990). About the Author in *Masnavi Ravayeh*. Lanham, MD: University Press of America.

CHAPTER 17
CONSCIOUSNESS

275 Combs, Allan L. (1990). *Concepts of Consciousness*. Unpublished paper.
276 Dewey, John. *Democracy and Education*. Quoted in White, John (Ed.) (1984). *Frontiers of Consciousness*. NY: Julian Press. p 91.
277 *The Origin of Consciousness in the Breakdown of the Bicameral Mind*. p. 84.
278 Ibid, p. 79.
279 Ibid, p. 34.
280 Jung, C.G. Quoted in *Beyond Ego*. p. 176.
281 Lambert, C. (1989). *The Chopra Prescriptions*. Harvard Magazine. September/October. 21-28.
282 Guenon, Rene. (1984). *The Multiple States of Being*. Burdett, NY: Larson.p. 120.
283 James, William. *The Principles of Psychology*. Quoted in Ornstein, R. (1984). *The Psychology of Consciousness*. NY: Penquin.p. 27.
284 *The Portable Jung*.
285 von Franz, Marie-Louise. The Transformed Berserk: Unification of Psychic Opposites. *ReVision*. 8, 20.
286 Thapa, K. & Murthy, V.N. (1985). Experiential characteristics of certain altered states of consciousness. *Journal of Transpersonal Psychology*. 17 (1) 77-86.
287 Cited in Kelly, E.F. & Locke, R.G.Pre-literate Societies. *Parapsychological Review*, 13 (3), 1-6.
288 Ibid.
289 Oxman, T.E., Rosenberg, S.D., Schnurr, P.P., Tucker, G.J. (1988). The language of altered states. *Journal of Nervous and Mental Disease*. 176 (7): 401-408.

290 Goodman, F.D. (1986). Body posture and the religious altered state of consciousness: an experimental investigation. *Journal of Humanistic Psychology.* 26 (3) 81-118.

291 Spielman, Arthur & Herrera, Charles. (1991). Sleep Disorders. in Ellman, Steven J. & Antrobus, John S. (Eds.) *The Mind in Sleep: Psychology and Psychophysiology* (2nd Ed.) NY: John Wiley & Sons.

292 Foulkes, D. (1964). Theories of Dream Formation and Recent Studies of Sleep Consciousness. *Psychological Bulletin.* 62, 234- 247.

293 Small, Meredith F. (1992). A Reasonable Sleep. *Discover.* April. p. 88.

294 *The Amazing Brain.*

295 Tart, C.T. (1965) Toward the experimental control of dreaming: a review of the literature. *Psychological Bulletin,* 64, 81-91.

296 Jung, C.G. (1938-1979). *Psychology and Religion.* New Haven, CN: Yale University Press. p. 26.

297 Stewart, K. (1967). Dream Theory in Malaya. In Tart, C.T. (Ed.) *Altered States of Consciousness.* Garden City, NY: Anchor Books. p. 167.

298 Rzyl, M. (1970). *Parapsychology: A Scientific Approach.* NY: Hawthorn. p. 6.

299 Price, George R. (1955). Science and the Supernatural. *Science,* 122, 359-367.

300 Humphreys, Christmas. (1935-1981). *Concentration & Meditation.* Albuquerque, NM: Sun Books. p. 22.

301 *Manifestations of Thought.* p. 9.

302 *Hidden Angles of Life.* p. 99.

303 *New American Medicine Show.* p. 22.

304 *The Origin of Consciousness in the Breakdown of the Bicameral Mind.*

305 *Hidden Angles of Life.* p. 89.

306 *Al Rasa'el.* p. 103.

307 *The Approaching Promise.* p. 4.

308 *The Mystery of Humanity.* p. 42.

309 Ibid, p. 47.

CHAPTER 18
RELIGION

310 Allport, Gordon W. (1960). *The Individual and His Religion.* Toronto: Macmillan Co..

311 Spilka, B., Hood, R. W. Jr., & Gorsuch, R.L. (1985). *The Psychology of Religion: An Empirical Approach.* Englewood Cliffs, NJ: Prentice-Hall. p. 61.

312 *The Individual and His Religion.* p. 51.

313 Ibid, p. 59.

314 Ibid, p. 67.

315 Jung, Carl Gustav. (1938-1979). *Psychology and Religion.* New Haven,

CN: Yale University Press. pp. 52-53.
    316 Ibid, p.72.
    317 Ibid, p. 70.
    318 Moberg, D.O. Religiosity in Old Age. (1979). In Brown, L.B. (Ed.) *Psychology and Religion*. Baltimore, MD: Penguin.
    319 Schuon, Frithjof. (1984). *The Transcendent Unity of Religions*. Wheaton, IL: Theosophical Publishing House.
    320 *The Individual and His Religion*. p. 70.
    321 Ibid, xii.
    322 *The Psychology of Religion*. p. 115.
    323 *The Individual and His Religion*. p. 24.
    324 *Psychology and Religion*. p. 72.
    325 *The Individual and His Religion*. p. 9.
    326 Johnson, Robert A. (1987). *Ecstasy: Understanding the Psychology of Joy*. San Francisco: Harper & Row. p. 50.
    327 Ibid, p. 50.
    328 *The Psychology of Religion*.
    329 *Nahj Al-Balaghah*.
    330 *The Secret Word*.

CHAPTER 19
TRUTH
    331 Cerf, Christopher & Navasky, Victor. (1984). *The Experts Speak*. NY: Pantheon.
    332 Fox, Jack F. (1973). *A Lesson in How to Double-Talk*. Sacramento Bee. November 23 .
    333 Becker Robert & Selden, Gary. (1985). *The Body Electric*. NY: William Morrow.
    334 *Subliminal Seduction*.
    335 Henry, Jules. (1969). In Suburban Classrooms. In Gross, Beatrice & Ronald. *Radical School Reform*. NY: Simon & Schuster.
    336 Machiavelli, Niccolo. (1985). *The Prince*. Chicago: University of Chicago Press.
    337 Orwell, George. (1949-1977). *1984*. San Diego: Harcourt, Brace, Jovanovich.
    338 Freire, P. (1973). *Education for Critical Consciousness*. NY: Seabury, p. 4.
    339 Gatto, J.T. *Confederacy of Dunces: The Tyranny of Compulsory Schooling*. Nevada City, CA:Community Endeavor News, 7, 6.
    340 *Al-Rasa'el*.
    341 *Dawn*. p.23.
    342 *Hidden Angles of Life*. p. 108.

343 Ibid.
344 See Pearson, E. Norman. (1990). *Space, Time and Self*. Wheaton, IL: Theosophical Publishing House. and Schwaller de Lubicz, Isha. (1954). *Her-Bak*. NY: Inner Traditions.
345 *Al Rasa' el*. p. 78.
346 Ibid, p. 80.
347 *The Mystery of Humanity*.
348 Ibid, p. 39.
349 Ibid, p. 47.
350 *Understanding Human Behavior*.

CHAPTER 20
LOVE
351 Eibl-Eibesfeldt, Irenaus. (1974) *Love and Hate*. NY: Schocken.
352 In Reynolds, Sarah E. (1983) "Limerance": A New Word and Concept. *Psychotherapy: Theory, Research and Practice*. 20, 107-111.
353 Fromm, Erich. (1956). *The Art of Loving*. NY: Bantam. p.70.
354 Ibid, p. 8.
355 Ibid, p. 11.
356 Ibid, p. 47.
357 Buscaglia, Leo. (1984). *Love*. NY: Fawcett Crest.
358 Ibid, p.141.
359 Reik, Theodor. (1959). *Of Love and Lust*. NY: Grove Press.
360 Sorokin, Pitirim A. & Hanson, Robert C. (1953). The Power of Creative Love. in Montague, Ashley (ED.) *The Meaning of Love*. NY: Julian Press.
361 Ibid, p. 155.
362 Jampolsky, Gerald G. (1981) *Love is Letting Go of Fear*. NY: Bantam.
363 Tanner, Ira. (1973) *The Fear of Love*. NY: Harper & Row. p. 14.
364 May, Rollo. (1969) *Love and Will*. NY: W.W. Norton.
365 *The Varieties of Religious Experience*.
366 Ibid, p. 271.
367 Ibid, p. 506.
368 Berscheid, quoted in *Life Span Development*.
369 Davis, K.E. (1985) Near & dear: friendship & love compared. *Psychology Today*, 19, 2, 22-40.
370 Montague, Ashley (Ed.) (1953). *The Meaning of Love*. NY: Julian Press.
371 Ibid, p. 8.
372 Ibid p.14.
373 Ibid, p. 17.
374 Ibid, p.19.
375 *Al-Rasa' el*. p. 98.
376 *Masnavi Ravayeh*.. p. 10.

377 Ibid, p. 15.
378 Ibid, p. 10.
379 Quoted in *Al Rasa' el*, p. 17.
380 *The Mystery of Humanity*. p. 32.
381 *Al Rasa' el*, p. 18.
382 *The Mystery of Humanity*, p. 38.
383 *Al Rasa' el.*, p. 103.
384 Smith, Margaret. (1984). *Rabi' a the Mystic and her Fellow Saints in Islam*. Cambridge: Cambridge University Press, p. 93.
385 *The Mystery of Humanity*, p. 37-38.
386 *The Secret Word*, p. 21.
387 *The Approaching Promise*. p. 5.
388 See *Al-Rasael* pp. 106-110, and *Hidden Angles of Life* pp. 109-110.
389 *Al-Rasael*, p 111.
390 Ibid, p. 111.
391 Sura 76:21.
392 *Masnavi Ravayeh*, p. 14-15.
393 *Al Rasa' el*, p. 18.
394 *Masnavi Ravayeh*, p. 4.

CHAPTER 21
LIGHT

395 *Al Rasa' el*. p. 86.
396 Ibid, p. 91.
397 Ibid, p. 99.
398 *Masnavi Ravayeh*. p. 9.
399 *Al Rasa' el,* p. 105.
400 Ibid, p. 105.
401 Ibid, p.111.
402 Ibid, p. 104.
403 Ibid, p. 109.

References

al-Ghazali. (1980).*The Alchemy of Happiness*. London: Octago.

Al-Muqaddisi, Shaykh Izzidin. (1980). *Revelation of the Secrets of the Birds and Flowers*. London: Octagon Pres, 1980.

Alba, Joseph W. & Hasher, Lynn. Is Memory Schematic? *Psychological Bulletin, 93*:2, 203-231.

Ali, Molana-al-Moazam Hazrat Amir Al-Mu'minun. (1980). *Nahj Al-Balaghah*. Tehran: World Organization for Islamic Services.

Allport, Gordon W. (1960). *The Individual and His Religion*. Toronto: Macmillan Co.

Angha, Molana Hazrat Salaheddin Ali Nader Shah. (1987). *Peace*, Verdugo City, CA: MTO Shahmaghsoudi Publications.

_____. (1988). *The Secret Word*. Los Angeles: Pacifica Radio Archives.

_____. (1992). *Wealth of Solouk*. Unpublished English translation.

Angha, Molana-al-Moazam Hazrat Shah Maghsoud Sadegh Angha.(1991). *Dawn*. Verdugo City, CA: MTO Shahmaghsoudi Publications.

_____. (1986). *Al-Rasa'el*. Lanham, MD: University Press of America.

_____. (1975). *Hidden Angles of Life*. Pomona, CA: Multidisciplinary Publications.

_____. (1988). *Manifestations of Thought*. Denham, MD: University Press of America.

Ardrey, Robert. (1970). *The Social Contract*. NY: Atheneum.

Arieti, Silvano. (1976). *Creativity*. NY: Basic Books. p. 293.

Assagioli, Roberto. (1965). *Psychosynthesis*. NY: Viking Press.

Attar, Farid Ud-din. (1984) *The Conference of the Birds*. NY: Penguin.

_____. (1990). *Muslim Saints and Mystics*. London: Arkana.

Barbe, Walter B. & Milone, Michael N. Jr. (1981) What we know about modality strengths. *Educational Leadership*, 38, 378-380.

Becker, Robert & Selden, Gary. (1985). *The Body Electric*. NY: William Morrow.

Belmont, John M. (1989). Cognitive Strategies and Strategic Learning. *American Psychologist 44*: 2,142-148.

Benjamin, Ludy T. Jr. (1988). *A History of Psychology*. NY: McGraw-Hill.

Benson, Herbert. (1984). *Beyond the Relaxation Response*. NY: Times Books

Bickerton, Derek. (1984).The Language Bioprogram Hypothesis. *Behavioral and Brain Sciences*, 7:173-188.

Bornstein, M.H. & Lamb, M.E. (1984). *Developmental Psychology: An Advanced Textbook*. Hillsdale, NJ: Lawrence Erlbaum Associates.

Bowlby, J.M. (1959). *Attachment and Loss*. NY: Basic Books.

Bowne, Borden P. (1886) *Introduction to Psychological Theory*. NY: American

Book Co.

Breithaupt, Helmut. (1979) Biological Rhythms and Communication. In Popp, Fritz Albert (Ed.) *Electromagnetic Bio-Information*. Munchen: Urban & Schwarzenberg. 1-23.

Briffault, Robert. (1921). *Psyche's Lamp*. NY: Macmillan. .

Bronson, David. (1977) "Towards a Communication Theory". *Teachers College Record*. p. 453.

Brown, P. (1973). *Radical Psychology*. NY: Harper & Row.

Brown, L.B. (Ed.) (1973). *Psychology and Religion*. Baltimore, MD: Penguin.

Bruner, Jerome. (1963). *The Process of Education*. NY: Vintage.

Burr, H.S. (1972). *The Fields of Life*. NY: Ballantine, 1972.

Buscaglia, Leo. (1984). *Love*. NY: Fawcett Crest.

Burns, David. (1991) . *The Feeling Good Handbook*. NY: Plume

Byrd, Randolph C. (1981). Positive Therapeutic Effects of Intercessory Prayer in a Coronary Care Unit. *Southern Medical Journal*. 7, 826-829;

Capra, Fritjof. (1980). *The Tao of Physics*. NY: Bantam.

Carroll, Lewis. (1965). Beatrice. *The Works of Lewis Carroll*. London: Paul Hamlyn.

Cerf, Christopher & Navasky, Victor. (1984). *The Experts Speak*. NY: Pantheon.

Chomsky, Noam. (1980). Rules and Representations. *Behavioral and Brain Sciences*. 3:1-61.

Cohen, David. (1975). Magnetic Fields of the Human Body. *Physics Today*. pp. 34-43.

Combs, Allan L. (1990). *Concepts of Consciousness*. Unpublished paper.

Coon, Dennis. (1983). *Introduction to Psychology* (3rd ed.). St. Paul, MN: West Publishing.

Davis, K.E. (1985) Near & dear: friendship & love compared. *Psychology Today*, 19, 2, 22-40.

Dewey, John. Democracy and Education. Quoted in White, John (Ed.) (1984). *Frontiers of Consciousness*. NY: Julian Press.

Diamond, Marian C. (1985). Paper given at The Human Brain Conference, San Rafael, CA.

Donne, John. (1951). *The Selected Prose and Poetry of John Donne*. NY: Modern Library.

Edwards, Betty. (1979). *Drawing on the Right Side of the Brain*. Los Angeles:J.P. Tarcher.

Efan, Lukens and Lukens, quoted in Howard, George S. (1991). Culture Tales. *American Psychologist*, 46 (3), 187-197.

Ehrenfeld, David W. (1975). *The Arrogance of Humanism*. NY: Oxford University Press.

Eibl-Eibesfeldt, Irenaus. (1974). *Love and Hate*. NY: Schocken.

Eich, Eric. (1984). Memory for unattended events: Remembering with and without awareness. *Memory & Cognition*, 12, 105-111.

Ellman, Steven J. & Antrobus, John S. (Eds.) (1991). *The Mind in Sleep: Psychology and Psychophysiology* (2nd Ed.) NY: John Wiley & Sons.

English, Horace B. & Ava C. (1976). *A Comprehensive Dictionary of Psychological and Psychoanalytical Terms*. NY: David McKay.

Foulkes, D. (1964). Theories of Dream Formation and Recent Studies of Sleep Consciousness. *Psychological Bulletin*. 62, 234-247.

Fox, Jack F. (1973). A Lesson in How to Double-Talk. *Sacramento Bee*. November 23 .

Frankl, Victor. (1969). *The Will to Meaning*. NY: Plume.

Freire, P. (1973). *Education for Critical Consciousness*. NY: Seabury.

Fromm, Erich. (1956). *The Art of Loving*. NY: Bantam.

Gatto, J.T. Confederacy of Dunces: The Tyranny of Compulsory Schooling. Nevada City, CA: *Community Endeavor News*, 7, 6.

Ghiselin, Brewster. (1952). *The Creative Process*. NY: Mentor.

Goodman, F.D. (1986). Body posture and the religious altered state of con sciousness: an experimental investigation. *Journal of Humanistic Psychology*. 26(3) 81-118.

Gowan, John C. (1978). The Facilitation of Creativity through Meditational Procedures. *The Journal of Creative Behavior*. 12,156-160.

Greeno, James G. A Perspective on Thinking. (1989). *American Psychologist*. 44(2), 134-141.

Greenspan, Stanley I. (1989). *The Development of the Ego*. Madison, CN: International Universities Press.

Guenon, Rene. (1984). *The Multiple States of Being*. Burdett, NY: Larson.

Gurdjieff, G.I. (1974). *Meetings with Remarkable Men*. NY: Dutton.

Hafiz, Shams-ud-Din. (1986). *Book of the Winebringer*. Paul Smith translation. Melbourne: New Humanity Books.

Hall, Calvin C. & Lindzey, Gardner. (1957). *Theories of Personality*. NY: John Wiley & Sons.

Hall, Calvin S. (1954). *A Primer of Freudian Psychology*. NY: World Publishing.

Hall, Edward T. (1959). *The Silent Language*. Garden City, NY: Doubleday.

_____. (1969) *The Hidden Dimension*. Garden City, NY: Doubleday.

_____. (1976) *Beyond Culture*. Garden Cilty, NY: Doubleday.

Hamilton, Vernon. (1983) *The Cognitive Structures and Processes of Human Motivation and Personality*. NY: John Wiley & Sons.

Hammer, Signe (1984). The Mind as Healer. *Science Digest*. 92, 47-49.

Hart, Leslie A. (1983). *The Human Brain and Human Learning*. NY: Longman.

Henry, Jules. (1969). In Suburban Classrooms. In Gross, Beatrice & Ronald. *Radical School Reform*. NY: Simon & Schuster.

Hesse, Katherine A. & Campion, Edward W. (1983) Motivating the geriatric patient for rehabilitation. *Journal of the American Geriatric Society* 31 (10), 586-589.

Hewitt, Paul G. (1981). *Conceptual Physics*. (4th ed.) Boston: Little, Brown and Co.

Hirsch, D.M.N. (1931). *Genius and Creative Intelligence*. Cambridge: Sci-Art Publishers.

Hoffman, et al. (1988). *Developmental Psychology Today* (5th ed.). NY: Random House.

Holt, John. (1969). *How Children Learn*. NY:Pitman.

Horney, Karen. (1942). *Self Analysis*. NY: W.W. Norton.

Horton, David L. & Mills, Carol B. (1984). Human Learning and Memory. *Annual Review of Psychology*, 35, 361-394.

Hoyenga, Katharine B. & Kermit T. (1984). *Motivational Explanations of Behavior*. Monterey, CA: Brooks/Cole.

Hujwiri, Ali, B. Uthman Al-Jullabi. (1911-1976). *Kashf Al-Mahjub of Al Hujwiri*. London: E.J.W. Gibb Memorial.

Humphreys, Christmas. (1935-1981). *Concentration & Meditation*. Albuquerque, NM: Sun Books.

Ibn Tufail, Abu Bakr Muhammad. (1982) *The Journey of the Soul*. London: Octagon Press.

Isaacson, R.L.& Spear, N.E. (Eds.) (1982). *The Expression of Knowledge*. NY: Plenum Press.

James, William (1892) *Psychology: Briefer Course*. NY: Henry Holt & Co..

_____. (1890) The scope of psychology. In *The Principles of Psychology, I*, 1-8. Reprinted in Bornstein, Robert E. (Ed.) (1973). *The Nature of Human Consciousness*. San Francisco: W. H. Freeman.

Jampolsky, Gerald G. (1981) *Love is Letting Go of Fear*. NY: Bantam.

Jaynes, Julian. (1976). *The Origin of Consciousness in the Breakdown of the Bicameral Mind*. Boston: Houghton Mifflin.

Johnson, Robert A. (1987). *Ecstasy: Understanding the Psychology of Joy*. San Francisco: Harper & Row.

Jung, Carl Gustav. (1962). *Modern Man in Search of A Soul*. NY: Harcourt Brace & World.

_____. (1971). *The Portable Jung*. NY: Viking Press.

_____. (1938-1979). *Psychology and Religion*. New Haven, CN: Yale University Press.

Kelly, George A. (1963). *A Theory of Personality*. NY: W.W. Norton.

Kelly, E.F. & Locke, R.G. Pre-literate Societies. *Parapsychological Review*, 13(3), 1-6.

Key, Wilson Brian. (1972). *Subliminal Seduction*. NY: Signet.

_____. (1976). *Media Sexploitation*. NY: Signet.

_____. (1980). *The Clam Plate Orgy*. NY: Signet.
Klein, David C. (1978). The Pineal Gland: A Model of Neuroendocrine Regulation. in Reichlin, S., Baldessarini, R.J., & Martin, J.B. (Eds.) *The Hypothalamus*. NY: Raven Press. pp. 303-327.
Koestler, Arthur. (1964).*The Act of Creation*. NY: Dell.
Kubie, L. (1958). *Neurotic Distortion of the Creative Process*. Lawrence, KS: University of Kansas Press.
Kunkel, F. & Dickerson, R. (1947). *How Character Develops*. NY: Scribners.
Ladd, George T. (1901). *Primer of Psychology*. NY: Charles Scribner's Sons.
Laing, R.D. (1967). *The Politics of Experience*. NY: Ballantine.
Lambert, C. (1989). The Chopra Prescriptions. *Harvard Magazine*. September/October. 21-28
Langer, Susanne K. (1951). *Philosophy in a New Key*. Cambridge, MA: Harvard University Press.
_____. (1957). *Problems of Art*. NY: Charles Scribner's Sons.
Laughlin, Charles D. & d'Aquili, Eugene G. (1974) *Biogenetic Structuralism*. NY: Columbia University Press.
Lawry, John D. (1981). *Guide to the History of Psychology*. Totowa, NJ: Littlefield, Adams.
Lazarus, Richard S. (1991). Progress on a Cognitive-Motivational-Relational Theory of Emotion. *American Psychologist*, 46, 819-834.
Leukel, F. (1972). *Introduction to Physiological Psychology*. St. Louis: C.V. Mosby.
Locke, Steven & Colligan, Douglas. (1986). *The Healer Within*. NY: New American Library
Luce, Gay. (1973) Biological Rhythms. In Ornstein, R. (Ed.) *The Nature of Human Consciousness*. NY: Viking. 421-444.
Luria, Alexander. (1982). *Language and Cognition*. NY: John Wiley & Sons.
Lynch, Gary & Baudry, Michel. (1984). The Biochemistry of Memory: A new and specific hypothesis. *Science*, 224, 1057-1063.
Machiavelli, Niccolo. (1985). *The Prince*. Chicago: University of Chicago Press.
Madsen, K.B.(1968) *Theories of Motivation*. (4th ed). Kent State University Press.
Marken, Richard. (1983). "Mind Reading": A Look at Changing Intentions. *Psychological Reports*, 53, 267-270.
Marler, P. (1977) Sensory templates, visual perception and development: a comparative view. In: Lewis, M. & Rosenblum, L.A. (Eds.). *Intention, Conversaton and the Development of Language*. NY: Wiley.
Maslow, A. H. (1973) *The Further Reaches of Human Nature*. NY: Viking\Esalen.
_____. (1968). *Toward a Psychology of Being*. (2nd ed.) NY: Van Nordstrand

Reinhold.

May, Rollo. (1969) *Love and Will.* NY: W.W. Norton.

McConnell, James V. (1983) *Understanding Human Behavior.* (4th Ed.) NY: CBS College Publishing.

Moberg, D.O. Religiosity in Old Age. (1979). In Brown, L.B. (Ed.) *Psychology and Religion.* Baltimore, MD: Penguin.

Montague, Ashley (Ed.) (1953). *The Meaning of Love.* NY: Julian Press.

Murray, Sir James A. H. (1933). *The Oxford English Dictionary.* Oxford: Clarendon Press.

Murray, David J. (1988). *A History of Western Psychology* (2nd ed.) Englewood Cliffs, NJ: Prentice-Hall.

New Oxford Annotated Bible, Revised Standard Version. (1973). NY: Oxford University Press.

Nizami. (1976) *The Story of the Seven Princesses.* London: Bruno Cassirer.

O'Keefe, John & Nadel, Lynn. (1978). *The Hippocampus as a Cognitive Map.* Oxford: Clarendon Press.

Ornstein, Robert & Thompson, Richard F. (1984). *The Amazing Brain.* Boston: Houghton Mifflin.

Ornstein, R. (1984). *The Psychology of Consciousness.* NY: Penquin.

Orwell, George. (1949-1977). *1984.* San Diego: Harcourt, Brace, Jovanovich.

Oxman, T.E., Rosenberg, S.D., Schnurr, P.P., Tucker, G.J. (1988). The language of altered states. *Journal of Nervous and Mental Disease.* 176(7): 401-408.

Oyle, Irvin. (1979). *The New American Medicine Show.* Santa Cruz, CA: Unity Press.

Perls, Fritz. (1969). *Gestalt Therapy Verbatim.* Lafayette, CA: Real People Press.

Pearsall, Paul. (1987). *Super Immunity.* NY: Fawcett.

Pearson, E. Norman. (1990). *Space, Time and Self.* Wheaton, IL: Theosophical Publishing House.

Peavy, R. Vance. (1979). Therapy and Creativity: A Dialogue. *The Journal of Creative Behavior.* 13,1.60-72.

Piaget, Jean & Inholder, Barbel. (1969) *The Psychology of the Child.* NY: Basic Books.

Powell, Linda. (1990). Paper presented at the American Heart Association Meeting in Dallas, Texas, November, 1990. *Merced Sun Sta*r, November 11.

Pratkanis, Anthony R. & Greenwald, Anthony G. (1985) How shall the self be conceived? *Journal for the Theory of Social Behavior* 15:3, 310-329.

Pribram, Karl. (1979). Holographic Memory. Interview in *Psychology Today.* 1979, Feb., pp. 71-84.

Price, George R. (1955). Science and the Supernatural. *Science*, 122, 359-367.

Reichlin, S.Baldessarini, R.J., & Martin, J.B. (Eds.) *The Hypothalamus.* NY: Raven Press. pp. 303-327.

Reik, Theodor. (1959). *Of Love and Lust.* NY: Grove Press.

Reynolds, Sarah E. (1983) "Limerance": A New Word and Concept. *Psychotherapy: Theory, Research and Practice.* 20, 107-111.

Rice, Mabel. (1989). Children's Language Acquisition. *American Psychologist,* 44:149-156.

Rodale, Maria. (1988). For Long Life and Happiness. *Regeneration., 1.*

Roediger, Henry L. (1990). Implicit memory: Retention without remembering. *American Psychologist,* 45, 1043-1056

Rogers, Carl. (1951). *Client-Centered Therapy.* Boston: Houghton-Mifflin.

Romijn, Herms J. Minireview: The Pineal, a Tranquilizing Organ? *Life Sciences,* 23, 2257-2274.

Rumi, Molana Jalaluddin Molavi Balkhi. (1926-1982). *The Mathnawi of Jalalu'd-din Rumi.* London: E.J.W. Gibb Memorial Trust.

_____. *Divan Shams Tabriz.* Translated in Angha, Molana Hazrat Jalaluddin Ali Nader Shah. (1990). About the Author in *Masnavi Ravayeh.* Lanham, MD: University Press of America.

Rzyl, M. (1970). *Parapsychology: A Scientific Approach.* NY: Hawthorn.

Sahakian, William S. (Ed.) (1965). *Psychology of Personality: Readings in Theory.* Chicago: Rand McNally .

Samuels, Frederick. (1984). *Human Needs & Behavior.* Cambridge, MA: Schenkman.

Santrock, J.W. (1989). *Life-Span Development.* (3rd Ed.). Dubuque, IA: Wm. C. Brown.

Schacter, S. & Singer, J.E. (1962) Cognitive, social and physiological determinants of emotional states. *Psychological Review,* 69, 379- 399.

Scheibel, Arnold B. Anatomical and Physiological Substrates of Arousal. in Hobson, J. Allen & Brazier, Mary A.B. (1980). *The Reticular Formation Revisited: Specifying Function for a Nonspecific System.* NY: Raven Press.

Schimmel, Annemarie. (1985). *And Muhammad is His Messenger.* Chapel Hill: The University of North Carolina Press.

_____. (1986). *Mystical Dimensions of Islam.* Chapel Hill, NC: University of North Carolina Press.

Schuon, Frithjof. (1984). *The Transcendent Unity of Religions.* Wheaton, IL: Theosophical Publishing House.

Schwaller de Lubicz, Isha. (1954). *Her-Bak.* NY: Inner Traditions.

Shah, Idries. *The Sufis.* London: Octagon, 1977.

Shakespeare, William. (1963). *As You Like It.* Act II, Scene vii, line 139. London: Rex.

Simonton, O.C., Simonton, S., & Creighton, J. (1978). *Getting Well Again.* Los Angeles: Tarcher.

Slobin, D.I. (1973) Cognitive prerequisites for the development of grammar. In: Ferguson, C.A. and Slobin, D. I. (Eds.). *Studies of Child Language*

Development. NY: Holt, Rinehart & Winston.

Small, Melinda Y. (1990). *Cognitive Development*. NY: Harcourt, Brace, Jovanovich.

Small, Meredith F. (1992). A Reasonable Sleep. *Discover*. April. p. 88.n.

Smith, Margaret. *Rabi' a the Mystic and Her Fellow-Saints in Islam*. Cambridge University Press, 1984.

Sorokin, Pitirim A. & Hanson, Robert C. (1953). The Power of Creative Love. in Montague, Ashley (ED.) *The Meaning of Love*. NY: Julian Press.

Spielman, Arthur & Herrera, Charles. (1991). Sleep Disorders. in Ellman, Steven J. & Antrobus, John S. (Eds.) *The Mind in Sleep*: *Psychology and Psychophysiology* (2nd Ed.) NY: John Wiley & Sons.

Spilka, B,, Hood, R. W. Jr., & Gorsuch, R.L. (1985). *The Psychology of Religion: An Empirical Approach*. Englewood Cliffs, NJ: Prentice-Hall.

Sternberg, Robert J. & Kaye, Daniel B. (1982). Intelligence. *The Encyclopedia of Educational Research*. (5th Ed., Vol. 2). NY: Free Press.

Sternberg, Robert J. . (1984). Toward a Triarchic Theory of Human Intelligence. *The Behavioral and Brain Sciences*, 7, 269-315.

Stewart, K. (1967). Dream Theory in Malaya. In Tart, C.T. (Ed.) *Altered States of Consciousness*. Garden City, NY: Anchor Books.

Tanner, Ira. (1973) *The Fear of Love*. NY: Harper & Row.

Tart, C.T. (1965) Toward the experimental control of dreaming: a review of the literature. *Psychological Bulletin*, 64, 81-91.

Taylor, Irving A. (1976). Psychological Sources of Creativity. *The Journal of Creative Behavior*. 10, 193-202.

Thapa, K. & Murthy, V.N. (1985). Experiential characteristics of certain altered states of consciousness. *Journal of Transpersonal Psychology*. 17(1) 77-86.

Thomas, Lewis. (1974). *The Lives of a Cell*. NY: Viking Press. .

Toal, Jeanne. The Seven Flavors of Intelligence. *American Health*, VI, 62-67.

Torrance, Paul. (1974). *Torrance Tests of Creative Thinking*. Princeton, NJ: Personnel Press/Ginn.

Tortora, Gerard J. (1983). *Principles of Human Anatomy* (3rd ed.). NY: Harper & Row.

Tyler, Leona E. (1984). Some possible implications of Sternberg's triarchic theory of intelligence. *The Behavioral and Brain Sciences* 7, 301-302.

Underhill, Evelyn. (1910-1974). *Mysticism*. NY: New American Library.

von Franz, Marie-Louise. The Transformed Berserk: Unification of Psychic Opposites. *ReVision*. 8, 20.

Walsh, Roger N. & Vaughan, Frances. (1980) *What Is a Person? In Beyond Ego*. Los Angeles: Tarcher.

Watts, Alan. (1972). *The Book*. NY: Vintage.

Wechsler, Rob. (1987). A New Prescription: Mind Over Malady. *Discover*, Feb., 51-61.

Weiner, Bernard. (1972) *Theories of Motivation*. Chicago: Markham Publishing Co.

Wertheimer, M.A.(1972). *A Brief History of Psychology*. NY: Holt.

White, John (Ed.) (1984). *Frontiers of Consciousness*. NY: Julian Press.

Wittrock, M.C. (1978). The Cognitive Movement in Instruction. *Educational Psychologist*, 13, 15-29.

Wundt, Wilhelm. (1912/1973) *An Introduction to Psychology*. NY: Arno Press.

_____. (1902). *Outlines of Psychology* (2nd Ed.). Leipzig: Wilhelm Engelmann..

Zukav, Gary. (1979). *The Dancing Wu Li Masters*. NY: Bantam.